Image Theory:
Decision Making
in Personal and
Organizational Contexts

WILEY SERIES IN
Industrial and Organizational Psychology

Series Editors:

CARY L. COOPER
University of Manchester Institute of Science and Technology, UK

NEAL SCHMITT
Michigan State University, USA

Image Theory: Decision Making in Personal and Organizational Contexts

Lee Roy Beach, University of Arizona, USA

Further titles in preparation

Image Theory:
Decision Making
in Personal and
Organizational Contexts

LEE ROY BEACH
University of Arizona

JOHN WILEY & SONS
Chichester · New York · Brisbane · Toronto · Singapore

Copyright © 1990 by John Wiley & Sons Ltd,
Baffins Lane, Chichester,
West Sussex, PO19 1UD, England

Other Wiley Editorial Offices

John Wiley & Sons, Inc., 605 Third Avenue,
New York, NY 10158–0012, USA

Jacaranda Wiley Ltd, G.P.O. Box 859, Brisbane,
Queensland 4001, Australia

John Wiley & Sons (Canada) Ltd, 22 Worcester Road,
Rexdale, Ontario M9W 1L1, Canada

John Wiley & Sons (SEA) Pte Ltd, 37 Jalan Pemimpin #05–04,
Block B, Union Industrial Building, Singapore 2057

Library of Congress Cataloging-in-Publication data:
Beach, Lee Roy.
    Image theory: decision making in personal and organizational
contexts/Lee Roy Beach.
        p.   cm. — (Wiley series in industrial and organizational
psychology)
    Includes bibliographical references.
    ISBN 0-471-92030-4
    1. Decision-making.   2 Decision-making (Ethics)   3. Imagery
(Psychology)   I. Title.   II. Series.
BF448.B42   1990
153.8´3—dc20   89–24781
                                                    CIP

British Library Cataloguing in Publication Data:
Beach, Lee Roy
    Image theory: decision making in personal and
organizational contexts. – (Wiley series in industrial and
organizational psychology)
    1. Decision making theories
    I. Title
    153.8´3

    ISBN 0-471-92030-4

Typeset by Associated Publishing Services, Petersfield, Hampshire.
Printed in Great Britain by Biddles Ltd, Guildford, Surrey.

To
Helmut Jungermann and Terry Mitchell

With special thanks to
Barbara Beach and Emily van Zee

Contents

Series foreword ix

Foreword xi

Preface. xiii

Acknowledgements xv

1   **INTRODUCTION TO IMAGE THEORY** 1
    Introduction 1
    An informal statement of image theory 3
    A formal statement of image theory 6
    Images and decisions in organizations and groups 10
    A request 14
    Summary 15

2   **THE IMAGES** 16
    Images in cognitive research 16
    The three images 23
    Sources of candidates for adoption to images 40
    Summary 49

3   **FRAMING AND DELIBERATION** 50
    Decision framing 50
    Decision deliberation 66
    Summary 69

4   **THE COMPATIBILITY TEST** 71
    The test 71
    The rejection threshold 76
    'Is it worth it?' 77
    From compatibility to profitability 78
    Research on the compatibility test 80
    Summary 103

5   **MORE ON COMPATIBILITY** 105

6 THE PROFITABILITY TEST 127
The strategy selection model.................................. 127
Research on the strategy selection model ....·................... 137
Summary 147

7 MORE ON PROFITABILITY 148

8 IMPLEMENTATION AND PROGRESS 173
Control 173
Progress decisions 175
Implementation and monitoring research...................... 178
A model for implementation monitoring 187
Summary 197

9 IMAGE THEORY APPLIED............................... 199
An image theory analysis of auditing decisions 199
An image theory analysis of childbearing decisions 207
An image theory analysis of the Cuban Missile Crisis............. 214

References 231

Author Index.. 247

Subject Index 252

Series Foreword

The purpose of this **Industrial and Organizational Psychology Series** is to provide a range of high quality books covering 'leading edge' and significant topics in both industrial and organizational psychology. This series will help develop both theory and research in topics of interest to industrial and organizational psychologists in industry, in academia and in private and public organizations. We hope to explore such themes as job analysis, employee recruitment, psychology in the unions, motivation, employee satisfaction, counselling at work, job design and a range of subjects of topical interest to the international community of industrial and organizational psychology. We hope this series will be used by applied practising psychologists, as well as by graduate students in psychology departments and business schools throughout the world

The first book in the series explores the area of decision making in organizations—built on the notion of image theory. It is hoped that this book and many others in this new series will contribute to the vastly expanding field of industrial and organisational psychology.

Cary L. Cooper
Neal Schmitt

Foreword

This book represents a culmination of many years of work by numerous contributors. As such, it belongs to many people. But throughout this evolutionary process Lee Beach has been the major force; the person who has stimulated the thinking, rethinking, research and writing that make up this volume.

The first time I saw an outline of image theory was when I was in Nags Head, North Carolina, sitting in the sun reading my mail. Lee sent me an outline for a paper which summarized much of his thinking about decision making. This occurred in the spring of 1984.

From one perspective, the ideas inherent in image theory represented a logical extension of our earlier work on a contingency model of decision strategies. We had come to realize that most people, most of the time, for most decisions used fairly unanalytic strategies. What was elusive for us was a good description of this non-analytic process.

From another perspective, it was clear that image theory provided a radical departure from the prevailing paradigm of rational decision making. Image theory used terms like images, values, principles, fittingness and argued that the domain of traditional decision theory was probably a poor description of most decision processes.

Lee knew right from the start that he was swimming upstream. He knew that it would be difficult to be heard, to get published and to do rigorous research on relatively new and somewhat fuzzy constructs.

But the theory 'felt' right. And everywhere we went people seemed to resonate to our presentations. So Lee pushed on, did the research, wrote up the papers, tested the intellectual waters and persevered.

This book represents a summary of these efforts. It is a major new way of thinking about decision making. As such, it will undoubtedly result in debate, controversy, research and revisions of the way we think about the theory in particular and decision making in general.

But most of all it is a very personal statement. It reflects the creativity, reflection, insight and effort of Lee Beach. It also reflects Lee's humor, his style and scholarship. The book is both enjoyable and stimulating and should be read by both academics and practitioners.

Terrence R. Mitchell

Preface

The purpose of this book is to introduce a new theory of decision making—image theory. I call it a new theory even though my colleagues and I have been working on it for a number of years. The theory seems to us rather commonsensical. It assumes that decision makers pursue plans in the attempt to achieve goals, and that decisions consist of accepting or rejecting new goals and plans in light of what the decision maker considers to be the right thing to do. That is, it assumes that most decisions are made in an attempt to do what is 'right', rather than in an attempt to maximize—where 'right' is defined in terms of the decision maker's values, ethics, beliefs, and morals, not all of which are necessarily admirable. Furthermore, the theory assumes that most decisions are made quickly and simply, on the basis of 'fittingness', and only in particular circumstances are they made on the basis of anything like the weighing and balancing of gains and losses that is prescribed by classical decision theory. The theory is not particularly moralistic, despite the foregoing description, but it recognizes that decision makers ordinarily are trying to satisfy much more basic and much more consequential considerations than the maximization of profit. Indeed, profit, in the usual sense, often is not considered at all.

The book begins with an informal description of the theory, followed by a formal description. The former is designed to reveal the theory's intuitive logic and the latter is designed to impose a clear, if somewhat oversimplified, structure on that logic. Chapter 2 presents a discussion of the nature of images in cognition and decision making, and how those images both influence the decisions that are made and themselves change as a result of those decisions. Chapter 3 contains a description of framing, by which decisions are placed in meaningful contexts, and how doing so influences the course of subsequent deliberation. Chapters 4 and 5 describe the theoretical and empirical foundations of the compatibility test, one of the two decision mechanisms of the theory. Chapters 6 and 7 describe the theoretical and empirical foundations of the profitability test, the other of the two decision mechanisms. Chapter 8 examines decision implementation and the monitoring of progress toward a decision's goal. Finally, Chapter 9 describes the application of image theory to examples of three different kinds of decisions: business decisions, namely decisions by an auditing firm about whether to accept a client and about the accuracy of that client's financial statements; family planning decisions, namely decisions by married couples about whether to have a (another) child; and political decisions, namely decisions by President Kennedy and his advisors about how to deal with the Cuban Missile crisis.

Readers of previous publications about image theory will note that the present version features three images rather than the earlier four. The 'projected image' has been merged with the 'action image' to create the 'strategic image'. This came about when my colleagues, Bill Silver and Terry Mitchell, were writing about the theory for a lay audience. To simplify presentation they simply left out the projected image. Their presentation worked so well that we had to reconsider the image's theoretical usefulness. We found that the projected and action images were so interrelated that it was appropriate, and convenient, to merge them.

This book represents the efforts of many persons—colleagues, students, friends, and strangers. The colleagues and students have helped shape the ideas and gather the data. The friends and strangers have worked to make this presentation of the ideas and data more intelligible. It would be awkward to try to thank by name everyone who has contributed, if only for fear of inadvertently leaving someone out. However, I should like to acknowledge some of the people who have been particularly helpful.

Major thanks go to Terry Mitchell, with whom I have worked closely for the past 15 years. Had we followed the original plan we would have co-authored the book, but the demands on Terry's time were too great and he had to withdraw before we really got started. The result is that the book is different from what it might have been—perhaps more self-indulgent and certainly more idiosyncratic. However, the basic ideas of image theory and the work on the strategy selection model are our joint efforts and I hope that this is reflected in the book. Indeed, I have used plural pronouns throughout the book in an attempt to make it clear that the work is not solely my own.

Additional thanks go to the teachers who introduced me to decision research, notably Kenneth Hammond and Ward Edwards; to my faculty colleagues, notably Fred Fiedler, Earl Hunt and Nancy Pennington; to encouraging friends, notably Barbara Beach, Emily van Zee, Jay Christensen-Szalanski, Kenneth Rediker, Karl Teigen, and Charles Vlek; and most especially to Helmut Jungermann, whose idea it was that this book be written. I thank you all.

Lee Roy Beach

Acknowledgements

Portions of the following publications are incorporated into the text of this book by permission of the copyright holders; Beach, Barnes, and Christensen-Szalanski (1986) and Beach, Smith, Lundell, and Mitchell (1988) by permission of John Wiley & Sons Ltd.; Beach and Mitchell (1987) and Beach and Strom (1989) by permission of Elsevier Science Publishers B.V.; Beach and Frederickson (1989) by permission of Pergamon Press; Beach and Mitchell (1978) by permission of the *Academy of Management Review*; Beach and Morrison (1989) by permission of Springer-Verlag; and Jaques (1982) by permission of the author.

I Introduction To Image Theory

INTRODUCTION

Since its inception (Edwards, 1954) behavioral decision research has been strongly influenced by classical decision theory. This theory derives primarily from economic theory and secondarily from statistical theory, and has generally been interpreted as both prescriptive and descriptive of decision making in personal and organizational contexts. The best known and most thoroughly examined model from classical theory is the subjective expected utility model.

In spite of its influence, for a long while there has been marked skepticism about classical decision theory's adequacy at the level of the individual decision maker. Starting with the now familiar criticisms by Allais (1953), Simon (1955), and Ellsberg (1961) for decisions by individuals working alone, and by Simon (1945, 1955), March and Simon (1958), and Cyert and March (1963) for decisions by individuals working in organizations, the tide of informed opinion increasingly has turned against classical theory as a descriptive theory, and perhaps even as a prescriptive theory.

There have been two responses to the waning influence of classical decision theory. One has been to retain the underlying logic, while modifying it to make it more descriptive—a line of work that we discuss in Chapter 6. The second response has been to reject classical theory outright and to seek a completely different theoretical description.

This second response has been strongest in organizational science, in large part because empirical research in organizations so clearly refutes the descriptive adequacy of classical theory. In much of this research decision makers, usually managers, have been observed as they do their jobs. The results show very little similarity between what classical theory prescribes and how decisions actually are made. In general it is found that decisions seldom involve explicit balancing of costs and benefits and the major consideration seldom is maximization of profit. Decisions seldom are conceived of as gambles, classical theory's favorite metaphor; the decision maker retains control of post-decision events and views decisions as vehicles for producing predictable change. Not only are decisions not gambles, they seldom even involve choices—most frequently only one option is considered at a time, and the decision about each is whether to take that option (change) or to remain with the status quo. Neither is the status quo regarded as just another option—it has a very special status and is not easily abandoned.

The research results also show that few decisions are conceived of as isolated or unique. Rather, they are seen as components of a larger scheme that is dedicated to the achievement of some desired state of affairs, with each component contributing a small thrust in the appropriate direction while offering protection against failure. In addition, it is often found that the decision process itself influences the generation and clarification of actions and goals, rather than merely making choices from among well-formulated actions in pursuit of well-formulated goals. Overall, the research presents a picture of decision making managers as promoters and protectors of their organizations' values and goals rather than as relentless seekers of maximum profits.

As a result of these findings, organizational decision researchers have offered numerous alternatives to classical decision theory. These offerings fall, although not neatly, into five classes. One class contains theories that view decisions as the by-product of social processes, with little or no delineation of the specific mechanisms by which this is accomplished (e.g. Gore, 1964; Weick, 1979). A second class stresses cybernetic processes and sees decisions as adjustive or compensatory actions, with little detail about the decision process that leads to selection of these actions (e.g. Steinbruner, 1974). A third class examines the constraints imposed by decision makers upon both the options that they entertain and upon the objectives that they strive for, again with little detail provided about what is involved in the decision itself (e.g. Lindblom, 1959). A fourth class offers typologies of decision strategies and the variables that define the typologies (e.g. Mintzberg et al., 1976). And, a fifth class focuses on the chaos that often surrounds group decision making and how various characteristics of that chaos influence the success or failure of decisions (e.g. Cohen et al., 1972).

All of the theories in each of these classes are instructive. They each cast light upon one or another important feature of decision making and upon the conditions that influence decisions, particularly the social conditions. However, few of them differentiate the decision process itself from the social processes within which it is embedded. Admittedly, social processes exert a powerful influence on decision making. However, failure to differentiate between them makes the theoretical enterprise unnecessarily complicated. It is our view that most of the features that are included in these theories are important and should be represented in a broad theory of decision making. However, we also think that the broad theory should describe the decision process in a way that transcends, is invariant over, the different social processes within which it occurs. A theory of social processes in relation to decision making is a legitimate undertaking, but it is not the same thing as a theory of decision process.

The theory to be described in the following pages, image theory, is an attempt to formulate the broad theory referred to above. On the one hand, image theory does not completely spurn classical theory—it accommodates the fact that while most decisions cannot be described by classical theory, some can. Neither does it argue with the assumption that decision behavior is self-interested, surely the motivating assumption of classical theory. Instead, it expands the definition of self-interest. On the other hand, image theory is not merely a synthesis of the many different organizational decision theories—it accommodates many of the features that they each emphasize while limiting itself to the decision process *per se* rather than confounding it with social processes. Even though most decisions are made in groups, the decision maker is viewed as having to make up his or her own mind; then the various group members' decisions are integrated in a way that depends upon the dynamics of the particular group. Thus the focus remains upon the decision process rather than upon the social processes that define the group.

In the next two sections of this chapter we present the general ideas that make up image theory and a formal statement of the theory. The final section contains a brief discussion of our views on decision making in group and organizational contexts. The remainder of the book will elaborate upon each of the central concepts of the theory, drawing examples from both personal and organizational decision making.

AN INFORMAL STATEMENT OF IMAGE THEORY

IMAGES

Image theory views the decision maker as possessing three distinct but related images, each of which comprise a particular part of his or her decision-related knowledge. One image defines how events should transpire in light of the decision maker's values, morals, ethics and so on. The second image is about the kinds of changes the decision maker wants for himself, herself, or the organization—an agenda of goals and related time-lines for accomplishing them. The third image consists of the plans the decision maker has for accomplishing those goals as well as the decision maker's projections of the effects of implementing the plans in terms of the chances of successfully attaining the goals.

FRAMING

Not all of the decision maker's sizable stock of principles, goals, and plans are relevant in every context. Identifying the relevant subset involves use of knowledge about what has led up to the present moment in order to establish what is going on and whether there are any problems that require attention; this is called 'framing' the context. When things are found to be going smoothly within the framed context, the decision maker need only monitor the situation in order to detect any difficulties that subsequently may arise. However, if things are not going smoothly or if difficulties in fact arise, the decision maker must intervene. Intervention consists of either doing what has worked before in this context, the use of policies, or of adopting new goals or plans for the images, thereby instigating new behavior to deal with the difficulties and, perhaps, dropping existing goals or plans from the images if they are the source of the difficulties.

ADOPTION

Candidates for possible addition to the goal agenda come from the need to satisfy principles ('We should adopt quality circles in an attempt to ensure that our products meet our quality criteria'), or from someone who suggests them (a consultant, a relative, a friend), or from their being naturally correlated with other goals ('As long as we are reorganizing the office, we should adopt a new computer system'). Candidate plans for possible adoption come from past experience ('This worked before and it might work again'), from outside sources (a counselor, a consultant), and, sometimes, from creative flashes and imaginative opportunism.

Adoption of a candidate goal or plan is based, first of all, on whether it is reasonable. That is, do its ramifications satisfy one's principles, does it fit well with one's other goals or plans? If it is not perfect, how unreasonable is it? If it is not too unreasonable it might work out all right, but there is some point at which it simply is too unreasonable and must be rejected.

If this initial screening process involves only one candidate goal, and if that goal is judged not to be unreasonable, it is adopted and the decision maker moves on to considering candidate plans for accomplishing it. If the process involves multiple candidates to be the goal and only one passes, the situation is similar to having started with only one candidate and having passed it—it is adopted and a plan is sought for accomplishing it. However, if more than one candidate goal is involved and if more than one survives the screening, something must be done to break the tie. This something involves choosing the best from among the survivors, usually on the basis of their relative merits.

Adoption of plans is similar to adoption of goals except that it also involves imagining what the plan might result in if it were adopted; that is, whether it might accomplish its goal. Thus, plan adoption is, in effect, a combination of the goal adoption process and progress monitoring.

PROGRESS

Progress monitoring involves trying to imagine what would happen if a to-be-adopted plan were to be implemented, or if the implementation of an already-adopted plan is continued. Will it create difficulties for other goals and plans? Will it fail to attain its goal? Will it violate relevant principles? If the answer to any of these questions is 'yes', the plan is not adopted; or, if it has already been adopted, the decision maker considers abandoning it and seeking a replacement. If a satisfactory plan cannot be found to attain a goal, then the goal has to be re-examined to see if it ought to be rejected. That is, if one cannot find an acceptable way to accomplish the goal, it may be necessary to abandon the goal.

Of course, all of this assumes that a decision has to be made at all. If a goal is found to exist in a familiar situation, a plan from the past may already exist to serve as a policy for accomplishing it. Thus, no decision is required— the policy merely needs to be implemented. If the situation is less familiar, but not too different from situations that are familiar, the plans that were used in those familiar situations can be melded and modified to provide a new plan for the new situation. It is knowledge about familiar situations, together with knowledge about events leading up to the present, that gives meaning to decisions by embedding them in a frame that makes them understandable.

DELIBERATIONS

Many decisions, perhaps most of them, are quite straightforward. They require little deliberation and sometimes seem almost to make themselves. This occurs when the screening process reveals that the potential goal or plan (or that progress) fits so well with clearly relevant principles, goals, and plans that there is no question about adoption.

Sometimes, however, decisions require more deliberation in order to clarify the relevant criteria and to identify the relevant characteristics of the candidate. This deliberation may be sustained, purposeful, and rational, or it may be fleeting, scattered, and fanciful. It also may involve strong emotions. Whatever it may involve, its purpose is to illuminate the decision, to provide perspective, and to help the decision maker know what is important and how he or she feels about the issues.

Deliberative thinking helps in the identification of the decision's consequences—the ways in which principles, goals, and plans might be affected by the ramifications of the decision. It allows the decision maker to imagine possible futures and to experiment with variations on how to attain desired ends.

A FORMAL STATEMENT OF IMAGE THEORY

Figure 1.1 contains a diagram of image theory.

IMAGES

Images are the cognitive structures that summarize the decision maker's knowledge about what must be accomplished and why, about how it is to be done, and about the results of efforts to do it (see Chapter 2).

The *value image* consists of the decision maker's prescriptive and proscriptive values, standards, ideals, precepts, beliefs, morals, and ethics which collectively are called *principles*. These are imperatives that serve as rigid guides for establishing the 'rightness' or 'wrongness' of any particular decision. Principles govern the adoption or rejection of goals as well as the choice of actions for achieving those goals. Principles serve both to generate new goals and actions and to guide adoption or rejection of *candidate* goals and actions that fit or do not fit the value image.

The *trajectory image* consists of the decision maker's agenda for the future, the strategic outline for where he or she should be going, the ends that are being pursued. It is what the decision maker hopes he or she will become and what he or she wants to achieve; the landmarks that characterize the decision maker's ideal future.

The constituents of the trajectory image are called *goals*. Goals can be concrete, specific events, such as getting a particular job. They also can be abstract states, such as being a success in one's field or being happy. Knowing when concrete goals have been attained is fairly straightforward. Knowing when abstract goals have been attained is less clear. In the latter

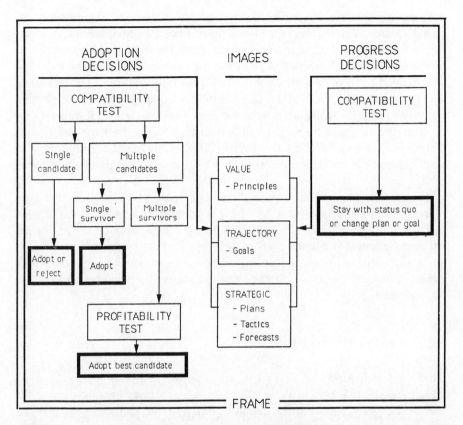

Figure 1.1 A diagram of image theory. From Beach and Mitchell (1987); reproduced by permission of Elsevier Science Publishers B.V.

case, concrete surrogate events, called *markers*, serve as indicators of goal attainment. For example, neither raises nor praise from one's boss actually are the goal of job success, but they are strong indicators of progress and may even indicate that the goal has been attained; often timely progress in the proper direction is itself the goal.

The *strategic image* consists of the various *plans* that have been adopted for attaining the various goals that the decision maker is pursuing. Each plan is a sequence of actions that begins with goal adoption and ends with goal attainment (Jungermann *et al.*, 1983). The decision maker regards the action sequence, the plan, as a unitary activity, described as 'trying to (prevent, achieve, acquire, avoid, forestall, accomplish) some event or state'. Examples are 'Trying to: increase my income, avoid bankruptcy, make my marriage work, prevent my kids from taking drugs'. It is the actions that are foreseen as being involved in 'trying to' that constitute the plan.

Plans are abstract strategies. Their concrete behavioral components are called *tactics*. Tactics are specific actions that are intended to facilitate implementation of a plan and to produce progress toward their goal. Some tactics are fairly well defined at the time the plan is adopted, others are less well defined but will become clearer as the plan unfolds. Some are dependent upon each other or must be executed simultaneously, and some are alternatives that are contingent upon what happens along the way. However vague or clear the tactical components of a plan may be at the time the plan is considered for adoption, the fact remains that tactics are the 'nitty-gritty' of goal seeking, the specific, concrete behavioral manifestations of the abstract plan.

Inherent in plans is an anticipation, a *forecast*, of the future that may result (1) if a particular candidate plan is adopted to attain a specific goal, or (2) if implementation of a particular plan on the strategic image is begun or, once begun, if it is continued.

As such the plan-based forecast serves as a measuring rod by which progress toward realization of the ideal agenda on the trajectory image can be evaluated.

TWO KINDS OF DECISIONS

There are two kinds of decisions, *adoption decisions* (see Chapters 4–7), which are about adoption or rejection of candidates as constituents of the value, trajectory, or strategic images; and *progress decisions* (Chapter 8), which are about whether a particular plan on the strategic image is producing satisfactory progress toward attainment of its goal.

FRAMING

In order to interpret events and to bring relevant knowledge to bear upon them, the decision maker relies upon recognition or identification of the present context to define a subset of the constituents from his or her images as relevant to the decision at hand. This is called *framing*. The frame's structure is defined by those constituents of the three images that are brought to bear on the decision; the meaning of the context is encompassed in the particular image constituents that constitute its frame.

If the necessity for action arises within a framed context, and if in the past some course of action proved successful, that same course of action, called a *policy*, will be used again. If no policy exists, appropriate goals and plans must be adopted.

TWO DECISION TESTS

There are two tests by which adoption and progress decisions are made. The *compatibility test* (Chapters 4 and 5) assesses whether the features of a candidate for adoption 'violate' (are incompatible with) the relevant (framed) constituents of the various images, and whether the forecasts based upon the constituents of the strategic image 'violate' the relevant constituents of the trajectory image. The *profitability test* (Chapters 6 and 7), which applies only to adoption decisions, assesses the relative ability of competing candidates to further the implementation of ongoing plans, attain existing goals, and comply with the decision maker's principles. The object of the compatibility test is to screen out the unacceptable. The object of the profitability test is to seek the best.

If a single candidate passes the compatibility test it is adopted without further scrutiny, except perhaps for post-decisional justification. In other cases, described below, candidates that pass the compatibility test are then subjected to the profitability test before the adoption decision finally is made.

Progress decisions (Chapter 8) require compatibility between the trajectory image and the forecast generated by the plans on the strategic image. If there is sufficient compatibility it implies that the plans could produce or are producing acceptable progress toward their goals and that their continued implementation is warranted. However, incompatibility between the two images implies that the plan would fail or is failing to produce progress and that something must be done to keep things on track toward the goals.

DECISION MAKING

For an adoption decision about a single candidate the compatibility test dictates that if the (weighted) number of violations exceeds the 'rejection threshold', the candidate is rejected; otherwise it is accepted. Violations are all-or-none (compatible/incompatible), and the rejection threshold is the upper limit of the decision maker's willingness to tolerate violations for the decision at hand.

For an adoption decision involving two or more alternative candidates, the compatibility test is essentially a screening process. If one of the candidates is sufficiently compatible (if violations do not exceed the rejection threshold) and the others are not, the compatible candidate is adopted and the others are rejected. If more than one candidate survives screening by the compatibility test, the survivors are passed on to the profitability test which chooses the 'best' from among them.

For a progress decision the compatibility test dictates that if the number of violations of the trajectory image by the forecast from the strategic image exceeds the rejection threshold, the existing plan is rejected and a new plan is sought to replace it; otherwise the existing plan is retained. The profitability test does not apply to progress decisions.

IMAGES AND DECISIONS IN ORGANIZATIONS AND GROUPS

Most decisions are made in collaboration with other decision makers; that is, in groups of two or more persons. These others may be a spouse, friends, fellow members of affinity groups such as sports clubs or hobby clubs, or fellow employees. In each case, like the decision maker, these people hold images that in part are unique to them and that in part are shared with other members of the organization.

In some cases the shared images exist merely because there is overlap between two or more persons' private images, which often is the motivation for having formed the organization or group in the first place (Zander, 1985). In other cases the images become shared as a result of shared experiences, often in the context of an ongoing organization, in which case the shared images often are unique to the members of that organization. In yet other cases the images are part of the organization when the decision makers join it, or are handed down to them by the leaders of the organization, and the members adopt them as part of the process of acculturation and functioning within the organization.

These shared images include the symbols that serve to illustrate the organization's principles, goals and plans, and which help communicate them to members of the group. They also include the shared norms that serve to prescribe and proscribe behavior and to emphasize the organization's uniqueness and unity. As such, they give direction to the efforts of the organization's members without requiring step-by-step instructions for every activity. This is because they provide a philosophical foundation for decisions, and in doing so they promote a complementarity among the decisions made by different members of the organization.

ORGANIZATIONS

Our view of organizational constraints on decision making is very like that outlined by Simon in his classic *Administrative Behavior* (1945/1976). Simon defines an organization as the pattern of communication and relationships in a group that provides each member with information and assumptions, goals, and attitudes that enter into his or her decisions. It also provides expectations about what the other members of the group are supposed to do and how they will react to what he or she says or does. That is, the individual's position within the organization determines both the information that he or she receives as well as the expectations he or she has about his or her own behavior and the behavior of others. 'A sales manager reacts like a sales manager because he occupies a particular organizational position, receives particular kinds of communications, is responsible for particular subgoals, and experiences particular kinds of pressure' (Simon, 1945/1976, p. xix).

Organizational influence upon decision making is exercised by (1) dividing tasks among its members, (2) establishing standard practices, (3) transmitting objectives throughout the organization, (4) providing channels of communication that run in all directions, and (5) training and indoctrinating its members with the knowledge, skill, and loyalties which allow them to make the decisions the organization wants made in the way the organization wants them made.

In short, by occupying a position in the organization, and by learning about the organization's purpose and its normal ways of doing things, the decision maker becomes able to contribute to the overall, relatively unified activity of the organization. Information about the direction that the organization's activity is to take, together with the specific expectations associated with the decision maker's position in the organization, constrain the activities that are open for consideration. Decision making at this level consists of selecting the actions that (1) conform to the aforementioned constraints, and (2) that are congruent with the activities generated by other positions in the organization.

For a specific decision maker, the relevant principles are those having to do with the organization's overall purpose, as seen from the decision maker's position in the organization, as well as principles specific to the position. For example, the human resources officer may include fairness and equal opportunity as principles that are unique to hiring, but also see them as desiderata that are congruent with the broader principles of the organization as a whole.

Similarly, for a specific decision maker, the relevant goals are both the general goals set down by upper management (if there is any) and the goals for his or her position. For example, if the general goal is to enter some high-tech market, the human resources officer's part of the goal involves finding adequately educated employees who can do the necessary jobs. If the general plan includes acquiring subsidiaries that can provide the necessary technical support for the organization's high-tech entry, part of that plan falls to the human resources officer, who must decide among various candidate plans for doing this successfully (e.g. shifting employees around to accommodate the acquisitions).

Decision making by top managers is no less constrained than decision making at lower levels, and is even more influenced by the organization's principles than is true at lower levels in the organization. Harrison (1972) examined organizational ideologies (principles) and concluded that they serve several functions. They specify the goals toward which efforts should be directed and by which its success and worth can be measured. They prescribe the relationships between the organization and its members—the social contract that states what each can expect from the other. They indicate what kind of control within the organization is to be regarded as legitimate and what is not. They define the qualities and characteristics of the organization's members that are valuable and those that are not, and how they will be rewarded. They indicate to members how they should treat each other— collaboratively or competitively, honestly or dishonestly, closely or distantly. And, they establish the appropriate manner for dealing with the outside world—exploitation, negotiation, etc. Harrison (1972) argues that the kinds of goals and plans that the organization and its members adopt are dictated in large part by these ideologies, and that the internal and external conflicts that are observed in organizations often are a result of these ideologies.

Beyer (1981) reviewed the literature on the influence of ideologies on organizational decision making and found strong support for Harrison's (1972) argument as well as the other points that have been made above. She summarized her findings thus:

> People define problems and perceive the situations surrounding them according to their ideologies and values. Organizations build ideologies and values into standardized solutions that then tend to define the problems to which they are applied. People's participation in particular decisions varies according to their interests and to their locations in organizational structures. People use ideologies and values to rationalize struggles for power. Organizations manage conflicts of ideologies or values affecting decision making by political mechanisms, by attending to interests sequentially, by misperceptions, and by decoupling. People use ideologies and values to simplify complex decision making situations. People use ideologies and values to structure and explain uncertain and ambiguous decision making situations.
>
> From these results it seems clear that decisions made in organizations can be affected in many ways by the ideologies and values of decision makers, or their perceptions of the ideologies and values of others to whom decision makers are responsive. All stages of decision processes can be affected by the ideological and value premises (a) that define the problems or provide available solutions, (b) that characterize the shifting configurations of participants with interests in the outcomes of decisions, (c) that characterize the environments to which decision makers try to fit organizations, and (d) that structure decision making situations. (Beyer, 1981, p. 187)

GROUPS

Of course, not all organizations are businesses or bureaucratic institutions, but most of what has been said above applies to less formal groups. Zander (1985) reports the stated purposes of 72 new non-business groups on which he kept records from newspaper reports. Of these, 18 were formed to generate changes in the customs of society, 14 were formed to make something, 13 were formed to change some other organization, 11 were formed to change the members themselves, and the remainder had various more specialized purposes. Thus, each group was formed to accomplish something—which one assumes is why any group is formed, businesses or otherwise.

Zander (1985) suggests that these groups' purposes are guided by what their members value, and that the purposes therefore become concepts of ideal kinds of behavior. This permits the individual, as a functioning member of the group, to assess the goodness or badness, the rightness or wrongness of the actions of other members of the group—as well as permitting him or her to decide about candidates for his or her own action. Zander (1985) states that a value (a principle) describes things that should be done or should be avoided without fail, not merely behavior that is attractive or disliked. It delineates moral efforts from immoral ones and is an absolute good under all circumstances.

INTEGRATION OF INDIVIDUALS' DECISIONS

The focus of image theory is upon individuals, either making personal decisions alone or, more often, making decisions in the context of organizations and groups of one or more other people. In the latter contexts, the decision maker's decisions may merely become integrated into the larger flow of the organization's activity with little in the way of comment or criticism from others. For example, the human resources officer's decisions about how to ensure a pool of technically trained job applicants may be regarded by others as his or her business; as long as things work out well little is to be said.

In contrast, many decisions in organizational and group contexts involve a good deal of consultation with fellow workers. In this case a major part of the process consists of argumentation (e.g. Bettenhausen and Murnighan, 1985; Rieke and Sillars, 1984) and negotiation (e.g. Bazerman et al., 1988; Pruitt and Rubin, 1986; Walsh and Fahey, 1986; Walsh et al., 1988). This provides the means to present the case for the decision candidate one favors, to gather political and substantive information for making or modifying one's own decision, and to allow the participants to reach a common decision that can guide everyone's subsequent actions. In some cases the common decision arises through consensus, in other cases it is arrived at through some form of voting, and in yet other cases it is determined by the decision of the most powerful participant.

This focus upon individual decision makers operating in organizations and groups is not, of course, unique to image theory. However, it is in marked contrast to the theories of, say, Cohen *et al.* (1972) or Weick (1979), and to other organizational theories. When observing multiple-participant decision making, it is often difficult to discern the difference between decision processes and social processes. Indeed, the decision frequently appears to be the product of the social process. The image theory view, however, is that decisions and decision processes occur within the individual members of the group and that social processes, at best, inform the individuals' decision processes or, at worst, interfere with them.

It seems somehow reasonable that social processes should serve as a vehicle for a synergism that would make the best use of the various members' knowledge and skills. However, the evidence indicates that this is true only insofar as the social process involves conveyance of relevant information; the 'purely social' aspects of the social process have a negative influence. Casey *et al.* (1984) were able to estimate the relative contributions of the informational and purely social components of social interaction to small groups' performance of a predecisional task. They found that information pooling accounted for an *increase* in group performance over individual performance of 20.5%, and that the purely social aspects of the group interaction accounted for a *decrease* in performance of 11.3%.

From this and related research on small-group performance, it may be inferred that social processes are not identical to decision processes and that the two ought to be treated differently in theory building. The results suggest that there is profit in pooling group members' information, the synergism of the group, but they do not suggest that the social process *per se* generates the group decision. Therefore, image theory views decision processes as properties of individuals and the group decision as a transform on the individuals' decision; the specifics of the transformation process, whether voting or something else, are reserved for some other theory to describe.

A REQUEST

It must be understood that the orderly, linear process suggested by the preceding discussion is an expositional convenience that does not obtain in reality. Research (Anderson, 1983; Axelrod, 1973; Bouwman *et al.*, 1987;

Isenberg, 1984, 1986; Kotter, 1982; March, 1978; March and Olsen, 1986, 1986; Mintzberg, 1975, 1978, 1987; Mintzberg *et al.*, 1976, and others) clearly shows that decision making proceeds by fits and starts. Opportunities (plans) beget goals. Goals are modified as plans are refined. Principles that at first seem to be irrelevant turn out to be relevant, often painfully so. Plans that at first seem straightforward turn out to be impossible to implement or to fall short of achieving their goal. Goals that look desirable become less so when the requirements for their achievement become clear. Moreover, there usually is more than one decision under consideration at a time, with deliberation switching from one to the other and back again. Sometimes things are left undecided, to be taken up again later, or to be forgotten as the press of events or changes in the situation make them obsolete and uninteresting.

No theory can include all of this and remain comprehendible. Therefore, in all that follows we will talk as though decision making is fairly orderly. The reader is requested to remember that this appearance of order is merely a fiction.

SUMMARY

In this chapter we began with an informal statement of image theory that was intended to give the reader an intuitive grasp of what the theory is about and how it relates to everyday behavior. Next, a more formal, more abstract, statement of the theory was presented. Then we discussed the role of the individual decision maker in organizations and groups, the concept of shared images, and the constraints that organizations and groups exercise on the decisions of their members. Finally, we asked the reader to keep in mind that the image theory description of decision making makes the process appear more abstract and more orderly than it really is and that goals and plans evolve and change as the process proceeds.

2 The Images

The value, trajectory, and strategic images are cognitive structures. Framing, the compatibility test, and the profitability test are cognitive processes that act upon these structures. In this chapter we examine the nature of images in general, and the nature of the images in image theory in particular. In subsequent chapters we will examine the processes and how they affect the images.

IMAGES IN COGNITIVE RESEARCH

KINDS OF IMAGES

Images play an important role in cognitive science, but there is often a great deal of confusion about just what they are. This is due to the failure to differentiate among the various kinds of images that people experience. Briefly, there are at least three kinds of images.

Visual images are experimental concomitants of physical stimulation of the receptors of the eye. Such experiences also have a large psychological component, without which they would be merely light without meaning. Nonetheless, there is a very close correlation between the physical patterns of stimulation and the visual experience.

Mental images are psychologically (centrally) generated quasi-pictorial events (Kosslyn, 1980; Pylyshyn, 1973, 1981). For example, you can call to mind your mother's face or you can create the mental image of an ice-cream sundae with a small brown dog sitting on top of it while wearing a dunce's cap. Moreover, these images can be mentally manipulated—imagine your mother starting to frown and then breaking into a big smile; imagine the small dog turning into a housefly (is the fly still wearing the dunce's cap?). Pylyshyn (1981) argues that the fact that mental images can be manipulated in this way demonstrates that visual and mental images are different things.

Cognitive images are even more remote from visual images, although they may retain some of the latter's pictorial quality (Simon, 1972). These images are a combination of mental images and non-image knowledge. That is, cognitive images have some features that are pictorial, some that are semantic, and some that are emotional (for surely emotions must be regarded as a form of knowledge).

To understand cognitive images, try to recall a conversation you had yesterday. Notice that, in part, the image you conjure up has a visual component—perhaps the setting or the faces of the other participants—although the image may be indistinct and fragile. (Perhaps you can even 'see' your own face, although unless you were facing a mirror at the time you could not actually have seen yourself during the conversation.) The image also consists of the content of the discussion, which is encoded semantically rather than visually. And, the image consists of the emotional tone that accompanied the discussion or that you added later when you thought about what had taken place. In short, the cognitive image is more than either of the other two kinds of images even though some of its visual-like components may in fact derive from them.

Pylyshyn (1981) argues that because the content of images can be described in words, the visual aspects are less important than they might at first seem to be. Ideed, he concludes that images can be reduced to a list of features without doing them substantive harm. This is a convenient conclusion because it makes images amenable to the kinds of analyses that are commonly done in cognitive research. We accept Pylyshyn's conclusion that, in principle, it is possible to construct fairly exhaustive prose descriptions of images, but we do not think that such descriptions wholly capture the essence of images. The striking thing about images is that they are so striking; the visual components often seem to have a far greater impact than do the semantic, or perhaps even the emotional, components. So, while we will settle for prose descriptions, or even lists, we retain the right to be uncomfortable about doing so.

IMAGES AS SCHEMATA

Once you reduce cognitive images to prose or lists, they can be recognized as a special case of a familiar concept, *cognitive schemata*. There are many other special cases: scenarios (Jungermann, 1985; Jungermann and Thüring, 1987; Thüring and Jungermann, 1986) and mental models (Johnson-Laird, 1983) are schemata that apply to forecasting the future and to problem solving; episode schemata (Rumelhart, 1977) and causal models (Einhorn and Hogarth, 1986) are schemata that apply to inferences about complex chains of events that lead up to some event of particular interest; scripts (Schank and Abelson, 1977) are prescriptions for actions in specific settings; prototypes (Rosch, 1976) and stereotypes (McCauley *et al.*, 1980) are schemata for classifying objects; self-concepts (Markus and Nurius, 1986; Markus and Wurf, 1987) are schemata that organize our knowledge about ourselves; and decision images (Miller *et al.*, 1960) are the schemata involved in planning and decision making. Indeed, the latter are the schemata that constitute the three images in image theory.

Piaget (1929) was one of the first theorists to use the schema concept—in his studies of the development of structured knowledge in infants and children. At about the same time, Bartlett (1932) used it in his work on structured memory: ' "Schema" refers to an active organization of past reactions, or of past experiences, which must always be supposed to be operating in any well-adapted organic response' (p. 201). Later uses have varied in precision and clarity, but the general idea seldom differs much from Piaget's and Bartlett's.

In our view, a schema consists of elements, concepts, and the relationships among them, that are pertinent in some sphere of interest to an actor. The schema defines the legitimacy of the elements that it encompasses. That is, the very fact that the schema includes those particular concepts and those particular relationships *means* that they are pertinent, at least for the actor who owns the schema. Relationships define the admissible interactions among the concepts—empirical violations of these prescriptions and proscriptions indicate that the schema is inadequate. To the degree that such violations are seen by the actor as important enough to heed, they require revision of the schema. Such revision involves either changes in or replacement of various of the schematic elements.

Images were identified as schemata by George Miller, Eugene Galanter and Karl Pribram (1960) in work that is the immediate ancestor of image theory. They, in turn, cite an even earlier ancestor, *The Image*, by Kenneth Boulding (1956), in which the implications of the image as knowledge are examined in various disciplines. Miller *et al.* describe Boulding's work as a 'tapestry of private and public Images, of personal and shared knowledge', but they complain that:

> [it leaves the actor] more in the role of a spectator than of a participant in the drama of living. Unless you use your Image to do something, you are like a man who collects maps but never makes a trip. It seemed to us that a Plan is needed in order to exploit the Image. (p. 2)

To better understand plans, Miller *et al.* turned to the work of Newell, Shaw, and Simon, in particular, and to simulation research and cybernetic theory, in general. According to Miller *et al.*:

> The Image is all the accumulated, organized knowledge that the organism has about itself and its world. The Image consists of a great deal more than

imagery, of course. . . . It includes everything the organism has learned—his value as well as his facts—organized by whatever concepts, images or relations he has been able to master. (pp. 17–18)

A Plan is any hierarchical process in the organism that can control the order in which a sequence of operations is to be performed. (p. 16)

[It is also] a rough sketch of some course of action, just the major topic headings in the outline, as well as the completely detailed specification of every detailed operation. (p. 17)

In short, a plan is 'quite similar to the notion of a program that guides an electronic computer' (p. 2).

The cybernetic part of the Miller *et al.* work was the famous TOTE system. The metaphor was that of a servomechanism. The actor *tests* the congruity between the existing state of affairs and the preferred state. If there is incongruity a plan is put into *operation* to correct things. The execution of the plan is guided by feedback from further *tests* until congruity is achieved, at which point the actor *exits* the system. Although TOTE proved to be the part of the work that most readers remembered best, it was in fact never fully developed. Moreover, thirty years later the TOTE system seems much too simplistic even to serve the purpose for which it was proposed.

Indeed, in 1976, Kreitler and Kreitler remarked of the Miller, Galanter and Pribram work:

. . . they have left unanswered most of those questions which are crucial for the theory's application. For example, they have not explained how the TOTE . . . unit, which represents the feedback principle, operates; how the 'image' which in the first test stage is matched against the newly formed representation, is retrieved; how the results of the test trigger those processes of which the 'operation' consists; what the nature of the 'operation' is on different levels; or how that kind of 'congruity' which makes 'exit' possible is attained. Moreover, the theory does not dwell at all on the functional relation between the 'images', which represent the sum total of knowledge in the individual's possession, and the set of instructions whose hierarchy constitutes the plan that controls behavior. . . . But the most crucial weakness is the fact that no directions about the use of the model in a concrete situation, say, in the framework of an experiment, are given. Even if a complete repertory of the plans of an individual or a group were available, it would not be possible to predict which plan has the best chance to attain the state of performance in a given situation. (1976, pp. 6–7)

Image theory is an attempt to remedy these faults and to bring the Miller, Galanter and Pribram ideas up to date.

IMAGES, SCHEMATA, AND FRAMES

Merely identifying images as schemata does not solve all problems by any means. One of the larger problems is defining what is included in a schema and what is not. Clearly, not all of the actor's knowledge is brought to bear on the focal task. Image theory deals with this via the framing process, in which only knowledge that is associated with recognized or identified contexts is regarded as pertinent.

In Chapter 1 we defined frames as that portion of the decision maker's store of knowledge that he or she brings to bear in a particular context in order to endow that context with meaning. This definition derives from theories of knowledge representation in artificial intelligence and linguistic processing (Dinsmore, 1987; Fauconnier, 1985; Schoenfeld, 1983), in which the total knowledge space of an intelligent system is partitioned into subspaces to which the system's logic can be locally applied.

Knowledge partitions

Dinsmore (1987) cites demonstrations by Cohen and Perrault (1979) and Martins (1983) to the effect that creation of a local subspace, a belief space, for a particular topic for a particular actor, makes it possible to apply the simulation system's general logic to simulate the actor's thinking in terms of deriving previously unlisted beliefs within that belief space. He also discusses the use of subspaces in simulations of reasoning about hypothetical or potential situations, which speaks to the creation of forecasts for progress decisions in image theory.

The advantage to artificial intelligence research of basing simulations upon partitions of knowledge is that it strongly delimits information that must be considered in making logical inference, thereby making inference simpler and requiring fewer steps than if the whole knowledge space were used (Dinsmore, 1987). This, of course, is exactly the advantage a decision maker needs in order to think precisely and economically about contexts and decisions. Moreover, in artificial intelligence work the meaning of a subspace is regarded as a propositional function (i.e. relationships, in our definition of schemata), '. . . which is assumed to have some applicability outside of that space'; . . . 'a specification of what must be true in reality in order for a proposition to be true in that space' (Dinsmore, 1987, p. 6). In short, ultimately the meaning of a subspace lies in the relationship between the truth of a proposition in that space and its truth in the real world. The value of such spaces is that they support efficient reasoning about complex information by limiting it to a specific context. Again, these are equally desirable conditions for a real, non-artificial, decision maker.

Thus we see that Miller, Galanter and Pribram's concern that images be connected to the real world, our definition of schemata as being subject to revision when their relationships are empirically violated, and the artificial intelligence assumption that the meaning of a subspace is dependent upon the truth of its propositions in the real world, all come together. In short, images, schemata, knowledge partitions, or whatever you wish to call them, ultimately derive their conceptual and theoretical value from the assumption that they bridge the gap between the actor's internal representation of phenomena and the empirical validity of that representation, and that this holds for subspaces as well as for the entire representation.

If the foregoing discussion of knowledge partitioning and subspaces seems a little cosmic, consider a more familiar example. The self concept is a schema, an image, that organizes our knowledge about ourselves. (While the self concept may have evaluative components, it is important not to confuse it with self esteem.) A little thought will reveal that each of us actually has several selves, and which self is on display at any time is dependent upon the situation in which one finds oneself. Thus we have a self for those we know and love, one for the office, one for the bowling team, etc. A thorough description of The Self, in the broadest sense, would include all of these selves. But in any particular context only one of the subselves is operational, and which it is depends upon how the context is framed. These subselves are called 'the working self concept' or the 'on-line self concept' (Markus and Nurius, 1986; Markus and Wurf, 1987). The idea is precisely the same as that of subspaces as partitions of the actor's total knowledge space. And it is precisely the same as that of frames as definitions of what is pertinent in different contexts. Moreover, at the time that any particular self concept is on-line, the user assumes that it is valid—that the propositions that constitute it have reference to external events.

Our point is that framing defines a subspace that consists of those constituents of the decision maker's value, trajectory, and strategic images that are deemed relevant to the context at hand. (Indeed, the frame *is* these relevant parts of the images—see also Yates (1985).) The frame not only defines the context, it supports efficient reasoning about that context by legitimizing the image components as valid descriptors of the context.

Frame representation

It may be accurate to describe frames as knowledge subspaces, and it may be appropriate to describe the knowledge contained therein as the relevant components of the decision images; but this description is all very abstract. What concrete form do frames take? More to the point, what is going through the decision maker's head? What are frames, really?

First, some frames must be rather simple, perhaps merely consisting of some naive impression that lacks much detail. However, there is evidence that in their full-blown, elaborated form, frames can be quite complex. Pennington and Hastie (1986) examined the way in which jurors framed the evidence that was presented to them in the course of a mock trial. They found that the information was economically organized into a story that was inferred from the testimony using the jurors' general knowledge about the world. The authors call this the Story Model of knowledge representation, a schema for giving meaning to information as it is presented in order to make a decision about the appropriate verdict. It appears that the verdict category that was most closely 'fit' by the story was the one that was decided upon—but different jurors chose different verdicts depending upon the particular story they constructed. It should be noted that the knowledge that jurors used to construct their stories was domain-specific (i.e. it often involved the juror's ability to imagine what he or she would do in the specific circumstances under discussion and how other people would be likely to behave in those specific circumstances). Morever, the stories were quite to the point; irrelevant information was not included. And, when information was lacking, the jurors made inferences based upon the parts of the story that they already possessed.

Pennington and Hastie (1986, 1988) show that the construction of stories as a method of organizing knowledge in a domain is compatible with other linguistic/comprehension models in cognitive research. They state that in contrast to classical decision theory, which tends to minimize interpretation and evaluation of information and to focus on direct relations among information and computations of judgment on a single dimension (usually expected utility), the focus ought to be on the interpretation component, in line with the results of their research.

We find ourselves in sympathy with Pennington and Hastie's (1986, 1988) conclusions, and we find their results compelling. It is our working hypothesis that the knowledge (image constituents) that constitutes a frame is largely represented in the form of stories, however fragmentary, and that it is this quality that gives continuity and meaning to the events that occur in that frame. It is, of course, difficult to talk in terms of complete stories at every step in the theoretical analysis of decision making. Thus, the images that make up image theory are the theoretical representations of the various kinds of components that make up the stories that the decision maker constructs in the process of framing a context and in observing events unfold in that framed context. In some larger sense, decisions are the twists and turns that the author of these subjective stories contributes to them, and this after all turns out to be the main point of interest in the study of decision making.

To summarize, images are schemata for decision making. These schemata are called frames when they consist of knowledge, usually in the form of domain-specific stories, that give meaning to contexts, and that permit inferences about information that is not immediately apparent. Framing defines the substance of the decision maker's total knowledge (image constituents), where the subspace contains the knowledge that is pertinent to the context that has been framed. That is, the frame is a schema that defines and that is defined by the image constituents that comprise it. Moreover, the three images in image theory are the theoretical representations of the components of the meaning-rich stories that comprise the frame. With all of this in mind, we turn now to an examination of each of the three kinds of images that make up image theory.

THE THREE IMAGES

THE VALUE IMAGE

The principles that are the constituents of this image define what one means when one speaks of such old-fashioned concepts as one's code of honour, ethics, and ideals, as well as one's fundamental standards of equality, justice, solidarity, stewardship, truth, beauty, and goodness, together with one's moral, civic, and religious precepts and the responsibility one assumes when performing one's mundane daily duties and in engaging in routine social intercourse (Mukerjee, 1965). Rokeach's (1968) view of beliefs fits well within our somewhat broader view of principles, and is instructive because it provides a way of defining different degrees of 'centrality' or importance of principles.

Rokeach (1968) reminds us of Jastrow's observation that the 'mind is a belief-seeking rather than a fact-seeking apparatus' (Jastrow, 1927, p. 284) and defines a belief as

> any simple proposition, conscious or unconscious, inferred from what a person says or does, capable of being preceded by the phrase 'I believe that . . .'. The content of a belief may describe the object of belief as true or false, correct or incorrect; evaluate it as good or bad; or advocate a certain course of action or a certain state of existence as desirable or undesirable. (p. 113)

Some beliefs are descriptive (I believe that the sun rises in the east), some are evaluative (I believe this ice-cream is good), and some are hortatory (I believe it is desirable for children to respect their parents).

Rokeach (1968) states that beliefs (principles) differ in the degree to which they are central or peripheral, with central beliefs being more resistant to change and having greater influence on other beliefs in the system. Centrality results from connectedness—central beliefs have implications for other beliefs because they tend to be existential ('basic truths' about physical and social reality and about the self), they derive from private experience (as opposed to being derived from instruction by an authority or other credible source), they are often broadly shared by others who have had similar experiences, and they are not trivial or arbitrary—they are not merely matters of taste.

These characteristics of beliefs are also the characteristics of principles—except that we refer to principles as primary and secondary rather than central and peripheral. However, there is a subtle but important difference: even more than is the case for beliefs, principles are imperative—prescriptions and proscriptions. They are ideals that prescribe what one 'ought' or 'ought not', 'should' or 'should not' desire, and they therefore exert a powerful influence on what goals (ends) one finds desirable and what plans (means) one finds acceptable. This means that potential goals and plans must promote the principles' prescriptions and comply with their proscriptions. Jacob et al. (1962) offer three cues for recognizing principles: (1) the decision maker makes 'ought' or 'should' statements in rationalization of actions, (2) the decision maker makes statements that reveal guilt, shame or diffuse anxiety about specific actions, and (3) the decision maker makes statements of moral indignation or approbation of actions on the one hand, and of esteem or praise on the other hand.

Principles are for the most part cultural products, even though each individual holds a private version that may be quite distinctive. Sociologists (e.g. Kluckhohn, 1951) have long argued that shared cultural principles, called norms, are the bricks and mortar of society. Indeed, within a culture there is a good deal of agreement about principles, and there is surprisingly large agreement between different cultures (Morris, 1956). It can be argued that to function successfully within a culture, be it only two people, as in a marriage, it is necessary for the participants to share principles and to be able to assume that there is a common ground (Beach and Morrison, 1989). But, as Kluckhohn (1951) points out, even though there is a convergence of the individual's principles toward group norms, no two individuals share identical principles. Each one adds a little here, subtracts a little there, makes this emphasis or that emphasis. It is this similarity without identity that makes it possible for us to function in society while allowing us to be individuals instead of cultural clones.

To say that the individual crafts his or her own distinctive set of principles does not necessarily mean that he or she is therefore capable of clearly identifying all of those principles. Some principles are implicit and rather fuzzy, albeit none the less powerful in their influence on decisions. Other principles are explicit, if only because society discusses them—the decalogue provides an explicit list for Christians, and many other religions provide similar guidance to their adherents. By the same token, principles are not all of equal importance. Some are primary and have vast influence on decisions while others are secondary and have less influence—violations of the former are serious while violations of the latter, while of consequence, do not have the same weight. Of course, what is primary and what is secondary is not absolute, it depends upon the frame that has been adopted. Implicit or explicit, central or peripheral, primary or secondary, the function of all principles is the same: they are the criteria for adopting or rejecting potential goals and plans. They are not the goals themselves, but they define what is and what is not desirable about goals; they are not plans themselves, but they define what are and what are not acceptable means for achieving goals.

Principles need not be virtues. Some imperatives are quite ignoble—greed may be as compelling as altruism, lying may recommend itself as much as honesty. Moreover, some are fantastic and unreal, a romantic vision that has never been and that may never be—one would be embarrassed to describe these principles to a friend (if one could even recognize them oneself), and that friend might well dismiss them as sentimental nonsense. However, the embarrassment and the dismissal would not diminish their power to influence. These principles were described best by Kundera (1984), in *The Unbearable Lightness of Being*:

> 'Kitsch' is a German word born in the middle of the sentimental nineteenth century, and from German it entered all Western languages. Repeated use, however, has obliterated its original metaphysical meaning: kitsch is the absolute denial of shit, in both the literal and figurative senses of the word; kitsch excludes everything from its purview which is essentially unacceptable in human existence. (p. 248)

> [As an example] Her kitsch was her image of home, all peace, quiet, and harmony and ruled by a loving mother and a wise father. It was an image that took shape within her after the death of her parents. The less her life resembled that sweetest of dreams, the more sensitive she was to its magic, and more than once she shed tears when the ungrateful daughter in the sentimental film embraced the neglected father as the windows of the happy family's house shone out into the dying day. (p. 255)

> For none among us is superman enough to escape kitsch completely. No matter how we scorn it, kitsch is an integral part of the human condition. (p. 256)

There are a few studies that demonstrate the link between the principles of the value image and behavior. Burke and Reitzes (1981) showed that the way in which college students describe themselves (competitive, responsible, sensitive, creative), which arguably are descriptions of what they see as their principles, is predictive of their educational plans and choices of social activities. Meyer (1982) provides examples of how different plans emerge from different sets of principles in the same environment—where the 'actors' were 19 hospitals dealing with an environmental threat (a doctors' strike), and the principles were the beliefs the decision makers in each hospital had about their hospital's priorities and functions. Beyer (1981) reviews the influences of organizational ideologies and principles on organizational decision making, reaching conclusions that are congruent with the present discussion. And, Hage and Dewar (1973) examined 16 organizations that offered rehabilitation services and found that the directions taken by each organization were predicated upon the principles espoused by the decision makers at the top of the organization.

In a study that extended work by Sloan (1983), Brown et al. (1987) interviewed workers in an office in order to find out the relative importance to them of various classes of principles. Later, the workers were presented with pairs of plans and asked to indicate which they would be most likely to implement. It was found that the prefered plan in each pair usually was linked to the decision maker's more important principle. In addition, the rated difficulty of deciding between the two plans was a function of the similarity in importance of the plans' respective principles.

In another examination of principles, Mitchell et al. (1985) studied the editorial reviewers for five journals in the field of organizational behavior. They obtained the relative importance to 99 reviewers of various standards for evaluating the acceptability of manuscripts that are submitted for publication. Figure 2.1 shows the mean relative importance of each of the standards for the 99 reviewers. Note that method and logic are nearly equally important, that presentation is least important, and that the importance of the topic is the most heavily weighted standard, with perceived contribution being the most heavily weighted component of importance. Certainly, reviewers' standards are principles, and they influence the decisions that strongly impact the professional lives of many of us.

The Mitchell et al. (1985) study also examined the principles that experienced and less-experienced researchers applied to the decision to strive to do research and publish. It was found that the experienced researchers, who probably tended to be older and who certainly were better established than the less-experienced researchers, had a high value for the intrinsic enjoyment of doing research and publishing for its own sake and a low value for doing it for the extrinsic rewards it brings. The less-experienced researchers had a higher value for the extrinsic rewards of doing research and publishing, and a lower value for intrinsic enjoyment and the search for answers. In short, the established researchers are in a position to realize their principles of

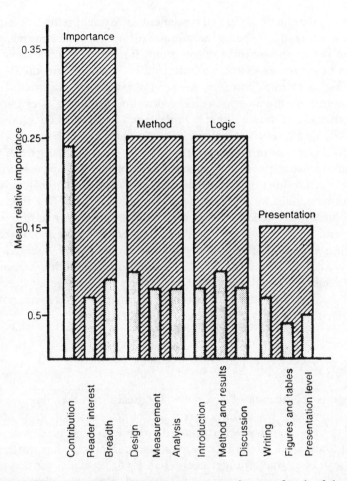

Figure 2.1 The mean relative importance to 99 reviewers of each of the standards for evaluating the acceptability of manuscripts. From Mitchell *et al.* (1985); reproduced by permission of Richard D. Irwin Inc.

enjoying what they do for its own sake, while the less-established researchers have to value the more tangible rewards that publication brings.

The observation that established researchers enjoy what they do for its own sake brings us to the final, and perhaps most important, role of the value image and its constituent principles in decision making. This role is, quite simply, that of motivating the entire process.

It is customary to think of decisions as involving the pursuance of desired outcomes, of the maximization of expected utility, of the attempt to end up better off after the decision is made than before it is made. Almost always the analysis begins with the potential contribution of the alternatives' outcomes to attainment of this advancement in fortune; seldom is attention given to what really is being accomplished by such advancement. Our contention is that the motivation for profit, for gain, for advancement and the values of outcomes that contribute to them derives from the degree to which those outcomes promote and comply with the decision maker's principles. Indeed, the most powerful motivation for action does not fit the profit-motive sort of thinking that is represented by classical decision theory. People often are personally altruistic and managers do not behave as single-minded maximizers of profit (Selznick, 1957). It takes a fair degree of logical contortion to make altruism and 'suboptimality' fit the classical maximization mold. But, such contortion is unnecessary because most people already know where the motivation for such behavior lies. It lies in the fact that getting things, doing things, making things happen gives intrinsic pleasure when it promotes and complies with one's principles. Introspection and observation provide clear evidence for the motivational strength of *autotelic* activity, that which is rewarding in and of itself (Csikszentmihalyi and Csikszentmihalyi, 1988). We submit that the intrinsic motivation for such actions, both the plans and the goals that they seek to attain, is provided by their compatibility with the decision maker's principles.

THE TRAJECTORY IMAGE

This image is the agenda of goals that the decision maker has decided to adopt and pursue. This definition requires closer examination of both the nature of the goals on that agenda, and the temporal aspects of that agenda.

It is odd how little of the literature on decision making has much of any depth to say about goals. Jungermann et al. (1983) remark that this may be because decision theory assumes well-defined problems; alternatives are assumed to exist and the focus is on their evaluation and on the subsequent choice of one of them. That is, the focus is on action, not goals; any analysis of goals is presumed as a precondition for the actual business of decision making, which is action selection. This last statement is true if only because, as Jungermann et al. state: 'we can think of no other way of defining the set of actions than to consider the goal or goals to be achieved' (p. 225).

The most thorough recent work on goals has been in action theory by Kuhl and his associates (Kuhl, 1983; Heckhausen and Kuhl, 1985). This analysis distinguishes between three levels of goals: action, outcome, and consequences. The first refers to action as a goal in itself—acting sheerly for the enjoyment or interest of the activity *per se*. The second refers to action outcomes that are inherently valuable. The third refers to desirable consequences that might arise from an achieved outcome. The analysis then goes on to focus on how motivation is generated by the relations among these three levels.

Kuhl's analysis, like virtually every other discussion of goals (e.g. Cyert and MacCrimmon, 1968; Galambos and Abelson, 1986; Lichtenstein and Brewer, 1980; Miller *et al.*, 1960; Simon, 1955) ends up with a hierarchy in which local, immediate goal seeking contributes to intermediate goal achievement, which in turn contributes to achievement of some sort of transcendent goals. One cannot argue with such hierarchical conceptions; they follow naturally from the use of the word 'goal' to describe the intended endpoint of every action. However, they lead to rather pointless and repetitious discussions that focus on which lower level goals contribute to which upper level goals and so on until some penultimate goal is reached—usually something that is only vaguely defined, self-realization or the like. Indeed, such discussions tend toward infinite regress and usually miss the rather obvious point that at any particular moment the actor is focused on a pragmatic and reachable goal, and only incidently, or in exceptional and extreme circumstances, is self-realization, or even survival, the immediate focus of attention.

In image theory we have attempted to structure the discussion of goals in much the same manner that Kuhl does—through identification of three levels in a hierarchy. However, rather than discuss each level as a different kind of goal, which makes the concept too vague, we have elected to treat each level as an image that has its own distinct character. Thus the value image corresponds, in some rough way, to the transcendent goals at the highest level of most goal hierarchies. The trajectory image corresponds to the intermediate level (e.g. Kuhl's outcome level). And, the strategic image corresponds to the alternative courses of action that usually constitute the lowest level in such hierarchies. Each kind of image is seen to contribute to the 'next higher level', but not by merely being a smaller version of some larger goal-seeking strategy. Rather, the plans, and their constituent tactics, that constitute the strategic image are seen as considerably different from the goals that constitute the trajectory image, and those goals are seen as considerably different from the principles that constitute the value image. In this way we have tried to break out of the trap imposed by using the work 'goal' too broadly.

The goals on the trajectory image are indeed the goals that people commonly refer to when they say that they are trying to achieve some specific thing. In large part this depends upon how the decision maker frames the problem in the first place, or on how the person who presents the problem to the decision maker frames it. In general, this focal goal, as contrasted with the plan that is aimed at achieving it, can be detected by asking the decision maker what he or she is doing. 'Why?' elicits the principles that support the goal, 'What?' elicits the goal, and 'How?' elicits the plan and its tactics.

In an informal study, Kenneth Rediker presented people with a 'lifeline', a graduated scale numbered from zero to 100. They were asked to regard the zero as the date of their birth and to mark the scale at their present age and at the age at which they expected to die. Then they were asked to list the major life goals that they had striven for in the past and the major life goals that they were striving for now. Then they assigned each of these life goals to a location on the lifeline to represent the age at which they had achieved (or given up on) past goals or the age at which they hoped to achieve future goals. It was found that all of the participants, who were merchants in a shopping precinct, found the task quite easy, suggesting that the goals and the time line existed before they were asked for. In addition, the reported events clustered most densely around the participants' present age and were fewer in number in the remote past and future. Too, older participants had fewer future goals than did younger participants, both because they had less time between the present and death and because they already had achieved many of the big goals for which people commonly strive. It was interesting, if understandable, that the goals that were elicited using this method tended to be concrete events (graduation from college, marriage, children, ownership of a business) rather than states like happiness, success, maturity and the like. We suspect that states, because they often are transient and ill-defined, are more difficult to recall than are events. However, we also suspect that they are more important and that events often are merely concrete markers that stand for achievement of desired states.

THE STRATEGIC IMAGE

Plans

The plans that are the constituents of the strategic image are adopted to achieve the goals on the trajectory image. Each plan has a temporal aspect in that it unfolds in time and culminates in successful goal achievement or is modified or abandoned when it is seen to be leading to failure. The strategic image represents the decision maker's overall time perspective in that different plans unfold simultaneously and in that different plans start and end at different times. Indeed, Jaques (1982) argues that one's time perspective is the result of one's multiplicity of extended plans, rather than being the prior condition for those plans. The role of action in the construction of psychological time will be discussed below, but the point is that the future 'is not what is coming to us but what we are going to' (Guyau, 1902, p. 33, in Lens, 1986).

A plan is an anticipated sequence of activities that begins with goal adoption and ends with goal attainment (Jungermann et al., 1983). Recall that the plan is the 'how' of goal attainment, the goal is the 'what', and the relevant principles are the 'why'. The 'how' is captured in statements such as: 'I am trying to avoid bankruptcy (get through school, join the Army, buy a house, etc.) by—' The plan is the list of steps that the decision maker provides to fill in the blank, what he or she anticipates having to do in order to reach the goal.

Tactics

Plans are abstract—'First I will call a meeting to discuss the sales figures' is not the same thing as actually calling the meeting or actually discussing the sales figures. The concrete behaviors that are implied by the plan are called tactics. At the time that a plan is being formulated, it is usually quite vague and sketchy. The decision maker may know the major tactics that will be required, but more will be revealed as the plan unfolds and implementation proceeds. Moreover, concrete tactics must be suited to local conditions at the time they are undertaken, and thus are not wholly pre-plannable. The result is that, at the time of adoption, a plan looks a good deal like the schematic in Figure 2.2. Some tactics are fairly well defined, designated T in the schematic. Some tactics are less well defined but will become clearer as the time for their execution approaches ('I'll cross that bridge when I come to it'), designated T^*. Some tactics are conditional upon execution of others (what Raynor (1969) has called a contingent path), or must be performed simultaneously, designated T_i and T_j. Some, designated T_{k1} and T_{k2}, are alternative actions contingent upon conditions at the time they are to be executed. The point is that plans are not 'carved in stone': they are merely general outlines—what March and Simon (1958) call 'loosely-coupled action programs'—in which component tactics are sensitive to, and molded to, existing environmental conditions as implementation proceeds.

Certainly, most plans are more complicated than the schematic in Figure 2.2. Moreover, this particular schematic is not the only way to show plans diagrammatically; for example, Jungermann et al. (1983) accomplish the same thing with a network schematic. The point is that, at the time of adoption, usually only the general outlines of the plan are apparent.

It is important to note that the sequence of tactics that comprise the plan may not be the same as the observed sequence of actions that constitute its implementation. The tactics of other ongoing plans may be interleaved with these tactics. There may be iterative loops necessitated by events that were

Plan

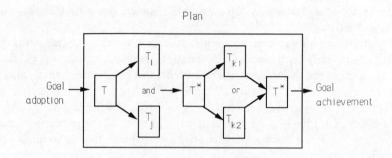

Figure 2.2 Schematic of a plan. From Beach and Mitchell (1987); reproduced by permission of Elsevier Science Publishers B.V.

not foreseen in the original plan. Activity sometimes goes into idle (Ryan, 1970), like a car motor idling, in that the plan's implementation is put on hold while attention turns to other things. Events that do not relate to the plan may intrude into the implementation. And, of course, plans may have to be revised in light of changes in the environment in which the tactics are executed, or when prior tactics fail to set up the necessary conditions for later tactics.

As implementation of the plan begins and the tactics at the beginning are executed, additional information becomes available in the form of environmental conditions and feedback about the tactics' degrees of success. This can be thought of as starting out on a trip toward a distant mountain peak (the goal). At first only the tops of the foothills between you and the peak are visible (the anticipated tactics in Figure 2.2). As you come to the top of the first foothill (i.e. execute the first tactic) the valley beyond comes into view. The valley may contain unsuspected small hills to be climbed or other problems that were not included in the original sketchy plan. Thus, the focus of the decision maker's attention turns to getting across the valley to the top of the next foothill, all in the service of reaching the distant peak.

Perhaps, in the process of focusing on getting across the valley, the decision maker may momentarily forget about the peak, but the peak still exerts its influence in that the decision maker continues on the path across the valley, and the next valley, and the next, in order to reach the peak. In this sense, execution of a plan consists of iterations of crossing valleys; because on the other side of every foothill there is another valley as yet unseen. Unless some valley proves to be too impenetrable or too diverting, the decision maker eventually will arrive at the peak.

One can think of plans as being formulated for environments that are either stable or unstable, either familiar or unfamiliar. That is, the environment may be expected to remain relatively unchanging during implementation, except as a result of the implementation itself. Or it may change spontaneously. Moreover, the decision maker may or may not have familiarity with the environment (what is in the hidden valleys). If it is stable and familiar, the environment is predictable. If it is stable and unfamiliar, it may be unpredictable. If it is unstable and familiar (i.e. if one knows what causes the changes or what they are going to be) it may be predictable. If it is unstable and unfamiliar, it is probably unpredictable. The question is whether comprehensive planning is the best way to approach both predictable and unpredictable environments.

We know of no empirical data that address this question on the level of the individual decision maker, but there are data for organizations that may also apply to individuals. Frederickson and Mitchell (1984) examined 27 firms that operate in unpredictable environments and found *negative* correlations between the comprehensiveness of their planning and their economic performance, a result also obtained by Bourgeois (1985) for another 20 firms. Frederickson (1984) performed much the same study for 38 firms that operate in predictable environments and found *positive* correlations between comprehensive planning and economic performance. Assuming that the decision makers in all of these firms were striving for the goal of successful economic performance, it is clear that too much planning in unpredictable environments is counterproductive and too little planning in predictable environments fails to capitalize on the advantages that predictability provides. It would appear that flexibility is necessary for unpredictable environments and that comprehensiveness is an advantage in predictable environments. Of course, one would assume that this relationship breaks down at the margins— compulsivity and disorganization may be equally bad. Insofar as these results apply to the individual decision maker's plans, it would appear that environmental predictability calls for plan comprehensiveness, but that flexibility is necessary for unpredictable environments.

Policies

Policies are preformulated plans that the decision maker can draw upon when a framed context is recognized as having been encountered before. Policies are much the same as Schank and Abelson's (1977) concept of scripts as preformulated programs for behavior in familiar situations. As Schank and Abelson repeatedly stress, scripts (policies) are not the same thing as plans:

> Plans describe the set of choices that a person has when he sets out to accomplish a goal. (p. 70)

Thus, plans are where scripts come from. . . . . The difference is that scripts
are specific and plans are general. (p. 72)

That is, scripts are essentially no more than highly stylized ways of executing
[plans]. . . . If a script is available for use then it is tried before a corresponding [plan] is tried. (p. 96)

Thus a [plan] is used whenever no script is available. If a [plan] is used often
enough, it will generate a script that eliminates the need for the [plan] as long
as the surrounding context stays the same. The difference between a [plan]
and a script is that a script is very specific to a situation with all details filled
in. In a restaurant one needn't plan how to get food, or consider what [plan]
to try in order to get the waitress to bring you some. It is all presented for
you. If you are familiar with a situation therefore you needn't plan it. A novel
situation (one where no scripts apply) requires planning. (p. 97)

Schank and Abelson (1977) also stress that neither plans nor scripts can be
understood without an understanding of the goals that they are designed to
attain. [In these quotations we have substituted the word 'plan' for the more
obscure word 'planbox', which is Schank and Abelson's term for a detailed
plan, much as illustrated in Figure 2.2. The 'details' of both plans and
scripts (policies) are the tactics in Figure 2.2.]

This distinction between plans and scripts continues in more recent work
on script theory. Thus, Galambos and Abelson (1986) state:

The boundary between scripts and plans is not altogether sharp. Both types of
knowledge structures encode purposive sequences of actions. The main distinc-
tions between the two are that scripts are more stereotyped, consensual, and
societally institutionalized. One can refer to *the* restaurant script, or doctor-
visit script, etc., in reasonable confidence that much very concrete detail is
thereby communicated. . . . Plans are coherent in a looser, more abstract way
than are scripts. One does not speak of *the* plan to win the heart of someone,
or even of *the* plan to get from New Haven to Indianapolis. The activity of
planning implies that there is a choice among alternative overall plans, and
often that subplans will need to be developed as well. . . . Despite their
flexibility, plans as knowledge structures are nevertheless highly constrained.
They are rule-bound. Understanders appreciate the relevance of particular
[tactics] to the achievement of particular goals or subgoals. If the goal of an
actor is known, certain actions [tactics] will seem sensibly interpretable as parts
of a plan for its achievement; conversely, otherwise cryptic actions [tactics]
may be explicable by assuming the presence of some goal they serve. The
structured relationships between goals and plans, therefore, have implications
for the processes of comprehension, of inference, and of explanation. (pp. 101–
102)

Indeed, in reference to the latter point, Lichtenstein and Brewer (1980)
found that when explaining behavior, observers gave reasons in which lower-

order behavior (tactics) was performed 'in order to' further higher-order progress (plans) toward goals. Indeed, participants remembered what the actor was 'doing' rather than precisely what the actor 'did'—the plan was remembered better than the tactics.

Galambos (1986) reports a series of reaction time studies showing that component acts (tactics) of specified scripts are more quickly identified as belonging to those scripts when they are necessary to performing the script, unique to it, and always part of it. For example, decision makers are quick to identify the 'raise the car' act as a component of the 'changing a flat' script because the act is necessary to the script, moderately unique to it, and always part of it. In short, scripts (policies) often are highly stereotyped and their component acts (tactics) are apparent to the decision maker at the time the context is recognized and the policy becomes available.

Finally, Lichtenstein and Brewer (1980) showed participants films and written descriptions of behavioral episodes. Then they asked what the various actions in the episodes were done 'in order to'. They found very high agreement (above 90%) about the tactical objectives of actions as well as the overall goals. Examination of participants' recall of actions showed that, when acts occurred at their 'proper' place in plans, they were recalled more easily than when they were at the 'wrong' place—or acts that were in the wrong place were recalled as having happened at the proper place. The authors conclude that participants 'share similar intuitions about how particular actions are related to other actions, and to achieving goals' (p. 443). These results are similar to those obtained by Abbott and Black (1986) and others for story comprehension—participants understand stories, and they can reconstruct the plans and tactics in the stories when they understand the actor's goals.

Even though policies are plans that have been tried and tested through past use (or acquired by instruction), they must be as flexible as any other plan. Just as one cannot step into the same stream twice, no context is exactly the same as any previous one, so no policy can be executed in exactly the same way every time (see Marken (1988) on policies and plans as control systems that are sensitive to environmental change). The larger tactics, the foothills in our earlier analogy, may be much the same, and the local conditions, the valleys, may be fairly predictable, but seldom will all conditions exactly replicate the past. Thus, tactics must be flexible enough to suit the idiosyncratic characteristics of the focal context, even though the policy may be fairly well worked out prior to implementation. Galambos (1986) points out, in reference to scripts, that a serial chain model is implausible on functional gounds because rigid representation of actions in a particular order does not take into account that many of the actions in a script may be iterated and that there is a good deal of flexibility about which actions can be performed in which order. This observation, of course, also pertains to policies and plans.

The strategic image contains many plans (and policies). The implications of this are well described by Jaques (1982) in his thoughtful essay on the psychology of time. He points out:

> . . . one of the outstanding characteristics of people is that they always are involved in more than one goal-directed course of action at any one time—we are multi-action creatures. Each person is engaged in many activities, in the pursuit of many goals at the same time—one activity being forwarded a little, then another, then the first again, then another, as opportunity or desire arises. Some activities are short and may be completed at one go, such as, for example eating a meal alone, or seeing a film, or having a particular and limited conversation with someone, say an interview. Other activities are extended in time and pursued intermittently, such as, for example, studying for exams, buying a house, or starting a club. And even many apparently continuous transactions are in fact intermittent when examined more closely. Thus, for example, a business lunch may be composed of two intermittent transactions—having a good meal, on the one hand, and forwarding the business conversation, on the other. (p. 136)

Because implementation unfolds over time, plans must be constructed on knowledge about the past, assessment of the present, and assumptions about the future. Returning to Jaques' (1982) analysis:

> [The past] is a highly selected past. It is the past of immediately relevant memory. Particular memories are somehow chosen [framing] and drawn from the great storehouse of memory—or somehow extrude themselves—to lend the current meaningfulness of the precipitates of earlier experiences to the handling of the present situation. . . . They inform the present with their accumulation of wisdom and knowledge (and of errors as well), and indeed sometimes press for particular outcomes. (p. 63)

> The active present is composed of all the behavioral episodes in which someone is engaged—all the intention-filled trajectories from their beginning to their final end state if achieved, or to a sense of failure if not achieved. It is how real life is experienced, and in particular organized. We arrange our activities, our plans, our hopes and expectations, our choices and desires around episodes; we bring various regions of our past experience into active play in relation to the current episodes in which we are involved. We set our priorities, our urgencies, our first things first, in terms of episodes. In short, we organize and actually live our lives in purposive episodes, in intentional trajectories, which are present, in existence, until they have reached their mark or have been dropped or transformed. That is the fullness of our active present: it is our sense of 'present-ness' extended to its widest active limit. (p. 113)

> And then, finally, there is the future, the seemingly nonexisting will-o'-the-wisp. It is the product of our experience of the things we intend to do, to

achieve, to create, to bring about. These things are the goals or objectives which we have in mind. . . . The future is a statement not of some actual event which has still to get here, but of our will or intention—whether to get a drink, . . . or to paint a picture or a house, or to take a holiday, or to create an export sales network, or to preach a sermon, or to land a man on the moon. (p. 63)

The remaining problem is to traverse the *path* which has been planned toward the attainment of the goal object, overcoming such *obstacles*—expected or unexpected—as may appear on the way, until the goal object is created or otherwise obtained, . . . or else it is abandoned and failure is experienced. (p. 113)

Temporal direction, then—the directionality from past to present to future— is nothing more nor less than the fusion of experience, of anticipation, of need and perception, and of memory, into a single force field in action toward an intended, desired, or willed goal. It is the sensing of the goal-directedness of our personal endeavors and behavior. (p. 63)

Forecasts

Of course, once having a plan, a path for attaining the goal, the decision maker must be able to determine whether that plan is working. That is, will continuing down the path eventually result in goal attainment? This involves forecasting the outcome of implementing the plan. A forecast is the result of projecting the future in light of the interventions that are anticipated in the plan. The forecast includes future events that are not under the decision maker's control as well as those that are—or at least appear to be. The result is a meld of both an external focus upon the unfolding future and an internal focus upon how the plan will influence that future in the service of progress toward goal attainment. It is by comparing the forecasted future with the desired future, the trajectory image, that the decision maker can assess the feasibility of candidate plans and, when those plans are adopted and implemented, their progress toward their goals. Once they are implemented, plans' satisfactory progress permits retention of the status quo (i.e. the plans on the strategic image and the goals on the trajectory image). Unsatisfactory progress requires replacement of failing plans or abandonment of unachievable goals.

Forecasting requires the ability to construct possible futures. Leslie (1987) has traced the development in childhood of the ability to pretend and to recognize when others are pretending. From the age of two years onward, pretend-like is recognized as different from reality. We would argue that this ability to discriminate the difference between what is pretend-like and what is real forms the basis for play, fantasy, imagination, the understanding of metaphor and analogy, *and* the ability to construct possible futures. With Sloan (1983), we suggest that this ability to construct possible futures is a central feature in decision making.

Forecasting the future usually consists of extrapolating the past and present to construct a plausible story about the future in which the decision maker is an active participant—a pretend-like, active, version of the story that constitutes the frame of the context. That is, the story is similar to the stories that Pennington and Hastie (1986, 1988) observed in jury decisions— except that their jurors' stories were constructed backward in time to permit inferences about how a subsequent event, the crime, took place. People's ability to construct extrapolating stories is easily demonstrated; interrupt someone who is reading a novel and ask them to describe what the characters will do and how the book will end. Or, read the beginning of a short-story to a subject and ask him or her to finish it. In neither case will the subjects have difficulty, although they may hedge a bit because they know that authors make stories interesting by springing surprises along the way. The point is, however, once one has grasped a fictional plot, one can make plausible forecasts about how the characters will behave, how the plot will develop, and about a reasonable denouement.

Let us consider how forecasts might be generated. In the decision literature, the stories that are constructed about events in order to forecast the future are called scenarios (Jungermann, 1985). Most discussions of scenarios focus on their use in goal adoption and planning. However, they are equally important in forecasting what will happen if adopted goals are pursued using existing plans—especially because scenarios are simulations of the future that can be modified in light of feedback as implementation of plans progresses.

Jungermann and Thüring (1987) presented a four-step model of cognitive scenario construction. In the first step the frame within which the decision maker is working, and the goal that is of interest within that frame, evoke relevant knowledge from memory. 'Relevant' means knowledge that permits inferences of if–then propositions, usually knowledge of causes or conditionalities.

In the second step, the if–then propositions are used to construct a mental model, which can be thought of as a causal network of propositions (Thüring and Jungermann, 1986). Construction uses both the known causal relationships that have been retrieved from memory, and inferred causal relationships. The latter rely upon four 'cues to causality' (Einhorn and Hogarth, 1982, 1986, 1987): covariation of events, their temporal order, their spacial and temporal contiguity, and their similarity—to which we would add a fifth, the intention (plan) to cause (or prevent) events to occur.

In the third step the mental model is 'run' by assigning plausible values to its various component propositions. Each unique set of values constitutes a scenario. Not all possible sets are admissible because the causal relations impose severe constraints.

In the fourth step, running the model produces a forecast. This is, in effect, an answer to the question: 'What if x were the case?' The x in the question is a scenario—a set of plausible starting conditions for the component propositions that make up the causal model. Assigning these starting conditions results in generation of the logical progression—given the model and given the starting conditions—that is the forecast. That is, the scenario yields a forecast about both the endpoint of the logic and about the propositional chain that leads to it. Moreover, if a different scenario (different starting conditions) is imposed upon the model, the resulting forecast can be compared with the earlier forecast, thus making it possible to select among scenarios, which makes it possible to select among the plans that are embedded in those scenarios.

To adapt the Jungermann and Thüring analysis to progress decisions, we first assume that the starting conditions assigned to the causal model's component propositions are dictated by the plan that is being implemented in pursuit of a specific goal. That is, the plan dictates the scenario that is run through the model. If the endpoint of the resulting forecast is compatible with the goal on the trajectory image, and if the endpoint and the chain of intervening events are compatible with the principles on the value image and the other plans on the strategic image, progress is assumed to be being made, and the plan-in-progress is retained. If incompatibilities are detected, the plan must either be modified or be rejected and another sought to replace it.

Evaluation of a candidate plan to replace a rejected plan, and evaluation of a wholly new candidate plan for a new goal, both proceed in the same way. The replacement plan, or the new plan, dictates the starting conditions for the model's component propositions and a forecast is generated. Again, the compatibility of this forecast with the various images is evaluated, where compatibility with the goal means forecasting its achievement. Sufficient compatibility leads to adoption of the candidate plan, and insufficient compatibility leads to rejection and a search for a replacement. If, after repeated attempts, no plan can be found that does not generate incompatible forecasts, the decision maker must re-evaluate the goal for which a plan is being sought. A goal for which there is apparently no acceptable plan will be deleted from the trajectory image. If the deleted goal was generated by principles that dictate that it be replaced, a new candidate goal will be considered for adoption; otherwise the decision maker will simply move on.

Precisely how a plan's scenario fails to forecast the goal can be diagnosed by varying the different components of the scenario until the forecast includes the goal. Then the plan can be revised to incorporate the variations that produce a successful forecast. Although there is not much research on this process, it is possible that decision makers are not very good at spotting promising variations for scenarios. Kahneman and Tversky (1982c) point out that scenarios can be varied by additions or deletions of causal links, or by merely altering values of the components of the scenario. Their research found that deletions were the most common revisions and alterations were least common. Wells *et al.* (1987) report that the kind of variations depended upon the circumstances, but that the first events in the scenario were most often varied. Unfortunately, these studies were done using simple descriptions of events about which the ending was known (a man leaves the office early and is killed in an accident—subjects think that if only he had left on time he might not have been killed), rather than forecasts of the future success of plans to achieve goals.

Finally, Lewicka (1988) has suggested that linkages within decision makers' causal models represent sufficiency but not necessity. Forecasts generated by such models are merely plausible. That is, there is sufficient linkage to provide a path from the initial values of the scenario to plausible results, but unless those linkages are also necessary, the logic is not iron-clad. Lewicka (1988) identifies sufficiency with prediction and necessity with explanation, and observes that many of the documented shortcomings of human reasoning occur in prediction tasks (see Chapter 5). Normative models (Barclay *et al.*, 1971) require both necessity and sufficiency, but when asked to make predictions, decision makers appear to require only sufficiency.

SOURCES OF CANDIDATES FOR ADOPTION TO IMAGES

CANDIDATE PRINCIPLES

Alexander Pope (1734/1980) observed that, 'Just as the twig is bent, the tree's inclined'. What he meant, of course, was that a child's early training and experience influence his or her later views about events, life in general, and the appropriate ways in which to behave. Pope's observation is particularly pertinent to the accretion of principles to the value image. Indeed, it is fair to say that most of the fundamental principles that determine the course of adult behavior, the goals deemed worthy of pursuit and the plans deemed acceptable for pursuing them, are acquired during childhood—at one's mother's knee, as it were. Later additions to, and deletions from, the value image are as rare as they are difficult.

The early acquisition of principles, and their later effects on behavior, lies within the purview of 'developmental psychology' and 'personality'. This is not the place to review these large literatures, but a few themes are relevant to our purpose.

It is generally held that the bedrock of future cognitive functioning, attitudes, and idiosyncratic viewpoints about the self and the world is laid down during childhood. Kohlberg's (1969) theory of moral development is one account of how this might happen. Freud's (1933) theory of personality development is another. All such theories see development as a series of cumulative stages in which earlier development is built upon by later development. Part of this evolution involves the person's basic principles about how people ought to behave, about how events ought to unfold, about how the world should be organized, and about what is incumbent upon him or her to make people and events and the world conform to these principles. Thus Kohlberg (1969), for example, discusses the developing sense of what constitutes moral, principled behavior; starting with the child's deference to authority, then reciprocity, conformity, duty, social contracts, and at the most mature level, self-selected ethical principles.

The bulk of the research related to principles involves their effects on later, adult behavior. For example, Ellis (1963) describes how 'shoulds', 'oughts', and 'musts' (principles) adopted early in life can prove dysfunctional later on. These 'irrational ideas', which once may have been rational, are seen as prescriptions and proscriptions that interfere with effective coping. Examples are: one ought to be loved by or approved of by virtually every other significant person in one's community; one must be thoroughly competent, adequate, and achieving in all respects; some people are bad, wicked, or villainous and should be punished; it is catastrophic if things are not as one would have them be; if something is dangerous or fearsome, one must worry about it; one must avoid certain difficulties and responsibilities; one ought to have someone strong upon whom to depend; one should become upset over other people's problems and strive to solve them for them; there always is a right, precise, and perfect solution to every problem and it is catastrophic if this solution is not found.

These, of course, are particular examples from Ellis' clinical experience; different people adopt different principles, not all of which are dysfunctional. However, people with similar backgrounds often have sufficiently similar principles to permit the outside observer to class them together. This permits inference of cause-and-effect relationships between childhood experiences and adult principles. For instance, Black (1987) describes current thinking about the effects on people's principles of growing up in a home in which one or both parents are alcoholics. It appears that children learn to deal with events that they do not understand and to structure the chaos and unpredictability in which they find themselves. The ways in which they do this often survive in later life as a set of principles for coping with everyday events. Thus, some children, often the eldest, become exaggeratedly responsible, protecting their siblings and trying to provide some sort of stability in the home. Others become chameleons, quickly adjusting to situations and trying to remain invisible. Others become peacemakers, striving to diminish family friction by placating all sides. As adults the responsible children may come to prize control, ambition, and accomplishment, sometimes to a pathological extent. The chameleons avoid responsibility and initiative and tend to walk away from unpleasantness. The peacemakers take care of everyone else, often to their own disadvantage. All of these personality types tend to have difficulty trusting other people and forming close relationships.

Of course, these types are generalizations to which exceptions abound, but together with Ellis' (1963) analysis and similar analyses throughout the literature, it provides insight into the sources of principles.

Internal sources

The children of alcoholics are not explicitly taught that they must be responsible, adaptable, or placating. They learn it in order to survive. However, once learned these principles color what happens afterwards; they constrain the kinds of principles that can be adopted later on. Moreover, these newer principles serve to bolster the older ones by the very fact that they are compatible with them. In some sense this mutual compatibility feeds back upon itself so that, even when the early principles cause difficulties later on, they are too much entrenched to be dislodged from the value image. In 'normal' homes the same thing occurs, but the early principles tend to be more advantageous in later life, less destructive and more realistic.

External sources

Parents, teachers, peers, and the media all provide instruction about which principles are to be adopted and which are not. Actions speak louder than words, and role models are influential (Bandura, 1986), but words also are important. Children are sent to Sunday School, or something like it, for moral instruction. Preschool often appears dedicated to teaching fairness and sharing and how to get along with other people. Parents teach their versions of the social graces through example and exhortation. Cultural norms are illustrated in movies, on TV and in books—by both positive and negative examples. Indeed, it could be argued that TV dramas, especially the soap operas that dominate each weekday afternoon, are the modern morality plays, instructing their audiences through exaggerated depictions of both good and evil.

Whether abstract and subtle, or concrete and heavy-handed, these sources all provide candidate principles, and in many cases they provide fairly clear instruction about which are to be adopted and which are to be rejected (Schwartz, 1970; Schwartz and Bilsky, 1987). Only psychopaths and sociopaths fail to get the message.

CANDIDATE GOALS

Like principles, candidate goals may arise either from internal necessity and invention, or from external necessity and suggestion. Moreover, they tend to be 'packaged' either as possible goals for which a requisite action is unstated, or as possible actions for which the goal(s) is unstated.

Internal sources

Goals arise from internal necessity either as a result of imperatives of the decision maker's principles or as a result of the need for a goal to complement existing goals. In the first case, imperatives, the diagnostic sentence is 'one should—', where the blank contains some good event or good state that is dictated by the decision maker's principles. Thus, for example, a decision maker who holds strict religious principles finds certain events or states proscribed, which engenders a goal of preventing them from occurring. And, he or she finds certain events or states prescribed, which engenders a goal of making them happen. Similarly, if a worker holds the principle that 'one should do the best job one can', it will engender the goal of high-quality job performance according to his or her lights about what constitutes high quality. Or, if an organization values customer relations, that principle engenders the goal of courteous and efficient service.

Goals also arise from internal necessity because goals are not necessarily independent of one another. Non-independence arises when attainment of one goal is a precondition for attainment of another goal, or when the goals enhance each other. The existence of non-independence is what has motivated discussions of goal hierarchies in the literature, but non-independence has a more specific meaning here. True, if one wishes to do so, the targets of the tactics can be viewed as subgoals for the plans, and the goals of short-term plans can be viewed as contributing to the goals of longer-term plans, etc., thus on up through some hierarchy. But, at the level of the trajectory image, the non-independence that engenders new goals is non-independence among similar-level entities. Thus, for example, a decision maker may have the goal of being a parent and also have the goal of being married, and may regard achievement of the former as contingent upon achievement of the latter. This does not mean, however, that being married is in any sense subordinate to being a parent. The two goals may have equal status even though the contingency is not symmetrical. So, if the parenthood goal were adopted, it might well engender the marriage goal if it did not already exist—both because of the necessity for a mate to facilitate achievement of parenthood, and, if the decision maker's principles make marriage a desirable state in itself as well as a necessary state for parenthood, because his or her principles require it. The point is that existing goals can give rise to new candidates for adoption as goals, and although the old and new goals may be linked, the new one need not be subordinate to the other in the manner implied by the notation of a goal hierarchy.

Goals can also arise from internal invention, both from spontaneous creativity and from opportunities that arise during plan formulation and implementation. We do not have much to say about creativity, if only because, for all that is written about it, creativity is not generally well understood. Suffice it to say that new goal candidates sometimes appear to spring from some internal recesses rather than from necessity or from external sources, but it is something of a mystery how it happens.

Opportunity is not much better understood than creativity as a source of goals, but is a good deal less mysterious. Mintzberg (1987) argues that the usual notion of planning as rational analysis leading to clear, explicit instructions for reaching a well-defined goal simply does not fit the facts. He argues that plans (which he calls strategies) often feel their way along, being clearer after the fact than before. He uses the metaphor of a potter working with clay:

> She knows exactly what has and has not worked for her in the past. She has an intimate knowledge of her work, her capabilities, and her markets. As a craftsman, she senses rather than analyzes these things; her knowledge is 'tacit'. All these things are working in her mind as her hands are working in clay. The product that emerges on the wheel is likely to be in the tradition of her past work, but she may break away and embark on a new direction. Even so, the past is no less present, projecting itself into the future. (p. 66)

Mintzberg goes on to discuss the emergence of goals as plans crystalize—how plans can *form* as well as be formulated. Indeed, he suggests that all planning is a mix of deliberate formulation and emergent form, and that neither alone would work well; the former is too rigid and the latter precludes control. But, the mix permits control and direction, as well as the freedom to seize upon unexpected turns of events and errors, what Köhler (1925) called 'happy accidents', and to use these opportunities to create new goals. Indeed, both the goal and the plan may be as much *found* as they are formulated, often emerging in the course of what the decision maker is doing (also see Beach and Wise (1980)).

Interestingly, Mintzberg notes that managing plans and their implementation consists mostly of managing stability rather than imposing change. If the status quo is working, if goals appear to be being achieved, change for its own sake is disruptive. The trick is to know when to change—when the status quo is no longer adequate or when plan implementation gives rise to an opportunity that should be adopted as a new goal, either in addition to or in place of the current goal.

External sources

The second way that goals arise is from external necessity and suggestion. External necessity means that problems arise in the external world that require solution, or that solutions (goals and plans) that are being pursued prove not to be viable. This is the starting point for most classical and organizational analyses of decision making—the external world is not as one would have it be, which provides the motivation for making a decision that will put things right. Although this is in fact merely one way in which goals arise, the role of unsatisfactory states of the external world in instigating decision making is quite significant. This is true if only because the definition of 'unsatisfactory' is that the external world is blocking the success of plans in attaining goals that are, ultimately, in the service of principles about how things *ought* to be. When progress decisions reveal that the status quo is not working, the decision maker moves to revise his or her images—to adopt new plans and goals—in order to keep things on an even keel. It is often the failure of the status quo that reveals changes in the external world.

Goals arising from external suggestion are also commonplace. Some of these are explicitly offered by other persons or by institutions as solutions to a problematic world. Others are offered simply as options—often passively received (as in the case of advertisements), but sometimes sought as advice. One must not underestimate the large part played by external suggestion— for example, role models are role models because they provide such suggestions, even when they do not mean to (as in 'setting a bad example'). Indeed, in much of our present discussion we talk as though candidate goals and plans arise as the result of external suggestion because it is such a commonplace occurrence and because it simplifies presentation owing to its familiarity.

In 1968, Locke presented a theory of goal setting and performance motivation. In the intervening 20 years a large body of research has examined the theory's primary theme: whether job performance is influenced by the adoption of a specific goal and what conditions promote adoption of the goal. Lee *et al.* (in press) have reviewed this work and have reached three major conclusions.

First, it appears to make little difference for performance whether the employee participates in setting the goal (internal) or if it is set by the supervisor (external) as long as the supervisor has legitimate authority, peer and group pressure favors pursuing the goal, the employee expects increased effort to lead to goal attainment, and both extrinsic and intrinsic rewards encourage goal attainment.

Second, performance is better when attaining the goal is difficult and when the goal is specifically defined. Thus, producing 60 widgets per hour is more difficult than producing 30, and setting the goal at 60 is more specific than merely telling the employee to do his or her best.

Third, as might well be expected, the key to all the other findings is whether the employee adopts the goal (i.e. accepts the goal and commits to attaining it). Indeed, when the employee rejects a goal but his or her job requires that it be pursued anyway, there is a negative correlation between its difficulty and the employee's performance (Erez and Zidon, 1984).

Because jobs consume so much of the average person's time, externally set goals turn out to be a major source of candidates for goal adoption. However, many other goals come from other external authorities like parents, teachers, and bureaucracies (building codes, licensing requirements, contractual obligations, etc.). Therefore, while the results of goal setting research are pertinent to image theory, we look forward to research in a broader range of contexts than just jobs.

Goal packaging

Goal candidates come packaged in three ways:

(1)   The goal is packaged alone, without a plan for achieving it.
(2)   The goal is unstated but implicit in a plan.
(3)   The goal is explicitly stated together with a plan for achieving it.

First, goals sometimes are suggested with only a minimum of accompanying information about how they might be achieved; for example, the goal of being married as contrasted with the goal of marrying a specific person. In the course of evaluating the candidate goal for adoption a rough plan may evolve (there is little reason for evolving a detailed plan if the goal may yet be rejected). If the goal clears the screening process and is adopted, it is not secure in its adoption unless a convincing plan for its attainment can also be adopted. This plan may not be all that detailed, but it must be promising enough to get through the progress decision's screening process—the forecast of its success must be sufficiently convincing to permit it to be adopted. Adoption of a plan temporarily assures security of its adopted goal. If a seemingly acceptable plan has been found, the goal can be deemed attainable, at least until events prove otherwise. However that may be, the point is that frequently the goal is itself the focus of the suggestion and the plan comes afterwards.

Second, goals also may be packaged implicitly in what otherwise looks like a suggested plan. If friends propose that you go with them to the circus, it is probably not the *going* that is important so much as it is the implicit goal of sharing an amusing evening with them. Sometimes it is difficult for an observer to discern the implicit goal in suggested plans, but the decision maker usually understands it, or, if not, he or she asks *why* the suggested plan should be adopted and implemented.

Third, goals may be suggested explicitly as part of a coordinated program ready for adoption and implementation. For example, high-school students are often urged both by parents and by teachers to go to college, and they may be carefully coached on how to achieve this goal. Schools in which the principle is 'prepare students for college' may start planning meetings for parents and students early in the freshman year. The meetings are but the beginning of step-by-step instruction that makes applying to college likely and that helps ensure achievement of the goal of acceptance.

CANDIDATE PLANS

As we have seen, plan adoption and goal adoption are intertwined. A goal may give rise to a plan, but unless the forecast for that plan offers promise of goal attainment, the plan will be rejected. If repeated attempts to find a new plan, either by modifying the old one or by considering totally new ones, prove to be unsuccessful, the goal will be rejected. In the course of the search, the goal may well be modified quite as much as the plan, thus changing the original goal–plan enterprise considerably. However, this complexity makes the discussion rather cumbersome, so for the sake of presentation we will talk as though a definite goal has been adopted and the task now is to find a plan for attaining it.

Candidate plans arise from internal sources: policies from past encounters with similar situations, utilization of existing skills to form new plans. They also arise from external sources: instruction from an external source, opportunism and happy accidents.

Internal sources

The first internal source, policies from past encounters with the current context, has already been discussed so we need not say much more here. However, it is important to note that the use of policies is not wholly automatic. If the policy consists of only a couple of simple tactics, it may be applied without much thought. But, if it is much more complex than that, it will be treated like any other candidate plan and used to generate a forecast for a progress decision. If the forecast is compatible with the decision maker's goal agenda, the trajectory image, and his or her value and strategic images, the policy will be implemented. If not, it will be rejected and another plan must be found that will offer greater promise of goal attainment.

The second internal source of plans is the repertory of skills that were discussed above. This repertory is something like a do-it-yourself store: some of the contents are preassembled and others are the basic parts that can be used to build new assemblages from scratch or used to link the preassembled parts. Everything in the store is defined by what it will do (i.e. the tactics that can be enacted by using it) and how it links with other parts. The plan is the blueprint that the decision maker uses when considering what parts to use and how to link them. Implementation of the plan consists of assembling the parts and actually using them in order to proceed toward goal attainment. Of course, not all of the parts have to be in place beforehand; it is possible to put successive parts in place as they are needed. This just-in-time procedure means that the plan remains flexible; it can generally follow the blueprint, but changes can be made if a part fails or if the unexpected is encountered. Mintzberg (1987) favored a potter as his metaphor, but we favor a do-it-yourself plumber who knows generally what is to be accomplished and how, but who must proceed one step at a time, selecting the next step in light of the success of the preceding step.

External sources

The first external source of plans is instruction by some external source, either as a role model or as a supplier of precise step-by-step instructions. Sometimes what is learned from the model or the instructions is applicable to only the goal at hand; for example, the instructions for assembling a complicated machine or children's toy. More often, what is learned adds to the decision maker's repertory and can be used for future planning. For example, after you have laboured through the tutorial for a new word processing program you have acquired some fairly complete plan components, such as how to move text. In addition, you have learned some smaller component skills that later can be molded into more complete components and into complete plans, such as how to write a book using the word processor.

Another form of instruction is advice from friends, often people who have sought a goal similar to the one the decision maker is pursuing or who are 'older and wiser'. Witness the amount of time decision makers spend asking for advice, sometimes even heeding it. If one believed the soap operas, an astonishingly large part of the average person's day is spent asking for advice; and even if this is not true, it is still clear that advice is a major source of instruction.

The second external source of plans is that suggested by Mintzberg (1987) and his potter metaphor (and by our do-it-yourself metaphor). Just as new goals may emerge as plans are formulated and implemented, so too may new plans emerge as things progress. An unanticipated way of accomplishing some part of the plan may become apparent, short-cuts may be discovered, happy accidents may occur that give insight to better ways of pursuing the goal, or a wholly new approach may become clear, especially if the old plan falters. Opportunity is an important side-benefit of plan implementation, both at the tactical level where local conditions require one to seize on opportunities in order to make progress, and at the blueprint level, where errors, mishaps, and unforeseen changes in the world offer both the specter of failure and new possibilities for success.

SUMMARY

In this chapter we have reviewed various definitions of images, particularly images as schemata for decision making. This led to consideration of frames as domain-specific knowledge partitions that give meaning to contexts. Frames are composed of those constituents of the value, trajectory, and strategic images that are pertinent to the context of interest.

Next, the discussion turned to each of image theory's three images and their respective constituents, linking the image theory view to other theories and the empirical literature.

Finally, the origins of candidate principles, goals and plans were discussed with attention given to both internal and external sources, again linking the discussion to the theoretical and empirical literature.

3 Framing and Deliberation

This chapter has two purposes. The first is to describe the mechanism and implications of decision framing. The second is to describe decision deliberation. Framing sets the scene for decision making by defining what the decision is about and delineating the issues that have bearing on it. Deliberation is the cognitive processing that goes on during decision making. It occurs within the frame to clarify the decision and the issues, to conceive of options and consider their implications, and to reach a decision.

DECISION FRAMING

To a remarkable degree, behavior is tailored specifically to each one of the vast variety of contexts in which it takes place. However, unless we are to construct a theory for every context, we must assume that the psychological mechanisms that generate these different behaviors are limited in number. Therefore, we begin with the assumption that the mechanisms of decision making are limited to those described by image theory, and that the varied results of their application are a consequence of their sensitivity to the characteristics of the contexts in which they are applied. It follows, then, that the decision maker must assess those contextual characteristics before applying the mechanisms that generate decisions. This is called framing.

To place things in perspective, the concept of framing has roots in two very different lines of inquiry. The sociological and social psychological line begins with the work of Bateson (1972) and Goffman (1974), and is reflected in script theory (Abelson, 1976) and other social schema theories. The cognitive psychological and behavioral decision line begins with the computer simulation work of Minsky (1968), and is reflected in artificial intelligence and expert systems research (Dinsmore, 1987; Fauconnier, 1985) and in prospect theory (Kahneman and Tversky, 1979). Unfortunately, neither of these lines is itself sufficient for the present purpose. The social definition of framing is very broad, encompassing the actor's perception of both the social context and its social demands. The cognitive definition is very narrow, concentrating on the ways in which specific characteristics of problems influence how they are interpreted by the problem solver and determine the means by which he or she attempts to solve them. The present definition acknowledges this entire spectrum of meaning for framing, but its focus is somewhere in the middle—on the framing of contexts that are more circumscribed than the social definitions admit and less circumscribed than the cognitive definition admit.

Imagine a decision maker arriving upon the scene with a store of knowledge about what has led up to it, what is going on and why, and what his or her role is to be in the proceedings: the scene is called a *context* (Beach *et al.*, in press).

We assume that the context has features, some of which derive from the knowledge the decision maker brings to it and some of which are unique to the moment. These features are the cues the decision maker uses to frame the context.

FRAMES

Building upon an old theory of recognition memory (Beach, 1964) as well as a new one (Hintzman, 1986) we assume that the features of the context are used by the decision maker to probe his or her memory. If the probe locates a contextual memory that has features which are virtually the same as those of the current context, the latter is said to be *recognized*. If the probe locates contextual memories that merely resemble those of the current context, these memories and all that is associated with them constitute an *ad hoc* definition of the present context, which is said to be *identified*. The difference between recognition and identification is a matter of specificity; both permit the decision maker to use existing knowledge from memory to understand the current situation and to act accordingly.

The nature of frames

A frame is that portion of his or her store of knowledge that the decision maker brings to bear on a particular context in order to endow that context with meaning. This definition derives from the theories of knowledge representation in cognitive science that were described in Chapter 2 (Dinsmore, 1987; Fauconnier, 1985; Schoenfeld, 1983). Recall that, for intelligent systems, the overall store of information is divided into partitions and each partition is keyed to an environmental context (domain). The meaning of a context is specified by the knowledge in its particular partition. The memory probe mechanism described above is image theory's way of accessing the appropriate knowledge partition (frame) for a given context.

Wagenaar and Keren (1986) provide an example of what follows from framing contexts in either one way or another. They instructed half of a group of subjects to frame a problem from the viewpoint of a public official and the other half of the group to frame the problem from the viewpoint of a parent. The problem was to decide whether children must wear seatbelts when traveling in an automobile. The impact of different kinds of information on the two groups' decisions, as well as the final decisions themselves, was considerably different under the two different frames.

In the same vein, Anderson and Pichert (1978) had subjects read a story and led them to frame it either as a burglar would or as a prospective homeowner would. The two different frames had a marked effect on the details of the story that were recalled. Similarly, Staw (1975) had subjects participate in groups that received bogus high-performance feedback or low-performance feedback. Then he asked the group members about the characteristics of their groups. There was a distinct 'halo effect', in that high-performance feedback led to more positive descriptions of group cohesiveness, communications, and openness than did low-performance feedback— even though actual performance was much the same. This suggests that the way in which the group members framed the situation led them to infer that high performance could occur only if the groups had certain characteristics; thus if the group performed well it must have had those characteristics. In the same way, Phillips and Lord (1982) and others have found that frames can lead observers of group interactions to recall details that are consistent with the frames but that were not actually present during the interaction. In short, the frames that are imposed upon a context have powerful consequences for the decision maker's reasoning about that context.

Perhaps the best known work on framing effects in decision making is by Tversky and Kahneman (1981). In one of their experiments two groups of students were given the cover story that is reproduced below. Then one group was given Form 1 of a problem based on the story and asked to make a choice, and the other group was given Form 2 and asked to choose.

The cover story was: Imagine that the US is preparing for the outbreak of an unusual Asian disease, which is expected to kill 600 people. Two alternative programs to combat the disease have been proposed. Assume that the exact scientific estimate of the consequences of the programs are as follows:

- Form 1—If program A is adopted, 200 people will be saved. If program B is adopted, there is 1/3 probability that 600 people will be saved, and 2/3 probability that no people will be saved.
- Form 2—If program C is adopted 400 people will die. If program D is adopted there is 1/3 probability that nobody will die, and 2/3 probability that 600 people will die.

In fact, all four programs (A, B, C, and D) have the same expected value. Classical decision theory would predict indifference between the two options in both of the two forms of the problems. However, that was not the result. Instead, 72% of the people in group 1 chose program A and 78% of the people in group 2 chose Program D. The finding is interpreted as demonstrating risk aversion when the problem is framed in terms of gain and risk taking when it is framed in terms of losses.

Bazerman (1984) warned that Tversky and Kahneman's (1981) framing results may have gloomy implications for behavioral research: '. . . many accepted findings may exist more because of the way researchers frame the problem than because of the presumed impact of the construct on individual behavior' (p. 333). As we shall see in Chapter 5, results obtained by Barnes (1984) justify Bazerman's concern. Barnes found that the phrasing and subject matter of word-problems similar to those reproduced above strongly influenced the frame that participants adopted. Depending upon the frame, participants used either statistical logic or causal logic to generate answers to the problems, all of which the experimenters framed as requiring statistical logic. Barnes suggests that much of the literature that appears to demonstrate the irrationality of human judgment is due to the mismatch between the participants' frames and the experimenters' frames—and it is the experimenters who interpret the data and publish the papers.

THE FRAME AS STATUS QUO

Neither contexts nor frames are static. Once a context is framed, events continue to unfold and the frame must be updated accordingly. At each point in the context's evolution, its current frame defines the status quo. That is, the partition of relevant principles, goals, and ongoing plans that constitute the frame are the backdrop against which further contextual change is evaluated. Contextual change is of two kinds: (1) new options or alternatives arise and either are pursued or are spurned, and (2) old options expire and must be replaced by new ones. Or, in image theory terms, (1) new candidate goals or plans are encountered and evaluated for adoption, and (2) existing goals and ongoing plans are accomplished, forsaken, or made obsolete by other developments.

The standard textbook presentation of decision making begins with a short, ambiguous statement about problem detection as the motivation for decision making. Basically we have no quarrel with this, but we think that problem detection is only part of the story: it is integral to the decision process itself, not separate and prior to it, and it is much more important and interesting than the textbooks would lead one to believe. In image theory, decisions serve to change the frame appropriately as the context evolves, either as a result of plan implementation by the decision maker or as a result of outside influences. Decisions also serve to change the course of context evolution so that it in fact remains congruent with the frame (i.e. so that the status quo is maintained). In neither case is the decision maker passive.

Change

The frame, the status quo, is the anchor or baseline against which all change is evaluated. Indeed, the status quo is not usually thought of as, nor treated as, a decision alternative in the usual sense. Rather, the adoptability of candidate goals and plans is determined by assessing how well they would fit with the status quo, the present frame. This, of course, is considerably different from the conventional theoretical interpretation of the status quo as the sure-thing option in a decision dilemma (Behn and Vaupel, 1982).

Candidate goals or plans usually address only a portion of the framed status quo. As a result, the degree of change brought about by an adoption is small relative to that frame and relative to the larger images that make up the decision maker's entire knowledge store. This together with the require-ment that candidates be compatible with the principles, goals, and plans that define the frame means that there is a strong tendency for things to stay pretty much as they are, with only small accretions and deletions to the frame rather than revolutionary changes.

The conditions described thus far define what can be called 'optional change'—the status quo can be retained with minor modifications to adapt it to new opportunities and an evolving context. When changes in the context are large, or when goals are achieved or abandoned, the status quo ceases to be tenable and the decision maker is faced with 'non-optional change' (Beach and Mitchell, 1990; Beach *et al.*, 1982; Davidson and Beach, 1981; Mitchell *et al.*, 1986).

The status quo can terminate either because it comes to a natural end or because it is no longer viable in light of feedback about progress toward goals. For example, graduation from college is a natural end to the college life context; new contexts with new status quos (frames) must take its place. In contrast, repeated failure on multiple fronts may signal that the piecemeal replacement of failing plans and unattainable goals will no longer serve to maintain the status quo and that a whole new approach is needed. Perhaps the decision maker has drifted into a dead-end job, a failing relationship, or dependence on alcohol, nicotine, TV, or junk food. The decline may go unnoticed if each step has been too small to trip the alarm for implementation monitoring and progress decisions. But, perhaps a boss, friend or family member sounds an alarm. The decision maker becomes aware that the present frame no longer fits the context, or that his or her principles demand changes in either the frame or the context, or both. For example, religious conversion or Very Good Advice can completely reframe a context. Whatever causes it, the decision maker no longer sees the status quo as viable, he or she no longer regards the present frame or the present context as appropriate—intervention is in order.

Major change can occur even when the decision maker thinks he or she is merely considering optional change (i.e. when continuing with the status quo is seen as viable). Suppose that into this pastoral scene a candidate for revolutionary change intrudes. Because the status quo holds such strong sway, such candidates usually are rejected out of hand and no further consideration is given to them. Occasionally, however, especially if the context has drifted away imperceptibly from the decision maker's frame of it, a revolutionary candidate can prompt reflection about the accuracy of the frame (i.e. the adequacy of the status quo). If contextual evolution has weakened the legitimacy of the frame, the candidate may not look so revolutionary after all—it may look quite conservative in that its adoption could bring the decision maker into closer alignment with his or her own principles. For example, the decision maker may be reasonably content with his or her career when a different career opportunity arises. The first reaction is to reject the candidate because it is incompatible with the status quo. However (especially if other people do not let the matter rest with mere rejection of the opportunity) further examination of the candidate, and further examination of the status quo may reveal that the possibility of a new career creates a new definition of the current situation, a new frame for the present context. At this point, what had been seen as optional change switches to being seen as non-optional change—not unlike a figure–ground reversal in which the status quo, which usually is the ground, becomes the figure and the center of attention. When this happens the new career and the present career become competitors within the new frame, and the task becomes to choose the best of the two (using the profitability test, Chapter 6.)

Certainly it is stressful to exchange the familiar status quo for a new, different status quo, even if the latter is highly compatible with our principles. Anyone who has changed careers, or merely changed places of employment, can attest that even corrective change can be difficult. Desirable changes, like quitting smoking, adopting better health practices, marriage and leaving the single life, divorce and re-entering the single life, and the other traumatic changes we inflict upon ourselves in the name of self-improvement, usually are a mixture of pain and gain. Seldom do we adopt revolutionary changes until long after most outside observers would have pronounced them both reasonable and necessary. We much prefer to stay with the familiar but not-quite-right status quo and hope that it somehow will get better. Or, we modify the ailing status quo in small, slow steps that frequently do not quite get the job done, which leaves us in vague disquietude, but which allows us to stay on an even keel and avoid the pain of change.

Primacy of the status quo

Samuelson and Zeckhauser (1988) experimentally examined non-optional and optional decisions and the tendency in the latter case to maintain the status quo. They presented a total of 486 business school students with questionnaires containing various versions of six decision problems. Each problem had two, three or four alternatives (candidates) and was presented in either of two basic forms. In one form change was non-optional—it was inevitable and the question was which alternative future was the best. In the other form change was optional—one of the alternatives was identified by the experimenters as the status quo and the others were alternatives to it. For the latter form the question for the participant was whether to remain with the status quo or to replace it with one of the alternatives. (Note that no participant got both forms of any one question, and in the optional change form, what was designated as the status quo was counterbalanced among the various alternatives across participants.)

All together there were 66 versions of the problems. For non-optional decisions, the percentage of participants electing each of the alternatives was about equal for all alternatives. For optional decisions, for 90% of the problems the alternative that was identified as the status quo was retained by a larger percentage of the participants than when the same alternative was not identified as the status quo. In short, there was a clear tendency to retain the status quo merely because it was the status quo. But, the tendency was not strong (the trend was strong but statistical significance was obtained for only 38% of the problems), perhaps because the status quo was given by fiat by the experimenters rather than evolving naturally in the participants' experience. A follow-up experiment in which the status quo was more meaningfully identified produced mixed results but supported the tendency to remain with the status quo, even when the alternative was more attractive.

Silver (1989) also examined the effects of designating one or another decision alternative as the status quo on subsequent decisions about the alternative. The vehicle was the Bazerman and Neale (1983) counterpart of the Tversky and Kahneman (1981) framing problem that was presented above. The cover story for this problem is: A large car manufacturer has recently been hit with a number of economic difficulties and it appears as if three plants need to be closed and 6000 employees laid off. The vice-president of production has been exploring alternative ways to avoid this crisis. She has developed two plans:

- Form 1—Plan A will save one of the three plants and 2000 jobs. Plan B has a 1/3 probability of saving all three plants and all 6000 jobs, but has a 2/3 probability of saving no plants and no jobs.
- Form 2—Plan A will result in the loss of two of the three plants and 4000 jobs. Plan B has a 2/3 probability of resulting in the loss of all three plants and all 6000 jobs, but has a 1/3 probability of losing no plants and no jobs.

Bazerman and Neale report that roughly 80% of the participants who were given Form 1 selected plan A, which is comparable to Tversky and Kahneman's figure of 78% for the gain condition of this experiment. Bazerman and Neale also found that only about 20% of the participants who were given Form 2 selected plan A, which is comparable to Tversky and Kahneman's 28%. Silver, using introductory psychology students, found 70% of the participants to whom he gave Form 1 selected plan A, which reflects the risk aversion that was found in the earlier studies. However, Silver found that 55% of the participants to whom he gave Form 2 selected plan A, which does not reflect the risk taking that was found in the other studies. These results for Form 2 are, however, highly similar to those (56% and 42%) reported by Fagley and Miller (1987) in two experiments. Fagley and Miller, like Bazerman and Neale and Silver, used a variant of the Tversky and Kahneman task. (Fagley and Miller's and Silver's failure to replicate Tversky and Kahneman's and Bazerman and Neale's results for the loss condition cannot but raise a question about the generality of the reflection component of prospect theory (Kahneman and Tversky, 1979).)

Be that as it may, the next manipulation is the one of interest here. In light of the Samuelson and Zeckhauser (1988) results, Silver reasoned that it should be possible to demonstrate the robustness of the status quo by pitting it against the effects of framing problems as gains or losses. To this end, Silver simply inserted the sentence 'The manufacturer has used this plan on similar occasions in the past' in front of the description of *either* plan A *or* plan B in Form 1 and Form 2. This resulted in two altered versions of Form 1, one in which plan A is designated as the status quo and one in which plan B is designated as the status quo, and two similarly altered versions of Form 2.

The expectation was that relative to the unaltered forms of the questions, when plan A was designated the status quo, there should be a strong tendency on the part of the participants to select it no matter whether the problem is in terms of gains or losses, and when plan B was designated the status quo there should be a strong tendency to select it. In short, the status quo should tend to be selected merely because it is the status quo.

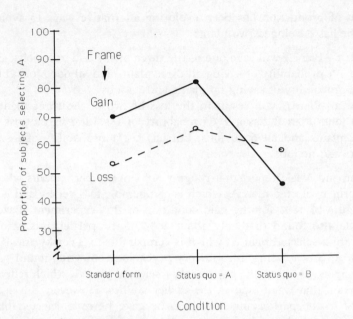

Figure 3.1   Results of the study by Silver (1989) which pitted the status quo against the effects of framing—gains and losses—on choice. Reproduced from an unpublished manuscript by permission of the author

Figure 3.1 shows the results. The graphs show the percentages of participants selecting plan A when the status quo was not designated (the 'neutral' phrasing given above), when plan A was designated the status quo, and when plan B was designated the status quo; the curve on the top is for Form 1 ('gain') and the curve on the bottom is for Form 2 ('loss'). For gains the results clearly support Silver's view—when it was designated the status quo, plan A was selected more than when it was neutral, and less when plan B was designated the status quo. For losses the same general pattern was found; but because the risk seeking result was not found in the first place (risk aversion dominates for all versions) the results are not as dramatic. In short, merely labeling one of the two alternatives as the status quo influenced the choice that was made. Moreover, for gains (Form 1) the effect of labeling an alternative as the status quo was as large or larger than the risk aversion effect about which so much has been made in the literature on framing of gambles.

Kahneman and Tversky (1982b) gave people the following vignette and asked which decision maker would feel the greatest regret about the negative outcome of his decision. Note that in the first paragraph the negative outcome occurs in the context of the decision maker having stayed with the status quo. In the second paragraph it occurs in the context of the decision maker having changed from the status quo to another course. In both cases, however, the negative outcome, the failure to realize a gain, is the same dollar amount.

- Paul owns shares in company A. During the past year he considered switching to stock in company B, but he decided against it. He now finds that he would have been better off by $1200 if he had switched to the stock of company B.
- George owned shares in company B. During the past year he switched to stock in company A. He now finds that he would have been better off by $1200 if he had kept his stock in company B.

Kahneman and Tversky report that most people think that the decision maker in the second paragraph, the decision maker who departed from the status quo, would feel the greatest amount of regret.

Landman (1987) expanded upon Kahneman and Tversky's (1982b) study by using three different vignettes and using both positive and negative outcomes (i.e. both realization of a gain and failure to realize a gain). She found that both judged-regret and judged-joy were greater for the condition in which the person in the vignette changed from the status quo than for the condition in which the status quo was maintained. These results suggest that people see both having good things happen and missing out on good things in the course of the status quo as simply part of the ongoing process, while similar events following change have something to say about (good or bad) luck, judgment, decision making ability or the like. However that may be, the point is that, like the results discussed above, these results underscore the unique status of the status quo—the events that comprise it are viewed differently from the events that comprise the alternatives to it.

Reframing

Contextual evolution requires the frame to be changed. Often the necessity is signaled by the failure of some action that is predicated upon the inadequate frame. As Christensen-Szalanski (1978) has pointed out, decision makers want to make the correct decision (decision theorists want them to make the decision correctly, which is quite a different matter): the essence of decision making is the effort to do the right thing, it has no other purpose. Failure to be correct can be quite jarring and usually prompts questioning about what went wrong. Subsequent investigation often reveals that the context was *misframed*; the context was incorrectly recognized or identified, or relevant knowledge was not included in the frame, or the context had changed so that the frame was no longer appropriate.

Misframing is revealed in statements like 'I misunderstood what was going on' or 'It didn't occur to me until later that I was overlooking the ethical aspects of it all' or 'I just thought we'd handle it the way we always have before, but I didn't realize how much things have changed since last time'. Such retrospective comments usually are accompanied by embarrassment and, sometimes, anger. For example, once when I was delivering my daily introductory psychology lecture, a young man entered at the back of the auditorium. He listened for a few minutes, raised his hand, was called upon, and then blisteringly denounced the proceedings as trivial and beside the point. At the end of his outburst, he stormed from the hall leaving everyone in stunned silence. Later in the term, a student who knew him explained that the intruder was acutely embarrassed by what had happened. It seems that he had mistakenly arrived at the lecture hall an hour early for what he expected to be a meeting of the American Civil Liberties Union. He was perplexed and outraged by the speaker's choice of topic (affectional systems in primates), and it was only after he had departed that it dawned on him what had happened (i.e. that he had misframed the context). Apparently, he lived in fear of being recognized on campus by somebody from the class.

Failure to include all relevant ethical knowledge is a common result of misframing. When the focus is on the concrete features of the context, and when ethical considerations have not played a major role in past encounters with this or similar contexts, the increased importance of ethics in *this* encounter may be underappreciated. Then, when the repercussions are felt somewhere down the line, it is often too late to repair the damage. For example, insider information may look much like other, lawful information in an investment-decision context, but having failed to recognize the danger of using it is not generally regarded as a mitigating legal defense.

Reframing is but one way to deal with incongruity between the frame and the context. A second way is to act upon the context to bring it back into line with the frame. This in turn can be done in either of two ways—use of existing policies or adoption of new plans.

POLICIES

Recognition of a context is possible because it, or contexts similar to it, has been encountered by the decision maker in the past. In many cases the encounter required the decision maker to take some sort of action in order to keep the context aligned with the frame (i.e. to maintain the status quo). This action is stored in memory along with the context and is thus available when the present context is framed. If the need arises, the action that was used before may be usable again. In the psychology of learning, these preformulated actions are called *habits*. In social psychology they are called *scripts*. In organizational science they are called *policies*; we have adopted the latter term.

Policies tend to be evoked automatically when a context is recognized, and this automaticity, while not completely blind, is complemented by a tendency toward inflexible implementation, at least until difficulties arise. In contrast, policies are unlikely to be evoked when the context is merely identified. That is, if the particular context has not been encountered before, and therefore is merely identified as being similar to some that have (Hintzman, 1986), the decision maker resists automatic application of a policy associated with any one of the similar contexts, if only because it is unclear which one to use. Instead, it is more prudent to think things through and to devise a new plan.

Actually, policies are seldom blindly followed; they are tempered by recent knowledge and current conditions. Similarly, new plans are seldom wholly new; they are a synthesis of policies that have worked in similar contexts in the past, the advice and example of other people and organizations, and the decision maker's creative efforts. Moreover, a policy may well be inappropriate for bringing the present context into alignment with the current frame. The appropriateness of the policy, which is a plan, must be reassessed at the slightest sign of resistance or failure. That is, if initial attempts to implement the policy do not produce progress toward the goal of maintaining the status quo, the policy must be abandoned and a new plan must be adopted in its place.

Plan adoption

In the absence of a usable policy for maintaining the status quo, the decision maker must adopt a new plan that offers success. This is done by drawing upon the advice of other people and upon the decision maker's repertory of tactics (the do-it-yourself shop mentioned in Chapter 2) to formulate a plan, to create a forecast of the plan's potential effects, and to evaluate the compatibility of these effects with the goal of maintaining the status quo. The mechanism for doing this is the compatability test (Chapters 1, 4, and 5) coupled with the progress decision process (Chapters 1 and 8)—where the progress is hypothetical and in the form of a forecast.

In some cases more than one candidate plan may emerge from this process, particularly if other people offer differing advice. When this happens, the choice among plans that all offer the promise of acceptable progress is made using the profitability test (Chapters 1, 6, and 7).

FRAMING, BY ANY OTHER NAME . . .

As was mentioned above, the concept of framing comes from various lines of inquiry, of which two are most easily recognized because they actually use the word 'frame'. The first of these is social psychology (Bateson, 1972; Goffman, 1974) and the second is cognitive psychology (Minsky, 1968; Tversky and Kahneman, 1981). However, under other labels, framing has played an important role in other areas. We will briefly point out some of these areas in order to illustrate the ubiquity of the concept.

Learning

In the area of learning, stimulus generalization and response generalization, which are well documented even though they are not much in fashion today, are simply older terms for framing and policy. When a rat or a person recognizes a familiar task, the commonly observed response is to do what has proved successful in that situation in the past. If the exact situation has never been encountered before but is identifiable as similar to some that have, the common response is to behave in much the way that worked in those similar situations. In short, if the present context can be recognized or identified, past experience can be brought to bear on dealing with it, sometimes in the form of a policy from the past and sometimes in the form of a new behavior that is built on policies from similar situations.

Problem solving

In the area of problem solving, 'set' is a contextually linked predisposition to use a particular frame. In his classic water-jar experiment, Luchins (1942) presented participants with a series of problems of the sort: 'If you had three empty jars that hold 21, 127, and 3 quarts respectively, how might you measure 100 quarts of water'. The easily discovered algorithm is to fill the second, the largest, jar and then take out 21 quarts using the first jar and six more quarts using the third jar twice. After the participants successfully solve several such problems using this algorithm, thay are given a problem with jars that hold 23, 49 and 3 quarts, and asked to measure 20 quarts. The majority of participants used their tried and true algorithm (policy), which worked—but a simpler method is to fill the 23 quart jar and then remove 3 quarts with the third jar. Other participants, who were presented this last problem first, could not recognize it as a problem for which a successful policy was available because they had never done the problems before; they used the simpler method. Thus, when the situation is recognized, the tendency (set) is to use a successful policy from the past to deal with it. When the situation is only identified (as a problem in an experiment), as when subjects were given the last problem first so they had no preformulated policy, the tendency is to shape the behavior to fit the unique situation.

Perception

In the area of perception, the perceptual constancies (color constancy, size constancy, etc.) also reflect framing. The constancies are necessary for keeping one's perceptual world in order. Without visual size constancy, for instance, every time an object approached the viewer, the increase in the size of its image on the viewer's retinas would be interpreted as an increase in its actual size rather than as a decrease in how far away it is. Instead, the viewer's perceptual system works on the assumption that most objects retain a constant physical size and that changes in retinal image size signal changes in distance. If, in the contrived conditions of a psychology laboratory or a circus funhouse, this size constancy frame proves inaccurate, the viewer tends to be startled and to become disoriented. On the other hand, if the viewer expects the object's size to increase, as when a balloon is inflated, the situation is framed accordingly, the size constancy frame is suspended, and the change in retinal size is regarded as normal. The point is, framing is fundamental to interpretation of what is going on in the world, from basic perceptual events to complex cognitive and social events.

CONFLICTING FRAMES

Because frames are linked to the individual decision maker's past experience, different decision makers may have quite dissimilar frames for the same context. An example of this was provided by Dearborn and Simon (1958), who presented the participants in an executive training program with a case that was widely used in business policy courses. The executives were all with the same manufacturing company, but they represented various departments within the company. Before class discussion of the case began, the executives were asked to write a brief statement of what they considered to be the most important problem presented by the case. Analysis of the statements showed that the problems that were identified tended to be the ones that were most highly related to each executive's own department within the company.

When conflicting frames prescribe different courses of action, the result is often discord. A famous example of this is the intra-board battle that took place at US Steel over corporate investment (Symonds and Miles, 1985). Board members whose careers had been in production, the 'steelmen', stressed production and investment in modern manufacturing facilities. Members whose careers had been in financial management, the 'money men', stressed high return from investments in promising ventures, even through diversifying away from steel. The resulting infighting was widely viewed as profoundly detrimental to the firm.

Much of the social interaction that precedes group decision making is devoted to ironing out differences in the participants' frames through the sharing of information and through negotiation (Bazerman *et al.*, 1988; Walsh and Fahey, 1986; Walsh *et al.*, 1988). However, if the individuals (or the constituencies they represent) cannot meet to negotiate, or if the constituencies are too large, too unorganized, or unwilling to negotiate, or if the conflicting frames are so different in substance that compromise or accommodation are impossible, the discord may result in paralysis.

A familiar example of the effects of irreconcilable differences in frames is provided by the ongoing feud between people who favor advanced technologies like nuclear power, and people who oppose such technologies. Both sides know that the issue is about the risks introduced by the technologies, but each side frames those risks so differently that rapprochement is virtually impossible.

Conflicting frames of the latter type were clearly illustrated by two papers on risk assessment that appeared together in *Science* in 1987. The first paper, by Wilson and Crouch (1987), framed the problem from the viewpoint of engineers and physical scientists, and the second, by Slovic (1987), framed it from the viewpoint of lay people in the general population. Each tried to educate the other's constituency about its own constituency's frame for risk and risk assessment. Each probably failed to produce any reduction in the discrepancy between the frames.

Wilson and Crouch (1987) explained that risks can best be assessed by calculating accurate probabilities of injurious events using relative frequencies from data bases, combinations of these relative frequencies in event trees, and estimations of the relative frequencies from experiments on animals. They also described methods of comparing, contrasting, and communicating the magnitudes of risks that these probabilities reveal. They further pointed out:

> The results . . . of performing the risk assessment must be sharply constrasted with the cultural values assigned to the results. Such cultural values will presumably be factors influencing societal decisions and may differ even for risk estimates that are identical in probability. (p. 267)

Slovic (1987) explained that lay people's assessments of risks are determined by considerably more than just the probabilities of occurrence, no matter how the probabilities are produced:

> When experts judge risk, their responses correlate highly with technical estimates of annual fatalities. Lay people can assess annual fatalities if they are asked to (and produce estimates somewhat like the technical estimates). However, their judgments of 'risk' are related more to other hazard characteristics . . . and, as a result, tend to differ from their own (and experts') estimates of annual fatalities. (p. 283)

Slovic's (1987) analyses of Americans' judgments about hazards revealed two factors—unknown risk (unobservability, unknown to those exposed, delayed effects, newness of the risk, unknown to science) and dread risk (uncontrollability, global, fatal, inequitable, catastrophic, impact on future generations, unreducible, increasingly risky, involuntary exposure). Similar factors have been obtained for Hungarians (Englander *et al.*, 1986), Norwegians (Teigen *et al.*, 1988), and Netherlanders (Vlek and Stallen, 1981)—although there are substantial cultural, subgroup, and individual differences between and within each of these populations.

Rayner and Cantor (1987) obtained data on the differences in the ways in which Public Utility Commissions (PUCs) and anti-nuclear public interest groups (intervenors) frame the problem of the acceptability of new nuclear power reactors. In general the PUCs view the question narrowly, in terms of economic risks arising from such things as unanticipated costs in building the utility or failure of demand to grow sufficiently to warrant the new capacity. They incorporate the health and safety risks into their concern that the public will view the plant's costs as outweighting its benefits. In contrast, intervenors frame the problem almost entirely in terms of health and safety, and in terms of the inequity of one group imposing these risks on other people. PUCs' frames are narrow, involving management and technology. Intervenors' frames are broad, involving the entire question of whether nuclear technology can be managed safely at all or whether its complexity makes it inherently unmanageable—they also see the regulators as too sympathetic with the nuclear power industry and as part of the larger problem. Rayner and Cantor (1987) suggest that acceptable risk cannot be defined in terms of how small the probabilities must be to convince people that a technology is safe enough. For the most part such probabilities and the magnitudes of the effects are irrelevant: 'The critical question facing societal risk managers is not "How safe is safe enough?", but "How fair is safe enough?" ' (p. 3). The authors' research suggests that the fairness of the distribution of risks and fairness in obtaining the consent of those who must bear the brunt of adverse effects are central to public decisions about technologies.

The conclusion is that different parties to technological decisions frame the context in fundamentally different ways. Moreover, until those parties can be brought to admit the legitimacy of their opponents' frames and to negotiate a common frame, the strife that paralyzes constructive discussion in this area will continue.

DECISION DELIBERATION

Decision deliberation is the cognitive processing in which the decision maker engages after the decision is framed, as the need for intervention is assessed, as goals and plans are adopted or rejected, and as implementation is monitored and plans and goals are retained or replaced in light of progress. In short, it is what the decision maker thinks about during decision making and decision implementation.

In image theory, deliberation is represented by the compatibility test and the profitability test, which are discussed in the next four chapters. However, the tests are theoretical abstractions that, of necessity, ignore some of the richness of what actually goes on in the decision maker's head as decisions are pondered and eventually made. So, before we launch into the abstract discussion, it is appropriate to put things in perspective by discussing deliberation in somewhat less abstract terms.

SOURCES OF MATERIAL FOR DELIBERATION

The most readily available material for deliberation comes from knowledge of the decision maker's own (or others') past successes and failures with similar decisions. Not only are such lessons vivid, they often have an emotional component that makes them particularly compelling. Another source of deliberative material is the views of other people who are involved in the decision, either co-decision makers or others who have some interest in the decision. When there are differences in views about what is relevant to the decision or about what the actual decision should be, information about these various positions can influence the decision maker's deliberations.

A third source of material for deliberation is inspirational or instructive stories or examples; the sorts of things that are presented in management seminars or published in magazines like the *Reader's Digest*. Additionally, reference works, news stories, testimonials, or conversations with uninvolved people may foster deliberation that provides perspective on the decision.

A fourth source of material for deliberation is rules and regulations (such as precedence, labor contracts and similar formalized obligations), or legal constraints or requirements.

No doubt there are many other sources, but these give the general idea. Decision makers tend to think in terms of examples from their own or other people's past experience, from their friends' examples of what has happened in the past or guesses about what might happen in the future, and from the suggestions and examples provided by outsiders. All of this is used in mulling over, in deliberating about, the decision—often it is used repeatedly at different phases of the decision, often it is reinterpreted or bought to bear on new points, often it is rejected as irrelevant only to be resurrected later. In short, decision deliberation involves exploration of the decision in terms of the lessons that can be learned from one's own and others' past experience and forecasts of the future.

FUNCTIONS OF DELIBERATION

Deliberation serves to identify and clarify issues, generate new candidates, evaluate those candidates, build confidence about the adopted candidate, and rehearse and refine the ways in which the decision is to be publicly presented and implemented.

The major function of deliberation is to identify and clarify issues. This occurs during framing and involves identification of the subset of principles, goals, and plans from among all of the constituents of the value image, trajectory image, and strategic image that is relevant to the decision as it is currently being framed. As has been said repeatedly, not all image constituents are strictly relevant to every decision, and working with subsets reduces the information processing load.

Deliberation also involves identifying the subset of the candidate's characteristics (or the characteristics of the focal goal and plan in the case of progress decisions) that are pertinent to the subset of image constituents that constitute the frame. Not all of a candidate's characteristics are relevant to any particular decision.

In the event, of course, the identification of the candidate's relevant characteristics and the identification of the relevant principles, goals, and plans are interactive processes. Identifying one places requirements and constraints on what is included in the other. While the initial frame defines the beginning phase of the process by classifying the decision as being of a particular kind, which means that it touches upon particular principles, goals, and plans, as the process proceeds the candidate's relevant characteristics modify the frame by determining what is added to or omitted from the initial subset and vice versa. This evolution of the frame occurs in the course of deliberation about examples of and analogies with previous decision experiences, and the latter help in the process of refining the frame.

The second function of decision deliberation is to generate new candidate principles, goals, and plans. These may emerge from such sources as contemplation of past experiences, arguments supplied by colleagues, fanciful ideas and creative thinking, or the perspective provided by constructing scenarios based upon environmental cues, personal life histories, or organizational experiences. Whatever the source, the emergence of new candidates is central to progress toward an appropriate decision.

The third function of decision deliberation is to enable the decision maker to use the examples and experiences that are thought about to make forecasts about the short-term and long-term implications of adopting a candidate (or of continuing to pursue a particular plan), and, thereby, to assess the desirability of adopting the candidate. This involves construction of forecasts and assessment of the potential difficulties as well as benefits that might result from adopting the candidate (or continuing to pursue the current plan). The existence of potential difficulties may serve to veto the candidate, and the existence of potential benefits is a necessary condition for it being considered at all. 'Benefits' means that the candidate satisfies the decision maker's principles, either directly or through enhancement of existing goals and facilitation of ongoing plans which themselves serve the principles.

The fourth function of decision deliberation involves confidence building and appraisal of the risk involved in the decision. Confidence and perceived risk are not identical to the subjective probabilities in subjective expected utility theory, in spite of years of effort to establish such an identity. They are, in fact, more fundamental and important than subjective probabilities. Among most decision makers' principles are requirements that candidates inspire some reasonable level of confidence and not involve undue risk. In the course of decision deliberation, forecasts of success, or forecasts that reveal possible (but tractable) difficulties in decision implementation, may increase the decision maker's confidence in the appropriateness of the candidate goal, or the potential of the candidate plan, thereby eliminating objections that otherwise threaten its adoption.

The fifth function of deliberation is to consider how the adopted candidate should be presented to other people and how to go about implementation. If the decision is a major one involving pronounced change, the decision maker will engage in a period of deliberation in which the manner of presentation of the decision to public view is rehearsed and refined. Adoption of a candidate goal triggers a new cycle of deliberative activity as attention shifts to implementation (Gollwitzer et al., 1987; Heckhausen and Gollwitzer, 1987).

The nature and purpose of deliberation changes throughout the decision. Premonitions of the need for a decision may be somewhat casual in character;

simple musings about possibilities that are not yet seriously considered. As the necessity for a decision becomes clearer, the decision maker becomes increasingly engrossed in rumination. Often this consists of, as William James (1890/1950) observed, 'the impatience of the deliberative state', which presses for a prompt decision, contending against 'the dread of the irrevocable', which presses for further deliberation: 'One says "now", the other says "not yet" ' (p. 530). Eventually, however, vacillation ceases and the decision is made: '[In this] transition from doubt to assurance we seem to ourselves almost passive; the reasons which decided us appearing to flow in from the nature of things and to owe nothing to our will' (p. 531).

EMOTIONS AND DELIBERATION

As James (1890/1950) makes so clear, the cognitive processes involved in deliberation are only part of what goes on in decision making. Decisions and their implementation occur within a matrix of sentiments, moods, perhaps even passions, that color and direct both the decisions themselves and the actions that follow them.

The decision-related emotions that most easily come to mind are those that arise during resistance to making any decision at all, as well as the 'impatience of the deliberative state'. Both of these appear to be concomitants of effortful, deliberative decision making—those moderately infrequent occasions when the decision maker is pressed by circumstances to take particular care in making decisions. Janis and Mann (1977) have examined the conditions that give rise to, and the results of, emotions in these special circumstances.

This discussion of framing and deliberation sets the stage for a more detailed discussion of the mechanisms by which decisions are made and carried out. In the next chapter we will discuss the compatibility test, and in the following chapter we will examine issues related to compatibility. In the subsequent two chapters we will discuss the profitability test and related issues. In the penultimate chapter we will examine the implementation of decisions. In the final chapter we will apply the theory to examples of real-life decisions.

SUMMARY

In this chapter we have discussed two topics. First, we examined the theoretical mechanism by which framing is accomplished, and some examples of the effects of framing upon subsequent decisions. This included a discussion of the frame as status quo, the difference between optional and non-optional change from the status quo, and the primacy of the status quo. This was followed by examination of reframing, policies, and conflicting frames.

Second, decision deliberation was discussed, for the same reason that the informal statement of image theory was presented in Chapter 1—to convey the richness of the deliberation process before plunging into the abstract theoretical description that is the subject of subsequent chapters. The reader should keep in mind that the theoretical description makes the deliberative process appear more abstract and orderly than it really is, and that goals and plans evolve and change as the decision process proceeds.

4 The Compatibility Test

The compatibility test serves to screen out adoption candidates that do not conform to the principles, or that adversely affect the goals and plans that make up the frame of the context within which adoption is being considered. For example, Dufty and Taylor (1962) describe a personnel decision for which the simplest plan was ruthless but legal. However:

> . . . there was no evidence that this course of action was even considered. So far as the personnel superintendent was concerned, he was not only fully aware of the probable dysfunctional consequences of such an action, but he would also have found it to conflict with his personal value system. (p. 115)

The compatibility test also serves to detect the possible failure of ongoing plans when the forecasted results of their implementation do not include their goals. For example, students drop courses in which they do not foresee acceptable grades. Businesses drop products when forecasted sales fall short of target. In both cases, the non-attainment of the goals derives its importance from the failure to promote or to comply with the decision maker's principles. Ultimately, it is their link to principles that gives value to everything else—to existing goals and plans, and to the compatibility of candidates and forecasts with these existing goals and plans.

THE TEST

The compatibility test involves violations, the rejection threshold, and the decision rule.

Violations

In adoption decisions, the compatibility test serves to evaluate the acceptability of a candidate by examining its 'fit', its compatibility with the image constituents that constitute the frame for the context. The candidate's compatability *decreases* as a function of the relevant principles, goals, and

plans that its attributes 'violate'. Violations are defined as negations, contra-
dictions, contraventions, preventions, retardations, or any similar form of
interference with the actualization of one of the image constituents that
make up the context's frame. Each violation is all-or-none. The impact
(weight) of a given violation is determined by the importance the decision
maker places on the image constituent that is being violated.

Rejection threshold

The rejection threshold is the critical (weighted) number of violations that
the decision maker will tolerate before rejecting a candidate for adoption or
before rejecting the assumption that progress toward the goal is proceeding
satisfactorily.

Decision rule

The compatibility test's decision rule is that if the (negative) weighted sum
of the violations exceeds the (negative) rejection threshold, the candidate is
rejected; otherwise it is accepted. That is, the default position is acceptance
of a candidate; violations degrade that position until it crosses a threshold
of untenability, whereupon the candidate is rejected. Quite simply, the
decision maker operates on the assumption that the candidate is acceptable
unless it is proved not to be so. We return to this point below.

   In progress decisions, the compatibility test evaluates the 'fit', the compatibility between the trajectory image and the forecast generated by the
strategic image. Here the violations are primarily of the trajectory image's
constituents (goals) by the strategic image's constituents (forecasts) because
the plan that is being examined for progress has already been accepted as
compatible with the value image and the other plans on the strategic image.
The decision rule is that when the weighted sum (negative) of the violations
exceeds the (negative) rejection threshold, the plan is discarded (rejected).
The operating assumption is that the plan is making progress unless it is
proved not to be doing so.

MEASURING COMPATIBILTY

For both adoption and progress decisions, compatibility is non-compensatory (Dawes, 1964; Einhorn, 1970; Keeney, 1980; Payne, 1976). Failure to
violate some image constituents does not balance out violations of other
constituents. Moreover, only the violations count in making the decision.

This is not to say that non-violations are ignored. As we shall see below, they play an important role in decision making. It is to say merely that the results of the compatibility test, which is to screen candidates, are determined solely by violations.

Based upon the research that will be described below, the compatibility test can be mathematically summarized as:

$$C = \sum_{t=1}^{n} \sum_{c=1}^{m} W_c V_{tc}; \; V_{tc} = -1 \text{ or } 0, 0.00 \leq W \leq 1.00 \qquad (4.1)$$

where the compatibility, C, is zero when a candidate has no violations and decreases (i.e. is more and more negative) as the number of violations increases; t is a relevant attribute of the candidate; c is a relevant image constituent; V is a violation of image constituent c by attribute t of the candidate; and W is the importance weight for each of the relevant image constituents—W is between and including 0.00 and 1.00.

Thus, while the violations are all-or-none (-1 or 0), violations of some constituents may count more than others (W_c) and compatibility is a continuous scale between 0 and $-mn$, where m is the number of relevant image constituents and n is the number of the candidate's relevant attributes (an attribute may violate more than one image constituent). For each candidate, a compatibility judgment is made with respect to each of the images; for example, a candidate plan is judged with respect to those constituents of the value image, the trajectory image, and the strategic image that are included in the frame of the context in which adoption is being considered.

Formally, the compatibility test is a special case of qualitative impact analysis (Maybee and Voogd, 1984). The latter is a multicriterion evaluation technique that is used in urban and regional planning to screen candidates on the basis of qualitative criteria. Its purpose is to weight the criteria such that an overall dominance score can be assigned to each candidate. Its decision rule is to adopt the candidate that has been assigned the highest dominance score (details in Voogd, 1982, 1983, 1988).

The compatibility test is a special case of qualitative impact anlaysis in two senses. First, it evaluates candidates sequentially, and thus only one at a time, and it only screens them; it does not choose, except by default when there is only one survivor of the test. Second, the compatibility test gives negative weight to criteria that *are not* met but gives no weight to criteria that *are* met; rejection is determined solely by failures to meet criteria—the violations. This means that the maximum-dominance decision rule does not apply. Therefore, the acceptability of the candidate must be determined by another standard, the rejection threshold.

Non-violations

Even if they determine the screening decisions that result from application of the compatibility test, violations are not the whole story. Certainly, the decision maker is interested in non-violations—in what the candidate is, not just in what it is not. However, while violations and non-violations are usually two sides of the same coin, as we shall see below it is experimentally possible to demonstrate their independent roles in screening, and the violations and non-violations appear to play very different roles.

What, then, do non-violations contribute to screening decisions? It is clear that decision makers attend to them—Gollwitzer and Heckhausen (1987) found that decision makers focused on positive aspects of decision alternatives early in decision deliberation but then changed to focus almost exclusively on negative aspects prior to making the decision. Czapinski (1987) had subjects make a decision about hypothetical persons on the basis of answers to questions about their characteristics. It was found that subjects began by asking positive questions ('Is he honest?' vs 'Is he dishonest?'), but when a negative answer (no) was received they tended to switch to negative questions. Negative information, a negative characteristic or the absence of a positive characteristic, allowed subjects to make a decision more quickly than positive information.

In the same vein, Beach and Strom (1989) presented 53 undergraduate business and psychology students with an exercise in which a hypothetical software company was trying to design a computer-aided job placement system. The system would compare the jobseeker's qualifications, interests, and criteria for a job (the pay, benefits, required travel, prospects for advancement, location, etc.) with the characteristics of each job. Then it would present the results for each job so that the jobseeker could eliminate those jobs that were unacceptable and retain the remainder for further consideration. As potential users of such a system, the participants were asked their preference for how the results for each job might be presented. The options were:

(1) to have results about the criteria the job did not satisfy (violations) presented first, followed by information about the criteria it satisfied (non-violations);
(2) the opposite order, with the non-violations first and the violations second; and
(3) a mixed order.

Of the 53 participants, 41 (77%) wanted information about non-violations first, only seven (13%) wanted information about violations first, four (8%) wanted a mixed order, and one (2%) disapproved of computer-aided job placement systems and refused to answer. In short, even in a task that focuses directly on screening, information about non-violations is important, perhaps especially so at the beginning of deliberation.

The desire for confirming information is not an uncommon finding in the study of cognition. In concept formation tasks, subjects often seek only information that confirms the hypothesis they are testing about a concept, thus tending to receive a good deal of non-diagnostic information that erroneously strengthens their belief in the rightness of their wrong hypothesis (Hovland and Weiss, 1953). Similarly, in problem solving tasks (Wason, 1960, 1968) there is a tendency to request hypothesis-confirming information to the exclusion of hypothesis-disconfirming information, although the tendency apparently is not as strong as it at first was thought to be (Farris and Revlin, 1989; Skov and Sherman, 1986). And, when subjects make evaluations of persons, objects, and events, the evaluations of individual attributes tend to be more positive than negative, but the overall evaluation is most heavily influenced by the negative attributes (Matlin and Stang, 1978; Peeters, 1971).

Insight into what lies behind these biases for confirming, positive information, even when it is not especially diagnostic, is provided by Peeters (1986). Peeters attempts to explain the asymmetric effects of positive and negative attribute evaluations on overall evaluations. He posits that people begin with the optimistic hypothesis that persons, objects, and events of interest are normally positive and that positive attributes are merely part of this normal state and they therefore add no real information. In contrast, negative attributes are informative because they define deviations from the normal state and they therefore differentiate the unique instance at hand from the common run. For example, Fiske (1980) found deviant information in general, and negative information in particular, was attended to more and was given primary consideration in a task involving judged 'likability' of target persons.

Peeters' view is reinforced by Lewicka (1988), who argues that affirmation is logically prior to negation since in order to negate one has first to positively identify the entity under consideration. Peeters' view is congruent, too, with results reported by Guzzo et al. (1986) who, in two experiments, found that subjects' evaluations of a group's performance were influenced by negative information about the group's interactive processes and the outcomes of that process, but positive information had no more effect than neutral information. Apparently participants regarded the positive and neutral information as uninformative, but negative information said something important about the group.

Peeters' view is congruent with that underlying the compatibility test—the decision maker begins with the assumption that a candidate is acceptable (normal state) unless and until information to the contrary is forthcoming. The first, and perhaps major, use of information about non-violations is to help the decision maker define generally what the candidate is. Within this, the violations help him or her define what it is not. That is, the violations then serve to limit the initial normative definition as it pertains to areas that would be negatively impacted if the candidate were adopted—the relevant principles, goals, and plans. (To use an analogy with science, one must define a hypothesis before it can be tested.)

The second use of information about non-violations is as a 'stopping rule' that curtails information search and decision deliberation when highly compatible candidates are encountered. In the extreme case, if the decision maker encountered a perfect candidate but deliberation only could stop when the weighted number of violations surpassed the rejection threshold, no decision would ever be made. Theoretically, deliberation would go on forever and the perfect candidate would never be accepted. Indeed, without some sort of stopping rule, *no* candidate would ever be accepted.

Clearly, if the rejection threshold is not reached, at some point decision deliberation must stop and the candidate must be adopted. One such point would be when all of the candidate's attributes or all of the relevant image constituents have been exhausted, or when all constituents with non-zero weights have been considered. A second point would be when the attributes or constituents have not been exhausted but violations are so few that it is not prudent to continue with the examination. However, in this latter case it is not at all clear how non-violations stop deliberation and lead to adoption of the candidate. As we shall see in the research to be discussed below, it does not appear that there is an acceptance threshold for non-violations that is the counterpart of the rejection threshold.

THE REJECTION THRESHOLD

Anyone who has ever waited until a boss (or a parent, or a spouse) was in a good mood before making some proposal can attest to the fact that rejection thresholds vary. This is inconvenient for theory, research, and in practice, but it must be accepted and dealt with.

We know of no research that is directly relevant to variations in the rejection threshold, but it is clear that it can change either across contexts or across time within a single context. Changes across contexts can be accounted for by changes in the frame. Thus decision makers may react differently to the same proposal depending upon differences in perceived contextual demands. Recall the study by Wagenaar and Keren (1986) in which subjects were asked to decide about whether to adopt a plan that would require children to wear seat belts while traveling in automobiles. Subjects framed the context either as one in which they were a parent

about it. It is only when there are multiple survivors that the process must be prolonged; the profitability test must be applied in an attempt to pick the best of the survivors.

The profitability test is the topic of Chapters 6 and 7, so this is not the place to discuss its details. However, this is the place to raise the question about what happens to the information that was used in the compatibility test (screening) when candidates are passed on to the profitability test (choice). Three obvious answers are:

(1) It too is passed on and used again, together with any additional information that may become available.
(2) It is discarded, perhaps because 'it has already been used'.
(3) There is some combination of the two in which the information is differentially weighted in the course of its use for screening and then again for choice.

There is no *a priori* theoretical reason to favor any one of these possibilities. On the other hand, there are (albeit slim) empirical reasons to suspect that, in the interests of reducing mental effort, decision makers might treat the compatibility test as one task and the profitability test as another task, and not carry forward information from the first task for use in the second task. The first 'empirical' reason is that in observing decision analysts one often sees them screen out 'inappropriate' alternatives before beginning the analysis, but one never sees them refer back to the reasons for doing so in subsequent consideration of the survivors of that screening. The second empirical reason comes from the literature on cascaded inference (Peterson, 1973). Cascaded inference refers to tasks in which participants must make an inference about the truth of a hypothesis on the basis of data that itself may or may not be valid. Normatively (i.e. according to Bayesian statistics), the task is one in which the inference about the data feeds directly into the inference about the hypothesis in the form of conditional probabilities. In contrast, at least in some cases, participants behave as though they are faced with two separate tasks. First they decide about the validity of the data. Then, behaving as if the first decision were correct, they move on to decide about the truth or falsity of the hypothesis. In treating the task as two tasks, the participants, in effect, drop the information they use to make the first decision; it is not passed on for use in the second task. This empirical result, however obliquely, suggests the possibility that, in the compatibility–profitability sequence, the information that serves the compatibility test may not be used again for the profitability test, although it could be argued rather convincingly that this is wasteful and, in some sense, suboptimal. Of course, the issue must be settled empirically, and the experiment that addresses it will be presented at the end of the following section.

RESEARCH ON THE COMPATIBILITY TEST

Most of what is known about compatibility and negative information in decision making comes from incidental findings in studies designed to examine other questions. For example, Anderson (1983) reports that, in the course of the Cuban Missile Crisis, decision makers were more concerned with plans that avoided negative outcomes than with plans that assured positive outcomes. Marshall and Kidd (1981) asked people whether they would prefer in general to know good news first or bad news first; approximately 80% preferred the bad news first. Ben Zur and Breznitz (1981), Wright (1974), and Wright and Weitz (1977) report that under time pressure decision makers focus more closely on negatives; but Maule and Mackie (1988) found that time pressure made no difference—decision makers always preferred negative information. There are, however, four studies that have examined the compatibility test specifically. We will examine each of them in some detail.

BEACH AND STROM (1989)

This study tested the image theory contention that screening decisions are determined solely by violations and that the rejection threshold is a plausible theoretical construct. It also examined the role of non-violations in terminating information search when few violations are observed; that is, it examined the evidence for an 'acceptance threshold'.

In terms of image theory, the experimental task required the sequential consideration of multiple adoption candidates (potential jobs). Each candidate was subjected to the compatibility test in an effort to either reject it or to pass it on to a pool of survivors from which the best could be chosen later using the profitability test.

The participants were 16 undergraduate students, each of whom participated individually. They each were asked to role-play a hypothetical person who was seeking a job after graduating with a Master of Business Administration degree. The person was described as holding a degree in marketing, accounting and finance, having experience with microcomputers, and having worked in sales and as a teaching assistant while in graduate school. Then a list was provided of the person's criteria for 16 aspects of jobs (e.g. geographical location, travel requirements, vacations). The purpose of having all participants role-play the same hypothetical person, and of giving so much information about the hypothetical person, was to make sure that they were all dealing with the task with the same level of knowledge. It would have been possible to key what followed to the private principles, goals, and plans of each individual participant, but it would have been very complicated and, therefore, not necessarily more precise than the method that was used.

The participant was asked to assume that the university's job placement service had compiled a pool of available jobs for which the hypothetical person was qualified. The person's (and the participant's) task was to screen the jobs in terms of which were acceptable for further consideration and which were to be rejected at once.

Each job description was written on a series of index cards. Participants looked at the cards one by one for each job. After looking at a card, the participant could choose either to obtain more information about the job by looking at the next card or to make a decision by telling the experimenter that the job was acceptable or unacceptable for retention for further consideration. There was no pressure for considering fewer than all of the cards or for considering all of them. Participants were told simply that for each job they could look at as many or as few of the cards as they wished before making a decision, and that it was possible that all of the jobs, some of the jobs, or none of the jobs would be acceptable.

Participants were allowed to refer to the information that had been given to them about the hypothetical person's qualifications and job criteria throughout the experiment. However, in order for the experimenter to know precisely how much information had been observed prior to a decision, they were not allowed to turn back to previous cards for a given job once they had turned to a later card.

After the participant had made a decision about a job, the experimenter recorded both the decision (no = reject, yes = accept) and the number of cards that had been inspected prior to the decision. At the end of the experiment, after having screened all of the jobs, participants were asked if they had placed more emphasis on some of the 16 job aspects than upon others. If they indicated that they had, they were asked to identify the five most important aspects and the five least important.

There were 14 jobs, the description of each of which was written on 17 separate cards which formed a small deck of cards. The first card in the deck for a job contained the job's title and its requirements in terms of education and experience (requirements that the hypothetical person met for all 14 jobs). The subsequent 16 cards each contained a single descriptive statement about an aspect of the job that was either a non-violation (called a positive statement) or a violation (a negative statement) of the hypothetical person's criteria for jobs. That is, each of the 16 cards contained a statement that was about one of the hypothetical person's 16 job criteria about which the participant had read earlier and to which he or she had access throughout the experiment. For each of the 14 jobs the order of the 16 job aspects was randomized; then within this each aspect was made positive or negative according to the following scheme.

There were three kinds of job descriptions—10 of the 14 job descriptions had eight positive and eight negative descriptive statements (mixed sequences), two had only positive statements (all-positive sequences), and two had only negative statements (all-negative sequences). The order of presentation of the mixed sequence jobs was randomized and the all-positive and all-negative sequence jobs were inserted into this order in every third position so that the final order of presentation of the 14 job descriptions was M, M, P, M, M, N, M, M, P, M, M, N, M, M; where M is a mixed sequence, P is an all-positive sequence, and N is an all-negative sequence. All participants saw the same order of sequences.

The mixed sequence job descriptions were designed to differ in the number of alternations between the eight positive and eight negative statements that they each contained. Thus, for example, the fewest alternations were in a job description in which the first eight statements were positive and the remaining eight statements were negative. At the other extreme were sequences in which positive statements alternated with negative statements. To control for order effects, every sequence had its mirror image; what was positive in one position in one sequence was negative in that position in its mirror image. The sequences are shown in Figure 4.1, in which each sequence in the column on the left stands for a job description and the minus and plus signs stand for the negative and positive statements in each sequence.

The data were analyzed first assuming that all of the 16 job aspects were of equal importance (weight) for all of the participants. Then a second analysis was done assuming that the weights were unequal, using weights derived from the differential importance that the participants reported for the job aspects at the end of the experiment. Finally, a sensitivity analysis was done to see if the obtained results are influenced by the weighting system that is used.

We begin with the equal weights analysis. First consider the two all-negative and all-positive sequences in Figure 4.1. In each pair of sequences the details of the job descriptions were different except that both jobs each consisted of 16 violations (A1 and A2) or 16 non-violations (B1 and B2). All 16 participants rejected both all-negative jobs; for A1 rejection occurred after an average of 4.97 negative statements and for A2 it occurred after 6.19 negative statements, which is an average of 5.58 for the two sequences together. Fifteen of the 16 participants accepted B1 after observing an average of 13.19 positive statements, and 14 of the 16 participants accepted B2 after an average of 12.28 positive statements, which is an average of 12.75 for the two sequences together. So, the first point to note is that, on the average, rejection decisions were based on far fewer observations than were acceptance decisions.

SEQUENCE	DECISION	MEAN TOTAL	MEAN NEG.	MEAN POS.
A1. (16) `----↓-----------`	No	4.97	4.97	/
	Yes	/	/	/
A2. (16) `-----↓----------`	No	6.19	6.19	/
	Yes	/	/	/
B1. (1) `+++↓+++++++++↑+++` (15)	No	4.00	/	4.00
	Yes	13.19	/	13.19
B2. (2) `++++++++++↓+↑++++` (14)	No	10.00	/	10.00
	Yes	12.28	/	12.28
C. (16) `--↓-----+++++++`	No	2.94	2.94	0
	Yes	/	/	/
D. (10) `+++++++↑+----↓---` (6)	No	13.40	5.40	8.00
	Yes	7.00	0.17	6.83
E. (12) `----++++↓++↑----` (4)	No	8.92	4.83	4.08
	Yes	11.75	4.00	7.75
F. (16) `++++-----↓--++++`	No	10.00	5.25	4.75
	Yes	/	/	/
G. (15) `---+↓+---+++--+↑` (1)	No	5.39	3.47	1.93
	Yes	16.00	8.00	8.00
H. (15) `+++---+++-↓-++-↑` (1)	No	11.26	5.44	5.99
	Yes	16.00	8.00	8.00
I. (14) `--++--++--↓+--+↑` (2)	No	10.71	6.00	4.71
	Yes	16.00	8.00	8.00
J. (16) `++--++--+↓--++--`	No	9.75	4.69	5.06
	Yes	/	/	/
K. (14) `-+-+-+↓+-+-+-↑-+` (2)	No	7.29	4.07	3.21
	Yes	14.00	7.00	7.00
L. (14) `+-+-+-+↑↓-+-+-+-` (2)	No	9.35	4.71	4.64
	Yes	8.00	3.50	4.50

Figure 4.1 The mean number of observations at each decision point. The parentheses contain the number of participants who rejected ('No' on top) or accepted ('Yes' on bottom) each job. Pluses indicate non-violations in the sequence of information about a job, and minuses indicate violations. The columns on the right show the mean number of observations that were made prior to the decision. From Beach and Strom (1989); reproduced by permission of Elsevier Science Publishers B.V.

For the group data in Figure 4.1, information search was not exhaustive for the two all-positive sequences, suggesting the existence of an acceptance threshold for searches that yield few or no violations. However, closer examination revealed that 17 (53%) of the 32 (16 participants × 2 sequences, B1 and B2) searches were exhaustive. Thus, if there is an acceptance threshold, roughly half of the decisions required 16 or more positive observations before it took effect. None of the 32 searches for the all-negative sequences was exhaustive.

Turning to the mixed sequences, if there is a consistent threshold number of violations for rejection of jobs, and if non-violations have little or no effect on rejection decisions, there should be lower variance among the number of negative statements than among the number of positive statements observed prior to rejection decisions for the 10 mixed sequences. Indeed, for the group data the variance of the means of the number of negative statements observed before a rejection was only 0.77, which is 5.5 times *smaller* than the variance of 4.34 for positive statements ($F(10, 10) = 5.64$, $p = 0.006$). This group result was also found for individual participants; for all 16 participants the variance of the number of negative statements observed before a rejection was smaller than the variance of the number of positive statements ($p < 0.001$, sign test). (There were not enough acceptance decisions for the group or for any individual to permit a reliable complementary analysis for acceptance decisions.) The mean number of negative statements observed prior to the participants' 174 rejection decisions (across all 14 sequences) was 4.80, which is an estimate of the average rejection threshold. The second point to note is that if there is a 'threshold' for acceptance as some function of the non-violations it is more variable than the rejection threshold in this experimental task.

The foregoing results support the image theory prediction that rejection decisions are based upon violations and that there is a fairly consistent threshold. They also show that information search for all-positive, non-violating, information frequently is non-exhaustive but that there does not appear to be as consistent an acceptance threshold for non-violations as for violations. The following analyses examine specific sequences in an attempt to further illuminate both of these issues.

First, if participants were basing their rejection decisions upon a threshold number of negative statements, and if that number is less than the eight negative statements that are present in each of the 10 mixed sequence jobs, then it is to be expected that decisions to reject those jobs should be significantly more frequent than decisions to accept. Of the 160 decisions (16 participants × 10 mixed sequence jobs), 142 decisions (89%) were to reject ($t = 15.78$, $df = 159$, $p < 0.001$). All of the 16 individual participants rejected more than half of the mixed sequence jobs ($p < 0.001$, sign test);

seven rejected all 10 jobs, three rejected nine jobs, four rejected eight jobs, one rejected seven jobs, and one rejected six jobs.

Further, the role of violations in rejection decisions can be examined by comparing the results in Figure 4.1 for sequences C and D, each of which begins with eight statements of one kind followed by eight statements of the other kind. If negative statements are the determinants of rejection decisions, participants should make negative decisions *early* in the sequence that begins with negative statements (job C) and *late* in the sequence that begins with positive statements followed by negative statements (job D), and they should reject both jobs. Indeed, all 16 participants rejected job C after observing a mean of only 2.94 statements. Ten of the 16 participants (62%) rejected job D after observing a mean of 13.40 statements—of which the first eight were positive statements and the remaining 5.40 were negative. The other six participants accepted job D after observing a mean of 6.83 of the eight positive statements at the beginning of the sequence, suggesting that these six people had an acceptance threshold of roughly seven for consistently positive observations. But, note the considerable difference between this mean of 6.83 for job D and the means of 13.19 and 12.28 for the all-positive sequences (jobs B1 and B2, respectively). If there is an acceptance threshold for non-violating, positive statements prior to acceptance decisions, it is not very consistent from one decision to another within the same experimental task.

Finally, consider the alternative hypothesis that participants' decisions are based upon a compensatory balancing (the net difference or net ratio) of the negative and positive statements, rather than upon simply the number of negative or positive statements. If this alternative hypothesis were correct it would predict that searches in frequently alternating sequences (jobs K and L) would tend to be long because successive statements in the sequences cancel each other and the net difference (or ratio) would always be small. On the other hand, this alternative hypothesis would predict that searches in less frequently alternating sequences (jobs E and F) should be shorter. In fact, the results obtained for these four sequences are the opposite of the alternative hypothesis' predictions: the mean number of observations for jobs E and F was *larger* than for jobs K and L, rather than smaller. Moreover, the mean number of *negative* statements observed by participants who reject jobs E and F was 5.07, which is roughly the same as the mean number of 4.50 negative statements observed by those who rejected jobs K and L, again suggesting a fairly consistent rejection threshold.

It is not necessary to go into the differential weighting analysis or the sensitivity analysis except to say that they did not make much difference. In fact, participants did not agree among themselves about which job aspects were most (or least) important. Moreover, analyzing the data after weighting the job aspects by each participant's unique specifications of what was most important (given the arbitrary weight of 1.5), least important (0.5) or in between (1.0) yielded almost exactly the same results as those reported above for equal weights. Moreover, a sensitivity analysis in which these arbitrary weights were varied over a wide range made no difference in the results except for the absurd case in which the weights were made to be exactly the opposite of what the participants told us.

In summary, the experiment's results support the image theory prediction that screening decisions (the compatibility test) which end in rejection do so as a result of the number of violations associated with the candidate, and that there is a fairly consistent rejection threshold within a single decision task. There also was weak evidence for some kind of acceptance threshold for sequences of non-violations—a rule that can prevent exhaustive search when the rejection threshold is not reached, and which therefore makes possible the adoption of highly compatible candidates. However, this acceptance threshold is not as well defined nor as consistent as the rejection threshold. The differential weighting analysis and the sensitivity analysis make it unlikely that the results obtained are an artifact of the equal weights that were used in the data analysis.

BEACH, SMITH, LUNDELL, AND MITCHELL (1988a)

The Beach and Strom (1989) experiment was a laboratory study using undergraduates and decision criteria that were introduced in the form of a hypothetical person who had to make screening decisions. In contrast, the present study examined compatibility in a field setting: participants were decision makers who were executives of three large commercial firms, and the decision criteria were the principles that actually guided decision making within each of the firms. The purpose of the experiment was to test the *descriptive sufficiency* of equation 4.1 for measuring compatibility.

The descriptive sufficiency of equation 4.1 was evaluated using a logical, rather than a statistical, test—the Turing test (Turing, 1950): If an outside observer would be indifferent between asking for assessments made by a real decision maker or assessments made by a simulation, the rule that determined the simulation's assessments is said to be descriptively sufficient. Thus, using equation 4.1 to guide the simulation, and applying the Turing test to results generated by the simulation and the results generated by actual decision makers, provides a way of testing the descriptive sufficiency of the equation. Note that descriptive sufficiency does not imply descriptive necessity; other descriptions may be equally sufficient. However, the fact that this particular equation is grounded in the larger theory makes its sufficiency of particular interest.

The simulation was written in Franz LISP and performed on a Sun 120 computer. (We thank our colleague, Earl Hunt, for his help with the simulation and for lending us the computer.) First, all relevant principles, obtained from interview, were entered into the simulation. Second, a goal was entered. Third, a list was entered of the tactics that were available to be used to construct plans for achieving the goal. Fourth, information was entered about which principles, if any, were violated by each tactic. Fifth, the computer derived all possible plans that can be constructed using the tactics that were provided. Because plans have various constraints (e.g. some kinds of tactics must precede other kinds), the number of constructed plans was less than the total number that can be constructed using all possible combinations of tactics. Sixth, after constructing a pool of possible plans, the simulation assessed the overall compatibility of each plan with the principles (i.e. the sum over the plan of the number of violations of the principles by its component tactics—recall that tactics are the components of plans). In the simplest case all violations would be weighted equally, as in Beach and Strom (1989). However, pilot work with the simulation demonstrated that this criterion was too strict in the present experiment. Seldom could plans be constructed that were compatible with every one of the principles. Instead, the pilot studies indicated that some principles were more important than others, and that relevant principles could be divided into primary principles and secondary principles. As a result, the weights in equation 4.1 were set to 1.0 for primary principles, 0.5 for secondary principles, and zero for irrelevant principles.

The purpose of the experiment was to see if the various plans' compatibility, as given by equation 4.1, was related to decision makers' assessments of the plans' compatibility with their own firm's principles. The simulation provided one measure of compatibility and the decision makers from a particular firm each provided another measure. The assumption is that the decision makers within a firm must assimilate their firm's principles in order to work together successfully. Failure to use similar principles in decision making leads to disagreements in the acceptability (compatibility) of candidate plans and to subsequent poor performance in goal achievement (Bourgeois, 1980). Our firms were selected to differ in the degree of agreement among the executives within a firm about what the firm's principles were. The hypotheses were:

- Hypothesis 1—If a firm's executives have similar perceptions of the principles that govern the firm's actions, there will be high intercorrelations among their assessments of the compatibility of various candidate plans (given a specific goal). If their perceptions are not similar, there will be low intercorrelations among their assessments.

● Hypothesis 2—If image theory's rule for compatibility measurement is descriptively sufficient, correlations between the executives' assessments of compatibility and assessments generated by equation 4.1 (the simulation) should be of the same magnitude as correlations among the executives' assessments. This, in the present circumstances, is the Turing test. That is, if equation 4.1 is sufficient and if the executives agree with each other about the plans' compatibility, then they should agree with the simulation. But, even if equation 4.1 is sufficient but the executives disagree with each other, then they should also disagree with the simulation. In either case, if the equation is sufficient the executives should agree with the simulation about as much as they agree among themselves. Careful thought about this rather unconventional way of testing experimental hypotheses will reveal that it is a logically more rigorous test of the rule's sufficiency than it may at first appear to be.

The participants in the first study were executives of two sports clothes manufacturing firms, nine from Firm A and ten from Firm B. During the period of the study, Firm A went through major internal change in response to increased foreign competition and a consequent decline in profits and in the price of its stock. Part of this change was in operating procedures and part was in personnel. As a result there was a good deal of turnover among executives as well as movement of executives within the firm. In contrast, Firm B remained stable throughout the study period. It maintained its market leadership, its high employee retention, and its efficient intra-organizational lines of communication.

The procedure consisted of visiting each firm twice. On the first visit, one of the experimenters interviewed six executives from each firm about their firm's internal structure and its market, what its 'image' was internally, and what was important in guiding its operations. The interview was far-ranging and not conditional upon any particular goal or specific course of action. The purpose was to identify the firm's primary and secondary principles. After the interviews at each firm, the researcher made a list of things that had been discussed. The list was examined by the rest of the research team and consolidated into five general underlying principles for each firm. Then, some of the principles were designated as primary or as secondary, based upon the interviewer's knowledge of each of the firms. For Firm A the primary principles were (1) product innovation, (2) being an industry leader, and (3) profitability; secondary principles were (4) innovative business practices, and (5) support and encouragement of employee initiative and drive. For Firm B the primary principles were (1) employee participation and teamwork, (2) being an industry leader, and (3) profitability; secondary principles were (4) craftsmanship and slow product evolution, and (5) conservative but assertive business practices.

Product design would be done completely in-house. Purchasing of materials would be done directly by [firm's name] employees, as would production of the product. Distribution would be handled partially by [firm's name] and partially by an outside agency. An advertising consultant would help formulate the promotional campaign which [firm's] advertising department would then execute with this agency's assistance

Extreme	Moderate	Mild	Mild	Moderate	Extreme

Incompatibility   Compatibility
with [firm's name]   with [firm's name]

Figure 4.2 An example of a candidate plan and the scale that was used to measure participants' EC by Beach *et al.* (1988a). Reproduced by permission of John Wiley & Sons Ltd

During the second visit to each firm, the original six executives plus four additional executives ($n = 10$ participants) were given a list of 10 different plans that had been generated by the simulation for introducing a new product (the specified goal). They were asked to rate each plan on a six-point scale, as shown in Figure 4.2 (these were reverse-scored to avoid confusion in subsequent analyses). These ratings were done at the executive's convenience and anonymously returned by mail. One executive from Firm A failed to return the materials.

The 10 plans that were given to the executives were selected from an original set of 243 alternatives. The original set was generated by specifying that a plan to introduce a new product (the goal) had to have five tactics and that each tactic could assume any of three different states ($3^5 = 243$). The tactics were (1) who is to design the product, (2) who will procure the materials for the product, (3) who will manufacture the product, (4) who will distribute the product, and (5) who will handle the advertising of the product. The three states were (1) the relevant in-house department of the firm will do the job, (2) the relevant department will work with an external consultant who will submit ideas that will be subject to the department's approval, or (3) the relevant department will contract with an external firm or agent for performance of the job. All three states were possible for each of the five tactics that comprised the plans, but they were not all acceptable in light of the firm's principles. For example, Firm B's conservative principles about product innovation and business practice would be violated by the use of external help (except for advertising), because it would mean reduced control over the firm's affairs.

Column #=	Study 1		Study 2
	1	2	3
Plan	Firm A	Firm B	Firm C
1	6.5	3.0	0.0
2	0.5	6.0	2.0
3	9.0	12.5	4.5
4	7.0	4.0	0.0
5	1.5	5.5	0.0
6	0.5	6.5	2.0
7	0.5	7.0	4.5
8	13.5	8.0	0.0
9	8.5	4.0	0.0
10	5.0	3.0	0.0

Figure 4.3 The simulation's calculated compatibility for each of 10 plans for each of the firms in the study by Beach *et al.* (1988a). Reproduced by permission of John Wiley & Sons Ltd

Each firm's five principles were entered into the simulation and labeled (weighted) as either primary or secondary. Then the researcher who had done the interviews judged the compatibility (or irrelevance) of *each* of the three states of the five tactics with *each* of the five principles. That is, the tactics that later constituted the aspects of the plans were separately evaluated for compatibility. These judgements were entered into the simulation. Then the overall compatibility of each of the 243 possible plans was assessed by the simulation, using equation 4.1. Violations were scored as −1 or 0 and weights were 1 for primary principles, 0.5 for secondary principles, and 0 for irrelevant principles.

Ten of the 243 plans were selected to be rated by the executives; 10 were deemed to be enough to produce the required data without taking up too much of the executives' time. The 10 included the four that were the most compatible for each firm together with six that were less compatible. Because the firms were quite different, it was impossible to create a single set of plans that had an equal range of compatibility for both firms; the 10 plans that came as close to this as possible were the ones presented to the executives of both of the two firms. The first two columns of Figure 4.3 contain the simulation's calculated compatibility for each of the 10 plans for both firms; the correlation between the values for the two firms is $r = 0.20$ ($p = $ n.s.).

To simplify presentation of the results, from this point we shall refer to the *simulation's calculated compatibility* for each plan as the *SC* for the plan

Column # =	1	2	3	4	5	6
	Firm A		Firm B		Firm C	
Participant	EC	SC	EC	SC	EC	SC
1	0.34	0.19	0.72	0.78	0.30	0.42
2	0.47	0.59	0.80	0.68	0.44	0.44
3	0.49	0.76	0.24	0.03	0.67	0.74
4	0.42	0.24	0.75	0.83	0.62	0.39
5	0.19	−0.28	0.65	0.92	0.64	0.69
6	0.20	0.41	0.72	0.59	0.66	0.81
7	0.34	0.20	0.62	0.34	0.58	0.50
8	0.47	0.65	0.67	0.57		
9	0.58	0.62	0.67	0.86		
10			0.73	0.71		
Mean	0.40	0.40	0.67	0.69	0.57	0.60

Figure 4.4 Columns 1, 3, and 5 contain the average correlations between each executive's ECs for the 10 plans and the ECs given by the other executives in the same firm. Columns 2, 4, and 6 contain the correlations between each executive's ECs for the 10 plans and the simulation's SCs for those 10 plans. From Beach *et al.* 1988a; reproduced by permission of John Wiley & Sons Ltd

and each *executive's rating of the compatibility* of that plan as the *EC* for the plan.

Hypothesis 1 was that if a firm's executives have similar perceptions of the principles that govern its activities, there will be high correlations among the different executives' ECs for candidate plans for achieving the given goal. Columns 1 and 3 of Figure 4.4 contain the average correlations between each executive's ECs for the 10 plans and the ECs given by the other executives in the same firm. Recall that Firm A underwent tumultuous change during the study period; hence the assumption that the similarity among its executives' perceptions would be lower than among those of the executives in Firm B, which was quite stable throughout the study. The validity of this assumption is reflected in the low mean correlations among Firm A's executives' ECs in column 1 (overall mean = 0.40), in contrast to the relatively high mean correlations for Firm B in column 3 (overall mean = 0.67). In short, when the firm was in flux its executives disagreed about the compatibility of the various plans it might adopt to attain a goal, presumably because they differed in their perceptions about the firm's principles. When the firm was stable, its members agreed about the plans, presumably because they had similar perceptions about its principles.

Hypothesis 2 was that if equation 4.1 is descriptively sufficient, the correlations between the executives' ECs and the simulation's SCs for each firm should be equal to the intercorrelations among the executives' ECs, no greater and no smaller. As shown in Figure 4.4, while there were individual differences, the mean correlations between each executive's ECs and the other executives' ECs (columns 1, 3) are very similar to the correlation between their own ECs and the stimulation's SCs (columns 2, 4). The mean EC–SC correlation for Firm A (column 2), 0.40, and for Firm B (column 4), 0.69, are both virtually identical to the mean intercorrelations among their executives' ECs (0.40 and 0.67, respectively). In short, the degree of agreement about assessed compatibility between each firm's executives and the simulation was neither more nor less than the agreement among the executives themselves; which is to say that an outside observer would be indifferent between asking for compatibility assessments made by an executive or assessments made by the simulation (Turing, 1950). This means that, in the present circumstances, the compatibility assessment provided by equation 4.1 is descriptively sufficient.

When this study was begun, the problems facing Firm A were not anticipated, although they became quite apparent during the first interview. It was because of these problems that hypothesis 1 was formulated and Firm B was added to the study. As a result, hypothesis 1 is somewhat *ad hoc*. Therefore, after the results reported above were obtained, it seemed prudent to see if they could be replicated using a third firm. To do this, Firm C was studied using the same method that was used before—with one exception, which will be described below.

Firm C was selected because it was between Firms A and B in terms of stability. It was not in trouble but it was undergoing rapid, orderly change. It was a fast-growing, highly successful producer of alcoholic beverages. It began as a small company, was purchased by a national conglomerate, was left largely to itself in terms of management as long as it did well, and was ambitious and aggressively expanding.

Four executives from Firm C participated in the initial interview. Three of these four also participated in the second part of the study, together with seven other executives. Of the latter 10, seven anonymously returned their materials through the mail.

The procedure for the simulation was similar to that described for Firms A and B. However, because the distribution of alcoholic beverages cannot be handled by the manufacturer in the state in which the firm is located, distribution was not included as a tactic in the potential plans. This reduced the set of potential plans from 243 to 81, of which very few were incompatible with the firm's principles. Figure 4.3 contains the SC values for the 10 plans that were selected for the study, but note that the 10 plans are not the same 10 that were used for Firms A and B, even though Firm C's primary and secondary principles turned out to be the same as Firm A's.

There was only one difference between the procedure used for Firms A and B and that used for Firm C. For the former, the researcher who had conducted the interviews judged whether the possible states of the tactics did or did not violate the firm's principles. For Firm C these judgements were made by the three executives who participated in both parts of the study, using a majority rule when there was disagreement. The rationale was that the participants probably knew better than the outside researcher about the compatibility of the tactics with the firm's principles. While this change in procedure had no obvious effects on the experimental results, it led to fewer judged incompatibilities than did the previous procedure, and this resulted in SC=o for all but four of the 81 candidate plans. As shown in Figure 4.3 the 10 plans that were used consisted of four with non-zero SC values plus six others with values of zero.

In the second part of the study the seven executives who returned their materials assessed the overall compatibility of each of the 10 plans using the six-point scale (again reverse-scored) that was used for Firms A and B.

The results for hypothesis 1 are shown in column 5 of Figure 4.4. The intercorrelations (mean = 0.57) among the executives' ECs lie between those for Firm A and Firm B. According to hypothesis 1 this is to be expected because the stability of Firm C was less that of Firm B and greater than that of Firm A.

Results for hypothesis 2 are shown in columns 5 and 6 of Figure 4.4. Each executive's mean correlation with the other executive's ECs (column 5) is similar in magnitude to the correlation between his or her ECs and the simulation's ECs (column 6). This replicates the results obtained for Firms A and B; the executives agreed with the simulation (0.60) to virtually the same degree that they agreed among themselves (0.57). In terms of the Turing test, an outside observer would be indifferent between asking the simulation or asking an executive for a compatibility assessment because the simulation's assessments and the executives' assessments agree to the same degree as the executives agree among themselves. In short, the simulation's assessments were as similar to any randomly selected executive's assessments of compatibility as the assessments by any other executive would be. This means that, in the present circumstances, equation 4.1 is a sufficient description of compatibility assessment.

Recall that descriptive sufficiency does not imply descriptive necessity. That is, equation 4.1 appears to be sufficient, but it might not be the only sufficient description. However, in the absence of a contending alternative, it is reasonable to tentatively accept equation 4.1 for image theory until further evidence indicates that it is insufficient. When this happens, the equation may have to be modified or replaced by some other description, particularly for circumstances that differ from those in this experiment.

REDIKER (1988)

In the third study of compatibility, 158 business school students each played
the role of the Chief Executive Officer (CEO) of a fictitious firm, American
Electronics Corporation (AEC).

The CEO's goal was to complete AEC's range of offerings in the business
data processing market. This was to be done by acquiring a computer
manufacturer. The firm had hired a consultant who had identified six
candidate companies. The process of acquiring any one of these companies
constitutes a candidate plan for attaining the CEO's goal. The CEO's task
was to evaluate the six candidates and to screen out the unsuitable ones,
retaining the remainder for further investigation.

Before performing the evaluations, participants were given information
about each candidate company as well as information about AEC's principles
(its 'culture') and about optional or non-optional change (defined in terms
of its economic environment). The candidate companies' characteristics were
keyed to AEC's principles.

Culture consisted of AEC's principles and the degree to which these
principles were shared by AEC's managers. The principles were (1) product
quality, (2) sales growth, (3) employee relations, and (4) use of debt
financing. The degree to which the principles were shared by managers was
manipulated as an experimental condition by presenting the results of a
survey of AEC's board members, its top executives, middle managers, and
first-line supervisors. For different conditions in the experiment the survey
showed high agreement about the principles (strong culture), or low agreement (weak culture). In short, this manipulation was the laboratory
counterpart of Firms A and B in the study by Beach *et al.* (1988a), described
above.

AEC's economic environment was described as either non-threatening or
threatening. A non-threatening environment meant that AEC could continue
operating in much the same way that it always had—the status quo could
continue and that change was optional. A threatening environment meant
that AEC's status quo was unlikely to prove successful in the future—that
change was non-optional. Threat was manipulated by varying (1) ease with
which other computer firms could enter AEC's market. (2) existing competition, (3) customer sophistication about computers and (4) the supply of
labor and raw materials.

The experiment was a 2×2 factorial design with strong *vs* weak culture
and non-threatening *vs* threatening economic environment. Within each of
the four cells of the design, the six candidate computer firms differed in
degree of compatibility with AEC's principles. This was varied by manipu-
lating the number of violations of AEC's four principles. Each candidate's

overall compatibility was the sum of its unweighted violations (−1 or 0); the sums were −3, −3, −2, −2, −1, and 0.

The dependent variables were the participants' (the CEO's) evaluations of the six candidate computer manufacturers. The first evaluation of interest is the mean ranked attractiveness of each of the six candidates as a function of their compatibility with AEC's principles. The second is which of the candidates were rejected and which were retained for further investigation.

The results showed that, across participants and conditions, as compatibility decreased, evaluated attractiveness also decreased ($r = 0.95$, $p < 0.01$). Moreover, on the average, the participants rejected the three least compatible candidate companies and retained the three most compatible for further investigation (one of the two companies with a sum of −2 was seen as less attractive than the other and was rejected more frequently—meaning that the equal-weights assumption was not wholly appropriate).

Culture strength (managers' agreement on principles) had a significant effect on the variance in evaluated attractiveness of the candidates, but the economic environment (optional *vs* non-optional change) did not. Weak culture resulted in a variance in attractiveness evaluations that was 1.81 times greater than the variance in the strong culture condition. Apparently, because the participants in the weak culture condition were less clear about the firm's principles, they varied among themselves in their evaluations of the candidates in terms of those principles.

Neither culture nor economic environment significantly affected rejection of specific candidates. However, both variables significantly affected participants' judgments about how much confidence AEC's top executives would have in their final decision, the time it would take them to decide, the difficulty they would have deciding, and (only for culture) the degree to which they would agree among themselves about the decisions. In general, these differences were what one would expect: weak culture and a threatening environment were judged to produce the most doubt, longer decision time, more difficulty, and less agreement. Strong culture and a non-threatening environment were seen to produce the opposite.

VAN ZEE, PALUCHOWSKI AND BEACH (1989)

This series of experiments addressed the question of what happens to the information upon which screening (the compatibility test) is based when candidates subsequently are evaluated so that the best can be chosen (the profitability test). The basic paradigm was the same for all of the experiments in the series, so we begin by describing it and then describe the variations as we consider each of the experiments.

Participants were undergraduates who were enrolled in an introductory psychology course. They were given a set of materials that consisted of (1) a cover letter, (2) a sheet that contained pre-screening information about five candidates (labeled A through E) and spaces for indicating screening decisions about the candidates, (3) a set of envelopes, each of which contained a sheet of paper on which was written both the post-screening information for one of the surviving candidates and a 7-point scale for rating the attractiveness of that candidate, and (4) a sheet for indicating a final choice among the candidates. The cover letter said: 'You have a friend who is moving to Seattle. Your friend has asked you to look at available housing and to put down a deposit on the best place you can find. Your friend's preferences are (in order of priority): rent of $200 per month or less, reasonably quiet without many parties, in a place that is in good repair, in a house or apartment with a large room, within a mile of the university. After looking at the ads in the newspaper and on the bulletin boards, you make some phone calls and come up with five possibilities.'

The pre-screening information consisted of information from the advertisements and phone calls about three of the friend's five criteria (distance from the university, rent, and noise/parties) for each of five candidate rooms, A through E. One candidate (C) violated all of the friend's three criteria, one candidate (E) violated none of the three criteria, and each of the other three candidates (A, B, and D) violated one each of the three criteria. After having read the information for all five candidates the participant indicated which of them he or she would take the time to go and see (i.e. the participant screened out the candidates that he or she did not want to consider further).

Each of the five envelopes was labeled with an identifying letter for one of the candidate rooms. Each contained post-screening information about its candidate on each of the friend's two remaining criteria (state of repair and size of the room). The post-screening information showed the candidate having either satisfied both criteria or having violated both criteria. Printed under this information was a seven-point scale on which the participant rated the attractiveness of the candidate (very unattractive to very attractive).

The choice sheet had five blank spaces, labeled A through E, and instructions to check a blank to indicate the final choice of a candidate room on which to make a deposit.

Experiment 1

Participants in group 1 ($n = 27$) were given the cover sheet and only the pre-screening information and were asked to rate the attractiveness of the five candidate rooms. Participants in groups 2, 3, 4, and 5 ($n = 24$ to 27) were given the cover sheet, the pre-screening information, were asked to screen the candidates, were given post-screening information for the survivors, and were asked to make a choice among the survivors. The difference among the latter four groups was in the post-screening information that they received for each of the rooms.

The first hypothesis was that the participants in group 1 would rate the attractiveness of the candidates on the basis of compatibility (i.e. the non-violating candidate as most attractive, the all-violating candidate as least attractive, and the other candidates somewhere in between).

The second hypothesis took the extreme position that the participants in groups 2–5 would treat the screening decision and the choice decision as two separate tasks and that the information used in screening would not be passed on for use in making the choice. This hypothesis leads to the expectation that the post-screening attractiveness ratings by groups 2–5 should be based *only* on the post-screening information and should not reflect the pre-screening information (as revealed by group 1's ratings). Moreover, because each of the four groups received different post-screening information, their post-screening attractiveness ratings should differ from one another, reflecting the particular post-screening information that was given to them.

A less extreme version of the second hypothesis is that the participants treat the two decisions as two separate tasks but that they pass on the pre-screening information, weighting it more or less heavily than the post-screening information in making their post-screening attractiveness ratings and their choices.

The results support the first hypothesis: Group 1's mean rating for the wholly compatible, non-violating, candidate (E) was 6.7; for the wholly incompatible, all-violating candidate (C) was 1.6; for the other candidates the means were 5.2, and 5.1, and 3.6.

The less extreme form of the second hypothesis was supported: Figure 4.5 contains graphs for each of the five groups of participants. The first graph contains the mean attractiveness ratings for group 1 ($n = 27$), which can be regarded as the pre-screening attractiveness of each of the five candidate rooms based upon the pre-screening information about them. The other four graphs are for groups 2, 3, 4, and 5 ($n = 26$, 26, 27, and 24, respectively). Under each of the bars in the latter graphs there is a plus or a minus to indicate whether the post-screening information for each of the candidates was positive or negative. Thus, for example, group 2 received negative post-screening information about candidate E, which had been the most attractive candidate before screening (see group 1's graph). The result was that the group 2 participants for whom E was one of the candidates that passed the compatibility test rated candidate E lowest of all the candidates. And candidate C, which has been the least attractive (all-violating), became

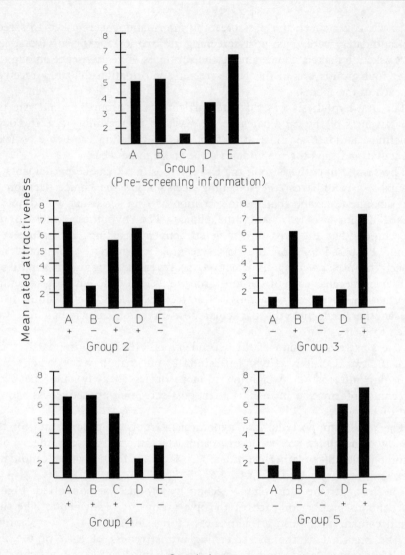

Figure 4.5 Results of experiment 1 by Van Zee *et al.* (1989). Reproduced from an unpublished manuscript by permission of the authors

very attractive after positive post-screening information was received. Indeed, observation of the high and low ratings for groups 2–5 suggests that attractiveness was most heavily determined by the post-screening information, and that the pre-screening information had considerably less influence on post-screening attractiveness. That is, the post-screening attractiveness ratings are high for positive post-screening information and low for negative post-screening information. However, when two candidates both received positive (or negative) post-screening information they were not rated identically. In fact, across groups 2–5, for 14 of the 16 pairs of candidates for which the post-screening information was identical, differences in their post-screening ratings are in the same direction as differences in group 1's pre-screening ratings ($p < 0.01$, sign test). This indicates that the pre-screening information was passed on. However, observation of the graphs shows that it clearly had less impact on post-screening attractiveness than had the post-screening information.

Of the 103 participants in groups 2–5, 23 (22%) screened out all but one candidate, 36 (35%) screened out all but two, 34 (33%) screened out two and kept three, four (4%) screened out only one candidate, and six (6%) did not screen out any candidates. (Most frequently screened out was the all-violation candidate, 91%, and most frequently passed was the no-violation candidate, 82%.)

After having seen the post-screening information for the candidates they passed and had rated, 100% of the final choices by the participants in groups 2–5 were of their most highly rated candidates.

If participants did not heavily weight the pre-screening information when making the post-screening ratings and choices because they could not remember it, it is to be expected that the ratings for single survivors would be different from ratings for multiple survivors. That is, one would imagine that participants could remember three simple pieces of information for a single survivor even if they could not do so for multiple survivors. However, the means of the post-screening attractiveness ratings for candidates that were single survivors, that were one of two survivors, and that were one of three or more survivors, were all essentially the same; they strongly reflected the post-screening information and only weakly reflected the pre-screening information.

In summary, in this first experiment the results for group 1 implied that rated attractiveness of the candidates depended upon compatibility. The results for groups 2–5 implied that, after screening took place, information that had been used for the compatibility test had only a minor influence upon the outcome of the profitability test. This in turn suggests that participants may have regarded the two tests as two fairly separate decision tasks. The next three experiments in the series looked at conditions that might prompt decision makers to weight the pre-screening information more heavily in their choices of the best of the surviving candidates.

Experiment 2

The procedure here was the same as for groups 2–5 in experiment 1, except that the post-screening information in the envelopes included one of two prompts. One prompt ($n = 25$) *told* the participant to consider all that he or she knew about the candidate before rating its attractiveness. The other prompt ($n = 31$) *asked* the participant if he or she had considered all that he or she knew about the candidate before making the rating. Results showed that neither prompt increased the weight of the pre-screening information in the post-screening ratings and choices. That is, the ratings primarily reflected the post-screening information, and choices were of the most highly rated candidates.

Experiment 3

In this experiment the pre-screening information was physically passed on for the participants ($n = 33$). That is, the pre-screening information was repeated along with the post-screening information in each envelope; printed directly above the rating scale. The supposition was that the participant could not avoid seeing the information but could either elect to read it again or ignore it if he or she did not regard it as particularly relevant to the rating and the subsequent choice. The results showed that, once again, participants' post-screening ratings reflected primarily the post-screening information; the physical presence of the pre-screening information did not cause it to be weighted more heavily than it had been in the previous experiments. Again, choices were of the most highly rated candidates.

Experiment 4

This was the crucial experiment. It involved two experimental groups that followed two slightly different procedures. One group followed the same procedure as groups 2–5 in experiment 1 ($n = 36$). That is, they saw the pre-screening information, screened, saw the post-screening information for each of the candidates that passed the screening, rated the attractiveness of those candidates, and made a choice among them. The other group did exactly the same thing *except* they did not screen ($n = 31$). That is, the second group saw the pre-screening information, then they opened the envelopes for each of the five candidates and saw the additional post-screening information for each of them, then they rated all five candidates and chose the best candidate.

The hypothesis was that, if the participants treat screening and choice as two separate tasks, and treat the information that was used for the first task

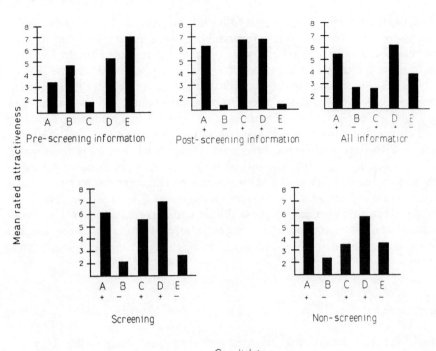

Figure 4.6   Results of experiment 4 by Van Zee *et al.* (1989). Reproduced from an unpublished manuscript by permission of the authors

as either 'used up' or of reduced relevance to the second task, then the ratings by the group that screened should reflect primarily the post-screening information and the ratings by the group that did not screen should reflect all of the information (i.e. a combination of the pre-screening and post-screening information).

Three control groups were included in this experiment. Participants in the first control group ($n = 38$) did not screen; they were presented with only the pre-screening information and were asked to rate the attractiveness of the five candidate rooms. The participants in the second control group ($n = 32$) did not screen; they were presented with only the post-screening information before rating the attractiveness of the five candidates. The participants in the third control group ($n = 40$) did not screen either; they were presented both the pre-screening and the post-screening information in two paragraphs and were asked to rate the attractiveness of the five candidate rooms.

The results, presented in Figure 4.6, show that the attractiveness ratings of the experimental group that screened are like those of the second control group that saw only the post-screening information, with overtones contributed by the pre-screening information. In contrast, the attractiveness ratings of the experimental group that did not screen are virtually identical to those of the third control group that saw all of the information.

The results of experiment 4 imply that the differential weighting of the pre-screening and post-screening information found in experiment 1 is brought about by the act of screening. It appears that screening decisions and choice decisions may be regarded by decision makers as separate tasks, and information used in the first is not given much weight is the second. The results of experiments 2 and 3 show that attempts to promote use of the earlier information in the choice decision using prompts and re-presentation of the earlier information were unsuccessful. On the whole, the results of these four experiments suggest that, when screening occurs, the information that is used to do it exerts relatively little influence on the attractiveness of the screened alternatives when it comes to choosing among them.

Experiment 5

The first four experiments used introductory psychology students and a rather simple task. In order to see if the results have generality, the fifth experiment in the series replicated experiment 4 using a more complex decision task and participants who were familiar with the task and its complexity. Borrowing from Rediker (1988), 112 business administration students were each asked to role-play the Chief Executive Officer of a fictitious 'American Electronics Corporation'. They were presented with a rather elaborate case study consisting of a two-page summary of background information about the company which included five of its principal values (annual sales growth, earnings per share, and debt/equity ratio, as well as a reputation for high product quality and a record of good management/ employee relations). The decision problem involved choosing one of five computer firms for acquisition by AEC in order to permit expansion into a new market. Pre-screening information for each of five candidate firms was related to three of AEC's five principal values, and post-screening information was related to the remaining two values.

As in experiment 4, there were three control groups: one saw only the pre-screening information and rated the five candidates ($n = 15$); one saw only the post-screening information and rated the five candidates ($n = 15$); one saw both the pre- and post-screening information combined and rated the candidates ($n = 15$). There were two experimental groups: one saw the pre-screening information, screened the candidates, opened envelopes to see the post-screening information for the candidates that passed the screening, and then rated those candidates and made a choice ($n = 44$); the other saw the pre-screening information and, instead of screening, immediately opened envelopes to see the post-screening information for all five candidates. Then they rated all five candidates and made a choice ($n = 21$).

The results were the same as for experiment 4. The experimental group that did *not* screen gave ratings that were virtually identical to those given by the control group that saw the pre- and post-screening information all at once. The experimental group that screened between the pre-screening information and the post-screening information gave ratings that were virtually identical to those given by the control group that saw only the post-screening information, although, as in the previous experiments, minor influences of the pre-screening information were discernible in the post-screening ratings. All of the participants in both experimental groups chose the most highly rated candidates.

Subsequent regression analyses, across all five experiments, of the relative contributions of the pre-screening and the post-screening information to the ratings made by groups that screened and by groups that did not screen were performed. The results simply underscored the findings reported above—when screening did not take place the ratings were nearly equally influenced by the pre- and post-screening information. When screening took place the ratings were almost wholly determined by the post-screening information, although the pre-screening information had a marginal influence.

To be sure, we are not so naive as to think that this series of experiments establishes that pre-screening information plays little role in subsequent choices. Clearly more evidence is needed, particularly non-laboratory evidence. For example, what happens to the information that is used to derive a 'short list' of job candidates? When there are many applications it is customary to pare (screen) the list down to two or three most acceptable (least unacceptable) candidates and then to interview them. Is the pre-screening information carried forward, and if it is, does it count as much in the final evaluations and choice as the post-screening (interview) information? Surely, this and other real-life decision tasks offer opportunities to extend the present studies.

Note that the five van Zee, Paluchowski and Beach studies only examine one of two cases involving the screening-choice sequence. Here additional information was provided after screening had taken place. In other cases, however, screening serves to eliminate unacceptable candidates, but no post-screening information is forthcoming. When this happens the choice must be made upon what is, in effect, the pre-screening information. It is intriguing to speculate about what may then take place. Perhaps, for example, screening uses only part of the information and choice uses the rest, a result that would be congruent with the results that were reported above.

SUMMARY

In this chapter we have examined the mechanism by which screening is accomplished, the compatibility test. Violations, the rejection threshold, and the decision rule were discussed and the results of four studies were presented in detail. These results demonstrate that image theory can be empirically tested and they answer some specific questions about compatibility. There remain, however, many other questions about compatibility and the compatibility test that must be answered before the image theory view of screening can be more adequately developed. Some of these questions are addressed in the following chapter.

5 More on Compatibility

The research described in Chapter 4 suggests that, in examining compatibility, the violations and the rejection threshold are useful theoretical constructs, and that equation 4.1 may be descriptively sufficient, at least in the circumstances in which it was applied, and that screening has a strong effect on how information is treated in subsequent choice decisions. However, many questions about compatibility remain, and it is the purpose of this chapter to examine some of them.

The first question to be examined involves the relationship between compatibility and Simon's (1955) concept of 'satisficing'. The second question involves the conceptual sufficiency of equation 4.1, and alternative ways of theoretically describing compatibility. The third question involves subjective judgments of violations, and the conditions that influence those judgments. The fourth question involves the way in which different modes of making forecasts lead to different results, and how these results relate to the heuristics and biases research of Kahneman, Tversky, and their colleagues (Kahneman et al., 1982). The fifth question involves the relationship between compatibility assessment and intuitive (and automatic) decision making.

There are of course many other questions that must be addressed as image theory is developed, but these will do for now. Insofar as it is possible to do so within the confines of existing research, we will address each question in turn.

QUESTION 1: HOW DOES THE COMPATIBILITY TEST DIFFER FROM SATISFICING?

The compatibility test and Simon's (1955) concept of satisficing have much in common, primarily because they both address non-maximizing decision behavior. That is, they are both proposed to account for the common observation that chosen alternatives often are not the choices prescribed by classical decision theory, even though the observed choices are not necessarily capricious or unreasonable. Whatever the similarities, however, the compatibility test and satisficing are different in important ways. Let us begin by looking more closely at satisficing.

Defining satisficing

Satisficing rests upon two assumptions (Simon, 1955). The first assumption is 'bounded rationality', which, like framing and knowledge partitions, means that the decision maker brings to bear upon the decision only a limited portion of his or her knowledge. This is an acknowledgement of the inability of the human mind to match the omniscience required by the Rational Economic Man assumption of economic theory. The second assumption is that, within this limited knowledge domain, decisions are sensible given local constraints. 'Sensible' does not mean optimal, either in terms of omniscience or even locally. Rather, it means that utility functions are step functions and that an alternative is satisfactory if its attributes lie on the high-utility side of the step. The satisficing model says that the first alternative encountered that is satisfactory in all attributes is the one that is chosen.

Through usage, Simon's (1955) precise definition of satisficing has became rather blurred. In March and Simon (1958) an alternative was said to satisfice if:

(1) there exists a set of criteria that describes minimally satisfactory alternatives, and (2) the alternative in question meets or exceeds all these criteria. (p. 140)

So definition in terms of utility functions is gone. By the time he had won the Nobel Prize, Simon's description had become:

One could postulate that the decision maker had formed some *aspiration* as to how good an alternative he should find. As soon as he discovered an alternative for choice meeting his level of aspiration, he would terminate the search and choose that alternative. I call this mode of selection *satisficing*. (Simon, 1979, p. 503)

Of course, one does not require an exact definition each time a term is used, and concepts evolve over time. Indeed, Simon's later usage is similar in spirit to the original. Without pointing fingers, however, it is the case that for other people who use the term, just about any deviation at all from classical theory's predictions, sensible or not, is 'explained' as satisficing.

The differences

There are three major differences between the compatibility test and satisficing. The first is that, while the compatibility test is a description of the process by which decisions are made, satisficing has ceased to be a description of process and, instead, has become a description of the end-state of the decision. That is, there appears to be a class of undefined mechanisms that all accomplish a similar end, satisficing. Thus, in his Nobel paper, Simon (1979) names nine theories of the business firm, the decision making aspects of which substitute the assumption of goals as targets for the traditional assumption of profit maximization. Simon states that these nine theories are therefore satisficing theories. If this is true (and who should know better than Simon?), given the difference among the theories, the only way in which they can all be regarded as members of the same class is if 'satisficing' defines *what* is accomplished rather than *how* it is accomplished. In this sense, what the compatibility test accomplishes can be called 'satisficing'. However, the compatibility test is more than that—it constitutes a specific theoretical description about *how* this satisficing is accomplished. Moreover, it describes the place of satisficing (compatibility) in the larger context of decision making; satisficing is not the whole picture.

Second, even if we go back to Simon's (1955) early definition of satisficing as a decision process, it still differs considerably from the compatibility test. According to the old definition, satisficing is a single-step choice process. In contrast, the compatibility test is the first step of a two-step process in which choice (the profitability test) is the second step. That is, in satisficing, the first alternative that meets or exceeds all the criteria is accepted. This may be a sufficient description of many decisions, especially decisions made in a hurry and under pressure. However, it is not descriptive of all decisions. Because the compatibility test is descriptive of a broader range of decisions, including those described by satisficing, the compatibility test logically is the preferable model.

Recall that in image theory the first step in decision making consists of the screening of alternatives using the compatibility test. If there is just one survivor, that survivor is adopted (satisficing) and the process stops after this single stage. However, unlike satisficing, the compatibility test can produce more than one survivor. These survivors are then passed on to the second step, the profitability test, where the best of them is selected for adoption. The question is whether this two-step view is empirically justified.

Payne (1976) presented six college students with the task of selecting an apartment to rent. Payne varied the number of available apartments (2, 6, 12) and the number of attributes of the apartments (4, 8, 12). Participants searched for information about the apartments' attributes before making their decisions. As they searched they talked about what they were thinking and what they were doing. The data analysis focused upon the patterns in the information searches and upon what the participants said.

The results were very clear, and they have been replicated by Olshavsky (1979) and Nichols-Hoppe and Beach (in press). As the number of available apartments increased, the decision makers first screened out those whose attributes failed to meet their standards, and then they chose the best apartment from among the survivors. The search patterns suggested that the first step, screening, was non-compensatory (acceptable attributes did not compensate for unacceptable attributes) and the second step, choice, was compensatory.

Payne (1976) presents excerpts from what some of the participants said as they searched and decided. If there were any doubt about the conclusions reached in the analysis of the search patterns, it is eliminated by the excerpts. For example:

> Apartment E. The rent for apartment E is $140. Which is a good note. The noise level for this apartment is high. That would almost deter me right there. Ah, I don't like a lot of noise. And, if it's high, it must be pretty bad. Which means, you couldn't sleep. I would just put that one aside right there. I wouldn't look any further than that. (p. 375)

> I'm going to look at landlord attitude. In H it's fair. In D it's poor. B it's fair, and A it's good. In L the attitude is poor. In K it's poor. In J it's good, and in I it's poor. So, one of them . . . is poor. So, that's important to me. So . . . that I'm living there. . . . So, I'm not going to live any place where it's poor. (p. 379)

Payne then remarks: 'After [the last statement], the subject never again examined alternatives, D, I, K, and L.' And finally, a third excerpt:

> So, eliminate those two [A & B], and decide between these two [J & H]. O.K., the kitchen facilities in H are good. In J they're fair. And that's about the same to me. . . . Landlord attitude in J is better than in H. And, that's important. . . . Quietness of the rooms. In H it's good. In J it's fair. And that's about the same. The rents are just about the same. In both of them the cleanliness is poor. In J the rooms are larger. So I guess, J will be better. (pp. 379–380)

These results, both the search patterns and what the participants said, indicate the existence of a two-step decision process. Satisficing may well coincide with the first step in some cases, but in its strong form satisficing requires that the first acceptable alternative be accepted. Payne's (1976) data, and that of the replications of his study, clearly show that most frequently more than one minimally acceptable alternative passes the first stage. Thus, the satisficing requirement that the first acceptable candidate be chosen is too narrow a description of what happens. Image theory, and the compatibility test, appear to be a more comprehensive description.

A third difference between the compatability test and satisficing is in the degree to which the two concepts are solidly grounded in a broader theoretical framework. What does it mean to say that a candidate (alternative) satisfices? Simon's (1955) original definition was that the candidate possessed levels of attributes that exceeded the steps in their respective utility functions. Later (Simon, 1979) this became level of aspiration. But, while these definitions account for what decision makers are observed to be doing, they do not explain why the decision maker has utility for the attributes (or aspirations) in the first place, or why the utilities are step functions rather than the usual curve. That is, satisficing is largely an atheoretical description of behavior. Other than the notion that satisficing is easier and less demanding than anything prescribed by classical theory, there is an absence of formal elaboration that would give it theoretical depth.

Let us be clear, this criticism can rightly be leveled at the satisficing concept, but it cannot rightly be leveled at utility theory. This is because utility theory is not a psychological theory, although it is often talked of as though it were. On the other hand, satisficing *is* a psychological theory, although it is often talked of as though it were not.

For utility theory, the ultimate measure of utility simply is the decision maker's willingness to pay to obtain something or to prevent its loss. The theory is not obliged to explain why, because its theoretical domain does not include why. In short, even though it is mathematically quite sophisticated, utility theory is a very superficial theory. Moreover, it may not even be particularly accurate in accounting for the phenomena for which it purports to account. As just one small example, applications of utility theory usually assume that money can be regarded as the common denominator for all value., and that it can be traded for all other goods (Anderson *et al.*, 1981). But it is a common observation that people are often unwilling to put a monetary price on things that they value.

In contrast to utility theory, both satisficing and the compatibility test are psychological constructs and therefore derive their theoretical solidity and depth from their relationship to other psychological constructs within the framework of a coherent psychological theory. The difference between them is that satisficing is anchored in part in non-psychological utility theory and in part in its own partially articulated psychological assumptions, which, because the two are so different, does not provide an adequately coherent framework. The compatibility test is wholly anchored in psychological theory, image theory, which provides a theoretical framework for understanding value. As we have stated above, the image theory definition of value is quite simple: every component of the theory, including compatibility, derives its value from its relationship, however indirect, to the decision maker's principles.

QUESTION 2: HOW MIGHT COMPATIBILITY BE DESCRIBED?

The research reported in Chapter 4 suggests that, within the limitations of the experimental conditions and materials, equation 4.1 is an empirically sufficient description of compatibility assessment. Indeed, because linear equations tend to be quite robust, it is possible that no alternative description could ever displace equation 4.1 if judged solely on its ability to fit empirical data. However, the equation is a very simple description—too simple. Its central mechanism is a variant of feature matching, where mismatches between a candidate's features and the features of relevant image constituents are counted as violations. This is not necessarily bad, but the description requires elaboration. In its present form, equation 4.1 does not deal with the more subtle indirect and abstract relationships between candidates and image constituents that an adequate concept of compatibility must encompass.

For example, suppose that if a particular candidate goal were adopted its attainment would necessitate diversion of effort from some other ongoing plan. If doing this would jeopardize the ongoing plan's attainment of its goal, thereby jeopardizing compliance with the relevant principles, the candidate must be rejected. Or, if a candidate goal's attainment would compromise or detract from the value of some existing goal being attained, the candidate must be rejected. In short, compatibility often involves indirect implications of considerable complexity and subtlety, and its description must be able to handle them. Simple feature matching is insufficient.

What form might a more sophisticated description take? Chiefly because of image theory's roots in the work of Miller *et al.* (1960), the present form, equation 4.1, is a simplistic control theory description. Thus, features of the value, trajectory, and strategic images serve as templates against which the candidate or forecast are compared. Differences are treated as violations and the rejection threshold is determined by external variables. We have already discussed the relationship between equation 4.1 and qualitative impact analysis (Voogd, 1988), which is a screening procedure that is logically comparable to the reasoning that led to equation 4.1. The present purpose, however, is to entertain two alternative descriptions that might reasonably supersede the equation. These certainly are not the only alternatives, but they are ones to which we have given some serious thought.

The first alternative description would retain the general idea of the present description of compatibility, but would enrich it using a modified version of Tversky's (1977) theory of similarity. The core of Tversky's theory is that perceived similarity is a weighted function of the intersection of the features of two objects, less the sum of a weighted function of the features that are distinctive to one of the objects and a weighted function of the features that are distinctive to the other object. The modification would change the emphasis from similarity to dissimilarity.

Even with this modification, this alternative ignores indirect implications and subtle relationships. However, Ortony (1979) has already modified Tversky's (1977) theory to include metaphors and analogies as well as simple matching. This suggests that further modification to include the relationships necessary for a richer description of compatibility could provide a model that is conceptually superior to equation 4.1, thus superseding the equation. The new model would have the advantage of being couched in the familiar logic and language of set theory.

The second alternative description comes from research on artificial intelligence and adaptive expert systems. It is neural network theory, which would be used to 'front end' a rule-based system; the neural network would assess compatibility and the rule-based system would constitute the compatibility test (Rosenfeld, 1987). Joining the two 'architectures' uses the strengths of both while overcoming their weaknesses (Fodor and Pylyshyn, 1988; Lachter and Bever, 1988; Rumelhart et al., 1987). An enriched form of feature matching would remain the underlying mechanism, but neural network theory would allow a great deal more flexibility than would, for instance, set theory. Moreover, because sophisticated computer models exist for simulating neural network processes and for using them in practical applications, this approach has much to recommend it.

Briefly, neural network models are abstract analogies to physiological neural networks. They begin with cells that are neuron-like assemblies which have input and output lines. Associated with each cell is a set of adjustable weights on its input lines and an adjustable threshold on its output lines. The function of the cell is to 'fire' when the input signals are similar to the values of its input weights. The output threshold determines how similar the signals must be to the weights. These cells feed forward to higher-order classification cells. When the classification cells receive sufficient, and properly ordered, signals from lower-level cells, they 'classify' the event that has aroused the system. The ultimate classification of the event depends upon which of the classification cells (or assembly of classification cells) ultimately is activated. By providing mechanisms for adjusting the weights and thresholds as a function of feedback and external conditions, the neural network can adapt—so-called 'learning'. Indeed, it can become highly proficient at performing complex classifications as a function of such experience (Reilly et al., 1982; Reilly et al., 1987; Rimey et al., 1986). Among the successful commercial applications of neural networks are financial risk assessment, the screening of industrial parts, and the screening of mortgage applications (Nestor Inc., 1988). These screening procedures might provide valuable heuristics for the utilization of neural network theory to formulate a conceptually rich description of compatibility and the compatibility test.

QUESTION 3: VIOLATIONS—HOW CLOSE IS CLOSE ENOUGH?

Violations occur when a feature of a candidate has the potential for inter-fering with the realization of a principle, the attainment of an existing goal, or the implementation of an ongoing plan. The question being examined here involves the measure that the decision maker uses to determine whether some degree of interference, etc., is too minor to bother about or too large to overlook. In short, what defines a violation, and is the definition different in different circumstances?

We know of no research that directly addresses this question, but there are studies that address it obliquely. These studies were prompted by Tversky's (1969) theory of lexicographic semi-orders. Tversky's theory was for choice decisions: the decision maker judges the features of two competing decision alternatives to be essentially equivalent if they are very similar on the underlying dimension of comparison, even if they are not exactly the same on the dimension. The assumption is that, if the features are essentially equivalent, they need not be considered further and the choice can be based on the remaining features. (This assumption is comparable to image theory's assumption about non-violations in the compatibility test.)

The research to be described consisted of a series of loosely related experiments on subjective judgments of equivalence. In all of the experi-ments, participants were presented with various mathematical and statistical problems and asked to predict the correct answers. Then they were asked to place intervals around either their predictions or the correct answers to the problems. The intervals are called equivalence intervals—EIs (Beach and Solak, 1969)—and they delineate the range of possible values that the decision maker regards as equivalent to the prediction that he or she gave or to the correct answer, which was usually provided by the experimenter. For example, if the participant were to make a prediction and then were told the correct answer by the experimenter, the EI would represent the degree to which the prediction could deviate from that correct answer and still be regarded by the decision maker as essentially correct. Similarly, if the correct answer turned out to be within the EI around the prediction, the decision maker would regard the prediction to be 'in the ballpark'.

Beach and Solak (1969)

In the first study, 54 college students were presented with 15 mathematical problems that required them to calculate percentages in their heads. Some of the problems were difficult ('What is 31% of 183?') and some were easy ('What is 25% of 1792?'), and the magnitudes of the quantities involved varied from as low as 17 to as high as 9306. After the participants had given their judgments, they were asked to cover their answers and the experimenter told them the correct answer for each problem. They were asked to indicate the upper and lower bounds around each correct answer within which their own judgment could lie and still be regarded as essentially correct ('in the ballpark').

It was found that the judgments were extremely accurate, but that is not the point. The important finding was that the relationship between the breadth of the EIs and the magnitudes of the correct answers was very well described by $EI/C = k$. That is, the breadth of the interval, EI, divided by the correct answer, C, was a constant, k; big Cs got big EIs and little Cs got little EIs, and the relative size of the EI was proportional (k) to C. Moreover, the value of k differed for difficult and easy problems; participants were considerably more demanding about what qualified as a correct answer for easy problems ($k = 0.02$) than for difficult ones ($k = 0.24$). (Note that $EI/C = k$ follows from Weber's law (Stevens, 1962) and is conceptually linked to subjective judgments of variance (Beach and Scopp, 1968; Hofstatter, 1939; Lathrop, 1967).)

Laestadius (1970)

Thirty-two college students were presented with 20 lists of 15 numbers; the means and variances of the numbers were different for the different lists. First they were asked to judge the means of the lists. They were then asked to cover their judgments, were given the correct answers, and were asked to place EIs around the correct answers. An additional 32 students were simply given the problems and the correct answers and asked to place EIs around the correct answers. The lists differed in the degree of variance among the numbers.

For both groups of participants, EIs were narrower for low-variance lists than for high-variance lists (which also was reflected in the first group's judgmental accuracy). In addition, those participants who had had experience making the judgments set significantly wider EIs than did those who had not had the experience.

Beach, Beach, Carter, and Barclay (1974)

The third study was a collection of five rather diverse experiments that examined the role of familiarity with the problem, and non-quantitative conditions that might make some degree of judgmental inaccuracy seem reasonable or of decreased importance (e.g. lack of expertise, too little information, lack of motivation). To summarize the rather complicated set of findings, EIs *decreased* as a function of familiarity of the task and relevant knowledge (as in Laestadius, 1970), as a function of increased information (sample size in a proportion estimation task) and decreased variance in that information (as in Laestadius, 1970). They *increased* as a function of the magnitudes of the numbers involved (judgments about people's ages, the seriousness of diseases, the seriousness of life events, and amounts of money) in the proportional way they did in Beach and Solak (1969), and they increased when judgments involved uncertainty (gambles). In short, the EI was related in an orderly way to numerous variables that increase or decrease the decision maker's willingness to disregard the difference between a judgment and a criterion and to treat the two as essentially equivalent for the purpose at hand.

Crocker, Mitchell, and Beach (1978)

In this experiment, 84 business students were presented with 20 pieces of information about each of eight hypothetical job candidates. They were asked to judge the probable job success of each candidate on a scale from 0.00 to 1.00, and to set an EI around their judgment such that it was likely that the true answer would fall within it. The definition of 'likely' was left up to the participant.

The information was presented sequentially and the orderliness ('trends') of the sequence was varied (orderly or disorderly) as was the credibility of the source of the information (high or low).

Analyses showed that the existence of orderly trends in the information sequences and high source credibility resulted in narrower EIs than when sequences lacked trends and sources lacked credibility.

Larson and Reenan (1979)

Sixty college students were asked to make three kinds of judgments: judgments of the number of marbles in each of five containers, judgments of the number of red discs in each of five tachistoscopically presented 10×10 matrices of red and blue discs, and judgments of elapsed time between two signals for each of five intervals. Half of the participants placed an EI around each of their judgments and half rated their confidence in the accuracy of each of their judgments on a 21-point scale. The correlations between the mean EIs and the mean confidence ratings for the three tasks were −0.72 for the marbles in the containers, −0.97 for the red discs in the matrices, and −0.92 for time intervals, indicating that as confidence increased the breadth of the EI decreased. Moreover, EIs also correlated with the degree of accuracy of the participants' judgments; –0.93 for the marbles, –0.89 for the red discs, and –0.96 for the time intervals.

So then, how close is close enough? The answer is: It depends. And, although the experiments were not specifically designed to study the assessment of compatibility, the results reported above suggest some variables upon which it may depend. Grant us license to generalize these results to the case of violations.

First, it may take a larger discrepancy to constitute a violation when the magnitudes involved are large than when they are small. If a decision maker were willing to pay $200 per month for a particular car but found that the required payment was $250, the additional $50 might constitute a violation sufficient to prompt rejection of the car. On the other hand, if he or she were willing to pay $1000 per month and the car payment turned out to be $1050, the additional $50 probably would not seem sufficient to prompt the car's rejection.

Second, unfamiliarity with a decision or forecast may affect judgments about violations. Thus, if the decision maker knows that because of his or her lack of knowledge or experience it might be difficult to attain a goal precisely he or she may be inclined to expand the definition of how close is close enough. This, for example, could lead to forecasts of near misses in goal attainment being regarded as close enough under the circumstances. So, too, for a new college graduate, a potential first job that pays less than what he thinks he is worth may still be regarded as close enough; or for a new assistant professor, student evaluations that fall short of her target may be regarded as an acceptable beginning.

Third, the ambiguity of the decision may influence judgments of violations. Ambiguity can be described by high variance in the information the decision maker has about the attributes being examined, by the absence of orderly trends in feedback or other forms of relevant information, by low source credibility, and by inherent uncertainty such as that found in gambling.

QUESTION 4: HOW DO DIFFERENT FORECASTING MODES INFLUENCE FORECASTS, AND HOW DOES THIS RELATE TO HEURISTICS AND BIASES?

Forecasting's important role in image theory raises two issues. The first is whether different ways of making forecasts result in different forecasts. The dominant model for subjective forecasting is the 'intuitive statistician' model, which uses statistical reasoning both as the metaphor for subjective forecasting and as the standard against which its adequacy is evaluated. The competing model is causal reasoning, which really is a collection of cognitive techniques for generating forecasts. The question of interest here is the degree to which the two kinds of reasoning generate similar or different forecasts.

The second issue is embedded in the first. The most well known research on subjective forecasting is that done by Kahneman, Tversky, and their colleagues. This work is based upon the assumption that statistical reasoning is in fact *the* rational way to approach subjective forecasting. Because their results demonstrate that decision makers' forecasts often fail to conform to statistical prescriptions, it is important to examine the implications of these findings for forecasting in general and for image theory in particular. The following discussion is based upon reviews by Loftus and Beach (1982), Jungermann (1983), Beach *et al.* (1986), and Beach *et al.* (1987).

The idea behind the 'intuitive statistics' model is that because humans are not omniscient they must make inferences about uncertain events in order to make decisions. Because probability theory and statistics were devised to make inferences in the face of uncertainty, the studies use them as *normative models*; that is, as prescriptions both for the methods of making such inferences and for the criteria for inferential accuracy (Barclay *et al.*, 1971).

In the original research agenda, deviations of humans' inferences from the prescriptions of these models were supposed to serve as a basis for changing the models so that they became descriptive of 'imperfect human inference' (Peterson and Beach, 1967, p. 30). In only a few cases, however, was a model ever changed. Instead, the focus of most research was simply upon documentation of the imperfection of human inference—usually referred to as 'suboptimality'. Nonetheless, upon reviewing the literature that had accumulated up to 1966, Peterson and Beach (1967) concluded that the normative models provided:

> . . . a good first approximation for a psychological theory of inference. Inferences made by subjects are influenced by appropriate variables and in appropriate directions. But there are systematic discrepancies between normative and intuitive inferences. (p. 42)

The discussion went on to list some of the discrepancies.

In the 20 years following that rather charitable conclusion, profound changes occurred in the study of inference. First of all, the term 'inference' was largely replaced by 'judgment' or by 'forecast' (we use the latter term). Second, the research results were increasingly viewed as instructive about the quality and nature of the non-laboratory judgments and inferences that are used in applied forecasting and decision making. Third, the research literature on the logic and accuracy of forecasts became exceedingly contradictory. Christensen-Szalanski and Beach (1984) found that 45% of the empirical articles on subjective forecasting and related topics showed that subjects performed something like intuitive statisticians, while 55% showed the contrary.

Given the stakes involved in the applied use of judgmental forecasts, and given the roughly equal split in the empirical literature, it is perhaps not surprising that two camps have emerged, each holding a different viewpoint about the quality of judgmental forecasts. Jungermann (1983) labeled these camps the pessimists and the optimists. The pessimists focus on failures of forecasting and the optimists focus on successes.

This is not the place to review the arguments on both sides of this controversy; Beach *et al.* (1986) presents such a review as well as a compromise framework for examining the literature. However, it is important to observe that, although the so-called pessimistic camp accommodates a diversity of people and opinions (e.g. Nisbett and Ross, 1980; Slovic *et al.*, 1985), its keynote has been the 'heuristics and biases' research (Kahneman *et al.*, 1982). That is, the pessimists do not claim that forecasts are haphazard or capricious. On the contrary, they infer from observed orderliness in the errors in forecasting experiments that participants rely upon cognitive short-cuts, heuristics, that produce systematic errors, biases, in the forecasts. The most commonly discussed heuristics are representativeness, availability, and anchoring and adjustment (Tversky and Kahneman, 1974), along with the simulation heuristic (Kahneman and Tversky, 1982c). The resulting biases are numerous—the law of small numbers (Tversky and Kahneman, 1971), the illusion of validity (Kahneman and Tversky, 1973), the regression fallacy (Kahneman and Tversky, 1973), the imaginability bias (Tversky and Kahneman, 1974), illusory correlation (Chapman and Chapman, 1967), the hindsight illusion (Fischhoff, 1975), the base rate fallacy (Bar-Hillel, 1980; Kahneman and Tversky, 1972), and the conjunction fallacy (Tversky and Kahneman, 1983).

The optimists' viewpoint has been advanced both by emphasizing the literature that demonstrates forecasting success and, to a greater degree, by questioning the foundations of the pessimists' evidence (Beach, *et al.*, 1987; Hogarth, 1981). The questioning has focused on two issues: (1) the appropriateness of the normative models that are used as criteria in the evaluation of forecasts, and (2) whether participants and experiments share the same understanding of the experimental tasks that are used in the research.

In the heuristics and biases literature, the way in which a task is understood, classified, or the like is called 'framing'—and, while narrower, it corresponds in part to what is meant by framing in image theory. In their studies of framing, Tversky and Kahneman (1981) have shown that apparently minor changes in how a problem is presented can strongly influence the answers that participants give to it. Indeed, this apparent lability of frames is regarded by the pessimist camp as yet another example of the generally low quality of human forecasts.

Alternatively, framing is seen by the optimists as having strong implications for those studies that report poor forecasting abilities. That is, if many participants are misframing the problems (from the experimenter's viewpoint at least), then what do the results mean? Does it make sense to infer from their forecasts that participants as a group used the so-and-so heuristic, thereby falling victim to the so-and-so bias, if in fact they did not see themselves as making that kind of forecast at all?

To illustrate how experimenters and participants can legitimately differ in their framing of a forecasting problem, consider the following hypothetical example. Suppose that an experimenter were to *randomly* select a church in the United States and visit it one Sunday afternoon in June, the traditional month for weddings in America. He stands outside and waits for the wedding party to emerge. Then he approaches the Best Man and asks: 'If I were to randomly select an American couple getting married this afternoon, what is the probability that they would still be married to each other ten years from now?'

Assuming that he knows the American divorce rate, the Best Man would probably give it, in probability form, as his answer. However, what if the experimenter asked instead: 'What is the probability that the newly married couple for whom you were Best Man will still be married to each other ten years from now'?

For the experimenter, the change in question does not change the problem—he randomly selected this couple and he knows absolutely nothing about them as individuals; for him they are mutually intersubstitutable with any other American couple getting married on that day, or on any other day for that matter. But, for the Best Man, the subject of this thought experiment, the change of question reflects a substantial change in the problem. The base rate (the prior probability of divorce) may influence his answer, but only if he is particularly cynical. (Indeed, if he really thought the base rate—about 0.50—accurately described his friends' chances of marital success, he might well have declined to serve as Best Man on the grounds that it would be a poor investment of his time.) Rather, his answer to the second question, the one that is specific to his friends as individuals, is properly based upon his knowledge about them and his theories about what leads to successful and unsuccessful marriages.

The optimists' view is that it is presumptuous to condemn the Best Man for not using statistical reasoning when answering the second question. That is, it is unreasonable to insist that the frame that is appropriate from the experimenter's point of view is the only admissible frame and use of any alternative is an instance of poor judgment and irrationality. The optimist would argue that it would perhaps be more to the point to investigate the circumstances under which statistical and causal reasoning are used, the differences in the forecasts that result from using the two different kinds of reasoning, and the degree to which those forecasts follow in a justifiable manner from the frame that is adopted and the reasoning that is used. The following experiment is, to our knowledge, the only empirical study to examine these questions.

Barnes (1984)

This experiment began with the assumption that there are two very different, and equally legitimate, reasoning modes for making forecasts for the kinds of problems that are commonly used in forecasting experiments. Building upon a suggestion by Tversky and Kahneman (1983; Kahneman and Tversky, 1982a), Barnes identified these modes as *aleatory reasoning* and *epistemic reasoning*, two modes that have long been recognized and differentiated. (See Hacking (1975) for a history and Hammond (1982) for use of the terms in forecasting research.)

Aleatory reasoning is the logic of gambling (an *aleator* is a dice player), and is the basis for modern probability theory. A major feature of this logic is the Principle of Extentionality which, in essence, states that all elements in a particular set are mutually intersubstitutable (Suppes, 1957). That is, statements about the characteristics of the element in question are based solely upon its class membership and not upon its unique properties. In gambling this means that knowing that the next throw of a die is in fact unique is regarded as irrelevant to statements about the probabilities of the possible outcomes of that throw—a five on one throw is the same as a five on any other throw.

In contrast, epistemic reasoning explicitly involves knowledge about the unique characteristics of specific elements and the reasoner's framework of knowledge, including the causal network and set of class memberships in which the elements' characteristics are embedded. In short, epistemic reasoning is the mode of reasoning that underlies scenarios and the causal logic of forecasting that was described in Chapter 2.

To be sure, both modes of reasoning can generate forecasts, although they do so in different ways. For example, when forecasting the probability of precipitation, a weather forecaster who uses aleatory reasoning depends entirely upon probability data, regarding present weather conditions as a member of a set of previously observed, similar conditions that have resulted in precipitation on a specific proportion of occasions. In contrast, a forecaster who uses epistemic reasoning might look at satellite photographs and mentally project the progress of various weather fronts and their subsequent influences on the local weather; the mental projection would rely upon the forecaster's knowledge about how fronts progress in the particular locale for which the forecast is being made, and upon his or her mental model about what causes precipitation.

Barnes' experiment was conducted using 10 undergraduates from an introductory psychology class who has never taken statistics and who were thus typical of the participants in most laboratory studies of forecasting.

The participants were presented with 15 word problems from the literature that have been used to demonstrate forecasting errors. Five of the problems had been used to demonstrate that forecasters tend to ignore sample sizes (the 'law of small numbers', Tversky and Kahneman (1971)), five to demonstrate that they ignore or underuse base rates (the 'base rate bias', Kahneman and Tversky (1972)), and five to demonstrate that they tend to judge the probability of the conjunction of events as higher than the probabilities of the constituent events (the 'conjunction fallacy', Tversky and Kahneman (1983)).

First, the participants read the 15 problems, sorted them into classes of similar problems, and labeled each class and described what was similar among the problems in it. The results were that the labels and the definitions of similarity did not reflect appreciation of sample size, base rate, or conjunction, the three aleatory concepts that the original experimenters had used to generate the problems. Instead, the participants' labels were based on concepts like 'math problems', 'problems about people', and 'other'. That is, the problems that experimenters frame as being of a specific statistical, aleatory, type got distributed among several of the participants' classes, indicating that the participants' frames were very different from the experimenters' frames.

The participants were also asked to make a forecast for each of the problems while 'thinking aloud' and what was said was evaluated according to whether it reflected aleatory reasoning, epistemic reasoning, a mixture of the two, or was unclassifiable. The results were:

- For the sample size problems, 74% of the forecasts were based on aleatory reasoning, 22% on epistemic reasoning, and 4% on a mixture or were unclassifiable.
- For the base rate problems, 50% were based on aleatory reasoning, 46% on epistemic reasoning, and 4% on a mixture or were unclassifiable.
- For the conjunction problems, 28% were based on aleatory reasoning and 72% were based on epistemic reasoning.

That is, the participants tended to use aleatory reasoning on sample size problems, epistemic reasoning on the conjunction problems, and both about equally on the base rate problems; only a small percentage of the forecasts were not clearly based on either of these modes of reasoning.

Participants were not rigid in their choice of forecasting modes, however. For example, for one of the five conjunction problems all of the participants used epistemic reasoning, while for another conjunction problem most of the participants used aleatory reasoning. Indeed, Barnes' results conform to conclusions by Nisbett *et al.* (1983) in that problems that encouraged recognition of chance, repeatability and the like tended to receive aleatory treatment, and those that involved individual persons tended to receive epistemic treatment. For example, two of Barnes' five base rate problems were about diseases in groups of people, and virtually all participants used aleatory reasoning for them. The other three base rate problems involved individual persons and most of the participants used epistemic reasoning.

These results show:

(1) that for these problems the two modes of forecasting, aleatory and epistemic, cover almost everything that the subjects did and that the evaluators could discriminate between the modes;
(2) that the evaluations were not biased toward one mode of reasoning or the other; and
(3) that not only are the participants able to use both modes of reasoning, the mode they used appeared to depend upon how they framed the problem.

Beach *et al.* (1986) explored the implications of Barnes' (1984) results for understanding the conflicting results that constitute the literature in judgmental forecasting. The analysis begins with the finding that participants and experimenters frequently disagree about the appropriateness of the aleatory forecasting mode for problems. This gives rise to the 2 × 2 matrix in Figure 5.1 in which experimenters' views about the mode of reasoning that is appropriate given the characteristics of the forecasting task are crossed with the mode of reasoning that participants view as appropriate.

Cell 1 contains studies in which the experimenters' frame for the forecasting task calls for aleatory reasoning and the participants' frame also calls for aleatory reasoning. The result is that the participants behave like 'intuitive statisticians'. This cell contains, for example, those research results that demonstrate that participants detect covariation (Crocker, 1981), observe the law of large numbers (Beach *et al.*, 1974), take base rates into account (Christensen-Szalanski and Beach, 1982), or revise probabilities in a manner that looks much like the prescriptions of Bayes' theorem (Murphy and Winkler, 1977).

Cell 2 contains studies in which the experimenters' frames call for aleatory reasoning, but the participants' frames call for epistemic reasoning. These studies constitute much of the heuristic and biases literature. For example, assessments of the probability that a person is a member of one or another professional group (the base rate fallacy) seem to involve epistemic reasoning since the assessments reflect the unique characteristics of that person and that professional group, rather than base rates. When an initial value (an

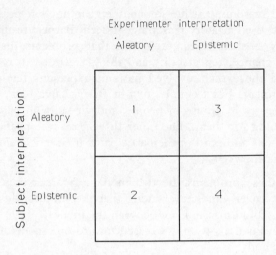

Figure 5.1 Experimenters' views about appropriate reasoning versus participants' views (Beach *et al.* 1986). Reproduced by permission of John Wiley & Sons Ltd

earlier forecast or a provided starting point) provides knowledge that is reflected in subsequent forecasts (the anchoring and adjustment heuristic), it evidences epistemic reasoning—events in a sequence may be related to each other in a causal manner.

Cell 3 contains studies in which experimenters, but not participants, think that epistemic reasoning is most appropriate for making forecasts about a single object, person, or event and that class memberships are not appropriate bases for forecasts about that individual. This cell contains studies of negative social stereotyping (e.g. Snyder *et al.*, 1977). For example, hiring decisions (performance forecasts) that use the unique characteristics of job applicants, such as experience, education, or training rely upon epistemic reasoning. But, hiring decisions that use stereotypes about applicants' gender or race rely upon aleatory reasoning (McCauley *et al.*, 1980), and ordinarily are condemned because epistemic reasoning 'should' be applied instead.

Cell 4 contains studies in which experimenters and participants agree that epistemic reasoning is appropriate to the task. Studies of psychotherapy may be examples of 'experimenters' and 'participants' sharing a common interest in epistemic reasoning—with emphasis being upon forecasting the progress of the individual client given a treatment method rather than upon the group of which he or she is a member. Another example is the knowledge structures found by Pennington and Hastie (1986) in their study of jury decision making. Indeed, the research on scripts (Galambos and Ableson, 1986; Schank and Ableson, 1977) and mental models (Jungermann and Thüring,

1987), and on related topics discussed in previous chapters provides examples for this cell.

These results leave things somewhat up in the air. It is difficult to know just what to make of the vast literature on heuristics and biases. Certainly, Barnes' results suggest that many of those so-called biases did not in fact result from application of the celebrated heuristics. They probably resulted from participants' application of an altogether different kind of reasoning. However, it is impossible to go back to the literature and sort out the studies that fall in one cell or the other in Figure 5.1, so we shall never know which studies really constitute evidence for the existence of heuristics and which do not.

The implication for image theory is also unclear. It seems reasonable to expect forecasts to vary in accuracy depending upon various circumstances, but it really is not altogether clear what those circumstances may be. Beach et al. (1986) present a contingency model that addresses this question, as well as the question of whether aleatory or epistemic reasoning will be adopted by decision makers in particular circumstances. However, the model is specifically designed for laboratory and applied forecasts that are similar to those used in the experiments that have been described. The forecasts in image theory are much richer and are done for the decision maker's own use, rather than in response to outside demands, and therefore the model may not be appropriate. At any rate, the role of forecasts in decision making is so important that future research must focus closely upon them, but that research must not be overly influenced by the heuristics and biases research lest it prejudge the adequacy of the forecasts.

QUESTION 5: WHAT IS THE RELATIONSHIP OF COMPATI-BILITY TO INTUITIVE DECISION MAKING AND AFFECT?

Isenberg (1984) studied senior managers as they made decisions on their jobs. He reports that intuition played a large role in their decisions, both in sensing that a problem exists (a gut feeling that something is wrong) and in applying their knowledge rapidly to diagnose and solve the problem. In addition, some managers use intuition as a check on more rational analysis:

> Most senior executives are familiar with the formal decision analysis models and tools, and those that occasionally use such systematic methods for reaching decisions are leery of solutions that these methods suggest that run counter to their sense of the correct course of action. (p. 86)

Part of intuition appeared to be the ability to recognize familiar patterns and apply a familiar solution from a repertory of solutions. Thus, Isenberg concludes that:

> . . . intuition is not the opposite of rationality, nor is it a random process of guessing. Rather, it is based on extensive experience both in analysis and problem solving and in implementation, and to the extent that the lessons of experience are well-founded, then so is intuition. (p. 86)

Isenberg's positive view of intuition is shared by Beck (1987), who describes its role in decision making as BankAmerica tried to redefine itself as a result of deregulation. In this role, intuition was identified with commitment to the organization, to action, and to innovation, and as a counterweight to 'analysis paralysis'.

Isenberg (1984) identifies intuition as the smooth automatic performance of learned behavior sequences. Barnard (1938) identified its prime qualities as speed and the inability to account for how the decision got made or precisely why, even though the decision maker is confident about its correctness. Simon began by regarding intuitive decisions as fast versions of non-intuitive decision making, which explanation he later termed as having 'finessed' the issue (Simon, 1987). When he re-examined the issue in light of advances in cognitive science (Simon, 1987), he noted:

> Experts often arrive at problem diagnosis and solution rapidly and intuitively without being able to report how they attained the result. . . . This ability is best explained by postulating a recognition and retrieval process that employs a large number—generally tens of thousands or even hundreds of thousands— of chunks or patterns stored in long term memory. (p. 61)

Mitchell and Beach (in press) have addressed the same issue from the point of view of image theory. Our conclusion is different from that arrived at by Isenberg, Barnard, and Simon. We differentiate between automatic decision making and intuition, on the basis of process and on the basis of the accompanying affect. What these other authors have identified as intuition, the application of specific learned experience to a problem, we identify as automatic decision making. We see this as the application of existing policies from memory that are keyed to recognition of a current context as having been encountered before. Thus automatic decision making is a direct function of framing, and the affect that accompanies it is a feeling of recognition of the decision problem and of knowing what to do.

Intuition, on the other hand, is considerably different. It occurs when the problem is not recognized, that is, during the compatibility test, when candidate solutions to some problem are being evaluated for their 'fit' with the ongoing flow of the decision maker's activities and his or her principles.

Fit is evaluated quickly and with minimal cognitive effort—and the accompanying affect is discomfort when fit is poor and comfort and confidence when fit is good, just as is reported for intuition (Beach and Mitchell, 1985, 1986). Of course, because framing determines identification and the principles, goals, and plans that are relevant to the decision, it therefore determines the criteria for 'fit', and thus is central to intuition as well as to automatic decision making.

The affect involved in intuition tends to be less obvious and less dramatic than that having to do with conspicuous indecision (see Chapter 3). However, it conveys a strong sense of conviction, often without supporting reasons. It is what one refers to when one says 'I decided to do it because it felt like the right thing to do', or 'I feel uneasy about it all—something isn't right', or 'I've tried, but I don't feel I'm getting anywhere'. In short, this is the affect that we berate as irrational even while using it as the ultimate criterion both for deciding whether to do something and for deciding whether our subsequent efforts are making progress toward achieving that something.

The compatibility test, the mechanism for making intuitive decisions, often is not part of conscious experience. Of course, consciousness includes only a small part of what goes on physiologically and psychologically. It is of limited capacity and it is usually devoted to those aspects of the internal and external environment that are in flux or that are suprising. Consciousness is a trouble-shooter that focuses upon incongruities, and for the most part it relies upon surrogates in order to 'know' when incongruities arise. Thus, for example, one's stomach receives little attention until it malfunctions or until it produces hunger pangs—the pain and affect arising from these states captures attention and focuses consciousness upon them, thereby providing a venue for their remedy. For the most part, when ongoing events fall within normal limits, consciousness is not directed to them.

We suggest that the affect related to the compatibility test serves as the surrogate that is monitored by conscious attention—as long as candidates' violations do not exceed the rejection threshold, they are adopted 'intuitively'. Thus intuition has a status akin to that ascribed by Polyani (1966) to the processes underlying perception; it is 'tacit' in that it is lawful and can be studied, but only its results ordinarily are part of conscious experience. Only incongruities and anomalies cause one to turn attention to tacit mechanisms, and even then one seldom has access to them.

In this sense, the compatibility test is the tacit mechanism underlying intuition. Our view is that affect constitutes a continuous (analog) system that indicates the ongoing state of the discrete results of the compatibility test. When the violations detected by the test are below the rejection threshold, attention is not engaged and adoption is intuitive and accompanied by positive affect and a sense of conviction. When violations exceed threshold, affect is negative and the candidate is rejected. If rejection is not possible (e.g. there is no contending plan for pursuing a goal), the discomfort accompanying adoption of the faulty plan is an increasing function of the plan's incompatibility. This, of course, is a hypothesis that has yet to be tested.

In closing this discussion, we note a curiosity. Decision researchers view analytic, 'rational' decision making as preferable to non-analytic, 'intuitive' decision making. The curiosity lies in the fact that satisfaction with a 'rational' decision seems to be determined by how acceptable it would be as an 'intuitive' decision, and not the other way around. Isenberg (1984) noted that, on the rare occasions when senior executives used formal decision analysis models for reaching decisions, they were leery of results that ran counter to their intuition. We suspect that, as a general rule, if intuition conflicts with analysis, analysis seldom wins.

6 The Profitability Test

The profitability test serves to identify the best candidate for adoption from among two or more candidates that have survived screening by the compatibility test. However, the profitability test is not a single, theoretically tidy strategy like the compatibility test. Decision makers in fact use many different strategies to make choices—from flipping a coin, to asking an authority what to do, to decision analysis. Different decision makers have different degrees of sophistication about available choice strategies—most know about coin flipping and asking advice, few know about decision analysis. Moreover, the same decision maker uses different strategies in different circumstances—coin flipping and advice may be appropriate for choosing a movie, and decision analysis may be appropriate for siting a power plant, but some other strategy surely is needed for choosing a spouse.

THE STRATEGY SELECTION MODEL

Beach and Mitchell (1978) proposed a general model for the selection of choice strategies. This model has since been merged into image theory as the profitability test (Beach and Mitchell, 1990). As part of the merger some features of the model and the names of some of its constructs have been changed to make them consistent with the theory, but the essence has remained unchanged. The components of the model are shown in Figure 6.1.

The purpose of the model is to describe how decision makers select a strategy for making a choice in particular circumstances. It is based on the assumption that strategy selection is contingent upon both the characteristics of the decision maker and the characteristics of the decision task. The decision maker is viewed as possessing a unique repertory of strategies from which one is selected to be applied to the decision at hand. The model is about how the decision maker makes a decision about how to make the decision. That is, the model is about a metadecision about which strategy to apply to the decision task. The metadecision is viewed as a single, theoretically neat process like the compatibility test. The selected strategy, however,

I. Decision strategies:
    Non-analytic
    Unaided-analytic
    Aided-analytic

II. Characteristics of the decision task:
    A. The decision problem
        Unfamiliarity
        Ambiguity
        Complexity
        Instability
    B. The decision environment
        Irreversibility
        Iterativity
        Significance
        Accountability
        Time/money constraints

III. Characteristics of the decision maker:
     Knowledge
     Ability
     Motivation

Figure 6.1 The basic features of the strategy selection model.

can be any of a broad spectrum of different strategies, depending upon the contents of the decision maker's repertory and upon the nature of the decision task—that is, upon the contextual frame.

The metadecisions follows a cost–benefit, subjective expected utility logic that balances the cost of using each of the relevant strategies in the decision maker's repertory against the expected utility (benefit) of making a correct decision. The relevant strategies are those that are considered by the decision maker to be appropriate for the context as it is framed at the moment the strategy is being selected, and a correct decision is one that will successfully yield outcomes that the decision maker anticipates it will yield. (As we noted previously, decision makers want to make *correct decisions*. Decision theorists want them to make *decisions correctly*, on the assumption that correct decisions generally follow from correct procedures—if perchance they do not, one should not mourn the failure because one did the best one could. This argument usually fails to impress decision makers as much as it does decision theorists (Christensen-Szalanski, 1978).)

The Beach and Mitchell (1978) paper laid out the framework for the strategy selection model, and Christensen-Szalanski (1978, 1980) formalized it. What follows is a mixture of the two, modified to fit into image theory.

DECISION STRATEGIES

Decision makers' repertories are assumed to contain a limited number of ways of making choices, some of which are approximations to formal decision methods (e.g. maximization of subjective expected utility) and some of which may be wholly unique to the individual. Beach and Mitchell (1978) divided these strategies into three classes, calling them aided-analytic, unaided-analytic, and non-analytic. Hammond *et al.* (1987) called them analytical, quasi-rational, and intuitive and described them as forming a continuum. We presently prefer our terms and the Hammond *et al.* continuum.

At the aided-analytic end of the continuum are strategies that require the decision maker to apply a prescribed procedure using tools such as mathematics, pencil and paper, calculator or computer, etc., in a guided, systematic attempt to analyze the various candidates and evaluate their potential outcomes. These strategies usually require training and frequently a technician is employed to help. Decision analysis, and the aid of a decision analyst, define the extreme at the aided-analytic end of the continuum, closely followed by all normative choice models that are considered optimal in some sense or other in economics, statistics, operations analysis, etc. Moreover, this end of the continuum contains many complex procedures that may or may not be wholly optimal, such as those used in siting of highways, power plants, and in similar large-scale institutional decisions. The latter are not necessarily optimal, but they are formalized, prescriptive approaches to immensely complicated and information-laden decisions and therefore are at the aided-analytic end of the continuum.

Somewhat less formal than the foregoing strategies, but still within the aided-analytic range, are strategies involving the listing and evaluation of outcomes that could occur if each of the candidates were the one chosen. These strategies typically involve decomposition of the problem through decision trees or some other diagrammatic representation of the candidates and their potential outcomes. Some, however, simply involve the listing of pros and cons of the various condidates and balancing the two against each other, a method called 'moral algebra' by Benjamin Franklin (Smyth, 1906).

Unaided-analytic strategies occupy the mid-range of the continuum. These are strategies for which an attempt is made to examine the candidates' potential outcomes, but for which no tools are used, and for which the decision maker restricts processing to the confines of his or her imagination. These are the strategies that have been studied most by behavioral decision researchers using the normative models from the aided-analytic end of the continuum as comparison models in order to evaluate the procedural adequacy of the unaided-analytic strategies (Barclay *et al.*, 1971; Peterson and Beach, 1967).

Examples of unaided-analytic strategies are the various approximations to the subjected expected utility strategy that decision makers perform entirely in their heads. In these strategies, the decision maker attempts to think about the outcomes that could result from selection of each of the available candidates as well as the chances of those outcomes occurring, and then chooses the alternative that seems in some way to offer the greatest potential. Gray (1975) found that third-grade children's choices of arithmetic problems to attempt appeared to be arrived at by this strategy, and Tversky (1967), Shanteau and Anderson (1969), Shanteau (1974), Holmstrom and Beach (1973), Muchinsky and Fitch (1975), and many others have found that adults can use something quite like it too. Research using the various versions of expectancy theory (Fishbein and Ajzen, 1975; Mitchell, 1974; Mitchell and Beach, 1976; Mitchell and Knudson, 1973), which are similar in conception to the subjected expected utility model, reinforces the plausibility of the idea that people sometimes attempt to use such strategies.

Tversky's (1969) special case of the lexicographic model (Fishburn, 1974) is a simple example of an unaided-analytic strategy. Here the decision maker selects the most important aspect of the various candidates and eliminates all candidates except the one that is superior to all others on it; if none are superior to the others on that aspect the decision maker drops it and moves to the next most important aspect; and so on until a single candidate survives. This and similar strategies (e.g Tversky's (1972) additive difference model) have the advantage of reducing the cost of information processing by restricting attention to only part of the available information about the candidates, but they have the disadvantage of introducing inconsistencies such as intransitivity of preference (Tversky, 1969).

Finally, the least structured of the unaided-analytic strategies involves the construction of mental movies (forecasts) of how things might turn out if this or that candidate were chosen. Then the candidate with the most favorable movie *relative* to the movies for the other candidates is the one that actually is chosen. Note the similarity between this process and the use of forecasts for progress decisions—the same underlying mechanism is involved in both of them.

Non-analytic strategies are at the opposite end of the continuum from the aided-analytic strategies. They are fairly simple, quick-and-easy ways of selecting one candidate from a set of two or more candidates. They require little information, little time, and little thought about the candidates' possible consequences. Examples are 'Eeny, meeny, miney, mo . . .', flipping a coin, or homilies. The latter might be used to decide about going sailing—'Red sky at night, sailors' delight; red sky in the morning, sailors take warning'.

Both 'Better safe than sorry' or 'A bird in the hand is worth two in the bush' represent conservative strategies in contrast to the riskiness of 'Nothing ventured, nothing gained'.

The major difference among the various strategies on the continuum is in the degree of analysis they involve, and, as a result, in the amount of resources (time, effort, and/or money) they require. Aided-analytic strategies use formal procedures to lay out the problem and to decompose it for analysis. They often require extensive information procurement; they rely on application of often complex logical procedures, usually mathematical, to break apart the potential outcomes for analysis, and to combine the analyses to provide a summary of the overall potential of each candidate. Then a decision rule must be applied to these summaries in a precise manner in order to make the decision. All of this requires the proper use of appropriate tools and it exacts a high cost in terms of the decision maker's time, effort, and/or money.

Unaided-analytic strategies require attempts to at least consider the different potential outcomes of the various candidates, but because no tools are used the degree to which this is done systematically and thoroughly is dictated by the abilities and tenacity of the decision maker. The limits of unaided human information processing preclude complicated analyses, and even simple analyses require substained hard work.

Non-analytic strategies require very little systematic thought, short of merely verifying that the strategy is applicable to the candidates of interest. These strategies are quick and require little in the way of resource expenditure.

Given that non-analytic strategies require so little in the way of resource expenditure, that unaided-analytic strategies require more, and that aided-analytic strategies require so much, why then would a decision maker ever choose anything other than a non-analytic strategy? The answer lies in the characteristics of the task and of the decision maker.

CHARACTERISTICS OF THE DECISION TASK

Because strategy selection is a subjective process, the influence of task characteristics on it is mediated by the decision maker's perception of those characteristics. Thus, while it is not possible to disentangle entirely task characteristics and decision maker characteristics, it is possible to separate them conceptually by defining task characteristics as the decision maker's interpretations of the demands and constraints imposed by the frame of the context in which the decision arises, and by defining decision maker characteristics as enduring aspects of the decision maker that are not task-specific.

Decision task characteristics can be further divided into two groups: those that are inherent in the *decision problem* itself (e.g. the number of possible candidates that must be considered), and those that describe the *decision environment* in which the decision task arises (e.g. the significance of the decision for the other areas of the decision maker's endeavors).

Characteristics of the decision problem

The characteristics of the decision problem that were identified in the Beach and Mitchell (1978) paper are probably not exhaustive, but they give the general idea.

Unfamiliarity is the degree to which the decision problem is foreign to the decision maker. When framing leads to identification of the context as similar to contexts that have been encountered in the past, it provides information about what might and what might not work for the present decision. But, if the problem is not very similar to past problems, its unfamiliarity demands more than average care and thought in order to reach a correct decision.

Ambiguity is the degree to which the problem is unclear to the decision maker. This includes the ambiguity of the candidates as well as the ambiguity of the demands and constraints imposed by the problem. It also includes the unavailability, unreliability, and imprecision of relevant information.

Complexity is the number of different components of the decision problem: number of candidates to be considered and amount of information about each to be considered. It also includes the degree to which the problem constrains future decisions; if one must choose the best alternative now as well as anticipate the consequence of that decision on later events, the problem is complex.

Instability is the degree to which the candidates and their outcomes change during the time the decision is being made as well as changes in the necessity of making a decision at all, particularly if these changes are difficult to predict.

Characteristics of the decision environment

Besides the specifics inherent in the decision problem, there are more general factors that influence the selection of a strategy.

Irreversibility means that the decision maker is held to his or her decision and cannot reverse it without great penalty. Contractual decisions are irreversible in this sense—joining the army, buying a business, getting married. Knowing that a decision is irreversible increases the motivation to make a correct decision.

Iterativity is whether the decision must be made in one pass or whether it can be made as a series of passes with adjustments each time in light of feedback. Connolly and Wolf (1981) suggested this addition to the list, and they call iterative strategies 'nibbling' strategies—tying them to Connolly's (1980) earlier idea of decision simplification by making decision trees into decision shrubs by snipping their branches. Clearly, iterativity is also related to irreversibility, which is a characteristic of the decision environment.

Significance means that the decision is of great magnitude, perhaps because of the size of the consequences and their implications for the future, perhaps because of the moral questions involved, perhaps because reputation and self-esteem are on the line, perhaps because the success of the decision is important to someone who is important to the decision maker.

Accountability means that the decision maker is to be held responsible for the results of the decision, both for its outcome and for the reasons for having made it. In some cases accountability is self-imposed, in other cases it results from being held responsible by other people.

Time and/or money constraints means that there sometimes are deadlines that must be met or limits on how much money the decision maker can invest in making the decision. There are few opportunities that do not expire, few decisions that must not be resolved before other things can progress, few persons willing to tolerate the decision maker's prolonged indecisiveness. When time is constrained, an upper limit is placed upon the resources that can be expended and, therefore, some strategies are eliminated from consideration. By the same token, if there are constraints on the amount of money the decision maker is permitted to spend on information procurement and/or decision technology, some strategies cannot be used.

CHARACTERISTICS OF THE DECISION MAKER

Again, the list suggested by Beach and Mitchell (1978) is not exhaustive, but it gives the general idea.

Knowledge is the decision maker's repertory of choice strategies. Usually aided-analytic strategies are only available through special technical training; most other strategies are learned in the course of experience or by informal instruction by parents, peers, and teachers. With knowledge about the existence of strategies come opinions about their appropriateness for different kinds of decisions and their relative likelihoods of yielding a correct decision.

As we shall see below, decision makers tend to regard the more formally analytic strategies as the ones most likely to yield correct decisions, even if they seldom or never use them. The explicitness and prescriptive authori-

tativeness of such strategies make them defensible and give the impression
of thoroughness and logical rigor. Of course, this faith is misplaced if the
strategy is the wrong one or if it is applied incorrectly, but the point here is
that decision makers perceive them as effective.

Ability is the competence to apply a decision strategy in a manner that
will produce a reasonable result. Of course, in addition to diminished
prospects, for someone who lacks the ability, the time and effort that must
be expended in the use of a particular strategy is greater than it is for
someone who has the ability. In short, the less able person not only risks
producing an unreasonable result, but to do so he or she must devote more
of his or her resources of time and effort to the task. Therefore, low-ability
people can be expected to be fairly unwilling to select demanding strategies
that require high resource expenditure.

Motivation is the tendency to expend the least possible amount of time,
effort, and money while still meeting the demands of the decision task. It is
not that decision makers are stingy and lazy; usually there are other demands
on time and energy. Sometimes there is a personal need to appear resolute
and decisive. Often there is a tendency to avoid the emotional aspects of
prolonged deliberation—the 'impatience of the deliberative state', which is
countered by 'the dread of the irrevocable' (James, 1890/1950). But, unless
the dread is awfully strong, the impatience to decide, to get the matter
settled and to cease working on it, is often a powerful motivator for selecting
the fastest and easiest strategies within reason.

At this point the model consists of the following proposition: The selection
of different decision strategies from the decision maker's repertory is contingent upon the characteristics of the decision problem and the decision
environment and the characteristics of the decision maker. Given the motivation to select the strategy that requires the least investment for a correct
decision, different strategies will be selected depending upon the problem,
the environment, and the decision maker. The next step is to link the parts.

LINKING THE PARTS

Figure 6.2 outlines the logic that links the parts of the strategy selection
model (Christensen-Szalanski, 1978). Recall, by the way, that the value of
candidates is determined, directly or indirectly, by their compliance with
the decision maker's principles. Thus, while the language that is used in
linking the parts of the model is the language of utility theory, utility is
defined here as compliance with principles.

Begin by defining:

● the utility of a correct choice of candidate as U_c;

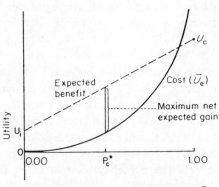

Figure 6.2 The relationship between cost and benefits in determining the optimal probability level (P_c *) for the strategy to be selected for a decision. From Christensen-Szalanski (1978); reproduced by permission of Academic Press and the author

- the utility of an incorrect choice of candidate as U_i;
- the cost of using a given choice strategy as $\overline{U}_e$;
- the subjective probability of a given choice strategy choosing the correct candidate as P_c;
- the subjective probability of a given choice strategy choosing the incorrect candidate as $1-P_c$.

Further, assume that decision makers believe that, in general, more analytic strategies have a higher probability of choosing the correct candidate, P_c, than less analytic strategies have.

Also assume that decision makers believe that more analytic strategies cost more to use, $\overline{U}_e$, in terms of time, effort, and/or money than less analytic strategies cost.

It follows, then, that the subjective expected utility for any strategy in a decision maker's repertory is:

$$SEU = P_c U_c + (1-P_c) U_i$$
$$= P_c (U_c - U_i) + U_i,$$

which is the equation for the straight line in Figure 6.2. The abscissa is a probability scale and the ordinate is a utility scale. The straight line in the graph extends from the utility of an incorrect adoption decision, U_i, which is virtually assured at $P_c = 0.00$, to the utility of a correct adoption decision, U_c, which is virtually assured at $P_c = 1.00$. (U_i is a positive number in the figure, but it could be negative if choosing an incorrect candidate would result in a loss.) The slope of the line is $U_c - U_i$, the difference between the utility of a correct choice and the utility of an incorrect choice.

The decision maker's repertory of choice strategies can be arrayed along the abscissa of Figure 6.2 according to the decision maker's subjective probabilities, P_c, that they will yield a correct adoption decision in the present context. On the left will be the simple, non-analytic, strategies, perceived to have low P_c, and on the right will be the aided-analytic strategies, perceived to have high P_c. The unaided-analytic strategies will be somewhere in the middle. Of course, which strategies are in the array and where they lie on the P_c scale depends upon the individual decision maker's repertory and his or her beliefs about the efficacy of each strategy.

Assuming that the strategies are arrayed from non-analytic to aided-analytic, and assuming that the perceived cost of using them varies from quite low for non-analytic strategies to quite high for aided-analytic strategies, results in the increasing cost curve, $\overline{U}_e$, in Figure 6.2 (The cost curve could be illustrated as negative utility, but doing so complicates the rather simple picture that the present method permits.)

The straight line in the figure represents the subjective expected utility (benefit) of each strategy on the probability scale. The cost curve represents the cost of using each of those strategies. The difference between the line and the cost curve represents the net expected gain of using each strategy. The optimal strategy for use on the adoption decision at hand is the one for which the net expected gain is maximal—which is the strategy that lies closest to the point at which the difference between the line and the curve is the largest. This point, called $P_c\,^{\star}$, is the optimal probability level for the choice strategy that is to be used. That is, using a strategy with a higher P_c would increase the expected benefit, but it would increase the cost more, thereby reducing the net expected benefit. Using a strategy with a lower P_c would decrease the cost, but it would decrease the expected benefit more, thereby reducing the net expected benefit.

Of course, the decision maker may not have a strategy in his or her repertory with a P_c that corresponds to $P_c\,^{\star}$, in which case he or she should select the strategy whose P_c most nearly corresponds to $P_c\,^{\star}$.

Note that at the moment that the strategy is selected, the decision maker need not know anything about the individual candidates under consideration for adoption. The utilities of making a correct (U_c) or incorrect (U_i) decision derive from the decision environment, rather than from the adoption candidates themselves. Thus, irreversibility, significance, accountability, and constraints on time and money induce a high utility for making a correct decision and a low (or negative) utility for making an incorrect decision. The decision maker's job is to balance these perceived utilities against the probabilities and costs associated with each of the strategies in his or her repertory in order to select the strategy that offers the best hope of success at the lowest cost in resource expenditure.

RESEARCH ON THE STRATEGY SELECTION MODEL

CHRISTENSEN-SZALANSKI (1978, 1980)

This research consisted of a series of experiments designed to examine the effects on strategy selection of the variables described in Figure 6.2. In the first study, 12 business school students were presented with a series of 20 decision problems and eight strategies that they could select for making the decisions. The 20 problems involved hypothetical business decisions. The eight strategies varied in the degree of analysis they required, from simple estimates to rather complex mathematical manipulations. For each problem, the decision yielded by the most analytic strategy was regarded by the experimenter as the correct decision.

The independent variable was in terms of points that the experimenter paid for a correct decision, U_c, which varies the benefit line in Figure 6.2. The dependent variables were (1) the selected strategy's rank in terms of analytic requirement (1 through 8), (2) the participants' confidence in the correctness of their decisions, an indirect measure of P_c, and (3) the time spent in applying the selected strategy, an indirect measure of cost, $\overline{U}_e$.

The results showed that, as the points paid (U_c) for making a correct decision increased, decision makers used more analytic strategies, took more time ($\overline{U}_e$) to make their decisions, and were more confident (P_c) in the decisions that they made. The curve fitted to the open circles in Figure 6.3 shows the relationship between mean confidence, P_c, and mean time spent, $\overline{U}_e$, for each of the five levels of points the experimenter offered for a correct decision. The curve shows the empirical relationship between the subjective probability of the selected strategy yielding a correct decision and the cost of using that strategy; it strongly resembles the theoretical curve in Figure 6.2. The cost of using strategies increases sharply as their probability of yielding a correct decision increases (i.e. as they become increasingly analytic).

The open circles in Figure 6.3 represent the relationship between cost and P_c at the beginning of the experiment when the participants were fresh and unfatigued. The closed circles represent the same relationship at the end of the experiment when the participants were fatigued. Clearly, the cost of applying the strategies increased as fatigue increased, and the participants tended to use lower P_c strategies—less analytic strategies.

A follow-up study showed that increases in confidence, P_c, with increases in the points paid, U_c, were mediated by the strategies that were selected, rather than reflecting a direct influence of points on confidence. In this experiment participants were given problems for which they were required to use either an analytic strategy or a non-analytic strategy, and points paid

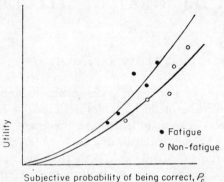

Figure 6.3 The change in the cost curve as a result of participants' fatigue in the study by Christensen-Szalanski (1978). Adapted by permission of Academic Press and the author

were varied. It was found that there was significantly higher confidence in the correctness of the decision when an analytic strategy was used than when a non-analytic strategy was used. However, when strategy was held constant, variations in the points paid for a correct decision had no influence on confidence.

Two subsequent experiments (Christensen-Szalanski, 1980) examined the effects of time constraints and analytic abilities upon strategy selection. Few decisions permit unlimited time for deliberation. Near deadlines tend to limit the decision maker to using non-analytic or simple unaided-analytic strategies. This means that when the most optimal strategy, the one having a P_c closest to P_c^*, cannot be used because it would require more time than is permitted by the deadline, the decision maker must fall back on the best strategy permitted by the time constraint and do the best he or she can. The result of having to use a less-optimal strategy should be reflected in reduced confidence in the correctness of the decision yielded by the strategy (i.e. lower P_c).

In the experiment on time contraints, participants were 10 business students who were given six decision problems in the form of four-page case studies. For each participant, three of the problems randomly were assigned five-minute deadlines and the other three were assigned 45-minute deadlines. Each participant had to read the case, write his or her analysis of the decision problem it contained, and make a decision within the assigned time limits. The points paid for correct decisions also were varied.

The dependent variables were the participants' rated confidence in the quality of their decisions, rated regret about the effects of the deadline on their decision, and stated preference for having used a more or a less analytic

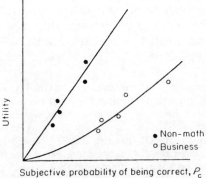

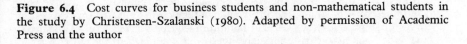

Figure 6.4 Cost curves for business students and non-mathematical students in the study by Christensen-Szalanski (1980). Adapted by permission of Academic Press and the author

strategy than the one that they actually had used.

Results showed that rated confidence was significantly lower in the five-minute deadline condition than in the 45-minute condition. Moreover, confidence did not change as a function of the points paid for a correct decision in the five-minute condition, but, as one would expect from the earlier experiment, it increased as the points paid increased in the 45-minute condition. Moreover, rated regret was significantly higher for the five-minute condition than for the 45-minute condition. Regret did not vary as a function of the points paid in the five-minute condition, but it did so in the 45-minute condition. Finally, in the five-minute condition, all participants expressed a preference for using a more analytic strategy than the one that they actually had used, but in the 45-minute condition no participant expressed a preference for any strategy other than the one that he or she had used.

In the experiment on participants' analytic abilities, 12 students from the Art and English departments were selected on the basis of their self-appraised lack of mathematical aptitude. They were given 10 of the 20 problems that were given to the business school students in the earlier experiment (Christensen-Szalanski, 1978) and followed the same procedure as the business school students in that experiment had followed. The hypothesis was that the cost of using analytic strategies would be higher for the non-mathematical students than for the business students, who generally score high on mathematical aptitude tests. The results in Figure 6.4 support the hypothesis. The open circles are from Figure 6.3 and the closed circles are for the present, non-mathematical participants. Clearly, the present participants found even moderate analytic requirements to be costly—and they tended to have considerably less confidence in the correctness of their decisions even thought they spent as much time on the decisions as the business school students did, and even though they used the same strategies the business school students used. Christensen-Szalanski's (1980) comments on these results are informative:

> As a result of the greater cost, the nonmathematical group might also be expected to spend less time thinking than the business group for a given level of [points paid]. This intuitively obvious conclusion, however, is not consistent with the obtained data or with the model's predictions because it ignores the role of strategy accuracy. Recall that the model proposes that the [decision maker] not only considers the [utility of a correct decision] and the cost of thinking, but also the potential accuracy of [the] several strategies that are available. . . . The amount of time the [decision maker] invests in a [decision] depends upon the shape of the cost curve; and the shape of the cost curve is determined by *both* strategy accuracy and strategy cost. Thus, for the two cost curves in [Figure 6.4], we see that nonintuitively for a given level of [points paid, a decision maker] appropriately invests more time when it is more costly to think and less time when it is less costly to think. (p. 118)

Subsequent analyses of the data from this experiment showed that, in spite of the differences exhibited in Figure 6.4, the model describes strategy selection by the non-mathematical students as well as it did selection by the business students. Moreover, the results showed that, like the business students, the non-mathematical students used increasingly analytic strategies to make decisions when the points paid for correct decisions were increased— thus supporting the model's assumption that people believe that more analytic strategies have a greater potential accuracy.

In summary, the results of Christensen-Szalanski's (1978, 1980) studies show that decision strategy selection varies as a function of the variables in Figure 6.2. These variables, of course, reflect the characteristics of the decision problem, the decision environment, and the decision maker. Next we turn to studies that have manipulated these characteristics specifically in order to ascertain their effect upon decision strategy selection.

HUFFMAN (1978)

This study was a 'bare bones' laboratory study for which the independent variables were the (high/low) familiarity and (high/low) complexity of decision problems presented in an environment that made the decisions (high/low) significant, in which the decision maker was (high/low) accountable, and the decision was (high/low) reversible. In addition, a (high/low) analysis decision strategy was described as being used for the decision in each combination of problem and environmental variables. This resulted in a $2^6 = 64$ cell factorial design, in which each cell was a description of a decision together with a strategy that the experimenter dictated would be used in making it. Each of the 64 decisions was described on a page in a booklet. Although each of the six variables was defined in detail for the participants at the beginning of the experiment, the description of the decision on each of the 64 pages of the booklet was minimal—for example, one decision was merely described as unfamiliar, simple, significant, low accountability, and reversible, with an informal (low-analysis) strategy having been chosen for making it.

The dependent variables were ratings for each of the 64 decisions of (1) the probability that the decision was correct, (2) the value of being correct, (3) the cost of making the decision in terms of time, effort, and money, and (4) the appropriateness of the chosen strategy for the particular decision.

The participants were 50 business school students.

Analyses of variance were performed for each dependent variable. The analysis for rated probability of the decisions being correct yielded significant main effects for the decision problem variables—problem familiarity and problem complexity (significance and accountability were also significant but accounted for very little variance). Significant interactions indicated that use of the high-analytic strategy resulted in a greater rated probability of a correct decision than use of the low-analytic strategy when the decision problem was unfamiliar and complex, and when the decision environment made the decision significant and reversible. Overall, the high-analytic strategy was rated as having a higher probability of resulting in a correct decision than the low-analytic strategy.

The analysis for rated value of making a correct decision yielded main effects for decision environment variables—significance, reversibility, and accountability. Rated value was highest when the decision was significant and irreversible, and when the decision maker was accountable (complexity and strategy account for significant but very small amounts of the variance, as did several interactions).

The analysis for rated cost of making the decision showed significant main effects for all six independent variables (along with several significant interactions which accounted for minimal variance). Rated cost was higher for the high-analytic strategy than for the low, for unfamiliar decisions than for familiar decisions, for complex than for less complex decisions, for significant and irreversible decisions and when the decision makers were accountable.

Finally, results of the analysis for rated appropriateness of the strategies were somewhat mixed, but generally in agreement with the other results. The interactions were important in this analysis, showing that the high-analytic and low-analytic strategies were, in general, equally appropriate for familiar, less significant, reversible, and low-accountability decisions (the low-analytic strategy was seen as significantly more appropriate for less complex decisions than was the high-analytic strategy), but the appropriateness of the high-analytic strategy increased significantly and the appropriateness of the low-analytic strategy decreased significantly when decisions were unfamiliar, complex, significant, irreversible and when the decision maker was accountable.

A follow-up experiment using much the same materials and design had another 50 business school participants rate the relative importance of decision problem and decision environment variables in the selection of decision strategies. Analyses showed that, for decision problem variables, unfamiliarity was rated more important than complexity. The three decision environment variables of significance, irreversibility, and accountability were all rated as about equally important. And, overall, the decision problem was rated as slightly more important than the decision environment—although if the demands of the environment were high and the demands of the problem were low, the environment was rated as more important.

In summary, these results are congruent with the strategy selection model:

(1) Decision makers' subjective appraisals of the strategies' probabilities of success and the cost of using them are higher for high-analytic strategies than for low-analytic strategies.

(2) Probability of success, P_c, is related primarily to characteristics of the decision problem.

(3) Value of making a correct decision, U_c, is related primarily to characteristics of the decision environment. Cost of making the decision, $\overline{U}_e$, is related primarily to the strategy that is used, but to a smaller extent it is also related to the characteristics of the decision problem and the decision environment.

(4) Appropriateness of the high-analytic and low-analytic strategies interacts with the characteristics of both the decision problem and the decision environment; the more demanding the characteristics of both, the more appropriate the high-analytic strategy and the less appropriate the low-analytic strategy.

(5) Unfamiliarity is seen as a more important problem characteristic than complexity, but significance, accountability, and irreversibility are seen as equally important environment characteristics.

(6) Overall, the decision problem is seen as slightly more important than the decision environment, but this varies with the demands of each.

It must be kept in mind, however, that results (5) and (6) may be particularly unique to the definitions of the problem and environment characteristics that were used in this experiment.

Huffman's (1978) experiment, while a beginning, was very unrealistic. Indeed, it was considerably less realistic than Christensen-Szalanski's (1978, 1980) laboratory experiments that were described above. However, it specifically examined some of the decision problem and decision environment characteristics that had been described in the original presentation of the strategy selection model (Beach and Mitchell, 1978). The next experiment to be described retained Huffman's focus on these characteristics while introducing increasing degrees of realism—starting with a very simple laboratory study and progressively increasing the participants' involvement in actually making the required decision.

McALLISTER, MITCHELL, AND BEACH (1979)

This study varied the same three characteristics of the decision environment that Huffman (1978) varied—significance, irreversibility, and accountability. Use of high and low levels of each of the three variables resulted in a $2 \times 2 \times 2$ within-subjects factorial design. The dependent variable was which of four decision strategies the participants selected for each of the $2^3 = 8$ cells in the design. Each cell constituted a separate decision and the strategies varied in the degree of analysis they required.

In the first two experiments, participants were given business cases and asked to play the role of the central decision maker in each case. The manipulations were built into the case. So, for example, in each case the decision problem was or was not significant, was or was not reversible, and the decision maker was or was not personally accountable for the outcome. In the first study the participants merely had to identify which of the four strategies was appropriate for each case. In the second study they actually executed the strategy they chose and made a decision.

Twenty-one full-time working managers who were taking evening courses in business participated in the first study and another 19 participated in the second study.

Analysis of variance results were the same in both studies: all three independent variables significantly influenced strategy selection and there were no significant interactions. When significance, irreversibility, and accountability were all high, the most analytic strategy was selected. When they were low the least analytic strategy was selected. Mixes of high and low conditions of the independent variables led to identification of and use of strategies that required intermediate degrees of analysis.

The first two studies were within-subjects designs in which the participants pretended they were the central decision maker in a business case. The third study was a between-subjects design in which the participants actually made their own decisions based upon their own evaluations. Each of 115 business students in an organizational theory class was given two decision problems from one of the cells of the $2 \times 2 \times 2$ factorial design. Participants were presented with two sets of three new kinds of sports products, asked to evaluate all of the products in each set, and required to select one product from each set as having market potential.

Four decision strategies were provided, varying in the amount of information they required and in the difficulty of the computations involved. To help participants formulate a P_c for each strategy, information was provided purporting to describe each strategy's past record for accuracy.

Significance was manipulated by telling the participants that the experiment was part of the experimenter's (McAllister's) dissertation and therefore of great importance to him, or that the experiment was a pilot supported by a group of consultants who did not expect it to be of much use. Accountability was manipulated by telling the participants that they would (would not) be asked to defend their decisions in front of the group at the end of the experiment. Irreversibility was manipulated by telling participants that they would (would not) be allowed to change their decisions at the end of the experiment.

The results were similar to those for the first two studies, but the effects were not as strong. Strategy selection varied significantly as a function of accountability, marginally as a function of significance, and insignificantly as a function of irreversibility, although all differences were in the expected direction. There were no significant interactions.

Overall, in spite of the weak results in the third study, this experiment, like the Huffman (1978) experiment, indicates that strategy selection is influenced by the decision environment characteristics that were identified in the strategy selection model (Beach and Mitchell, 1978).

SMITH, MITCHELL, AND BEACH (1982), AND WALLER AND MITCHELL (1984)

Because these last two studies primarily extended the work described above, they will be described only briefly. Smith et al. (1982) extended Christensen-Szalanski's (1980) work on the effects of time contraints on strategy selection. It explores the implications of assuming a range of feasible execution times for each decision strategy, given the decision situation, and of assuming that the subjective probability of a correct decision, P_c, in addition to being influenced by the variables described above, is influenced by the decision maker's perception that he or she will be able to implement the strategy in question properly and completely.

Sixty-four business graduate students participated in an experiment in which complexity, significance, and time constraints were varied in a $2 \times 2 \times 2$ between-subjects factorial design. The task required participants to make investment decisions using one of five strategies of varying degrees of analytic requirement.

Analysis of variance results showed that, while participants favored more analytic strategies for complex decision problems, they also favored these analytic strategies even more for less complex problems—which does not fit with either the original model (Beach and Mitchell, 1978) or Huffman's (1978) results. Decision significance was not manipulated sufficiently to produce significant results.

The result that was most important, however, was that time constraints affect decision makers' confidence in their ability to execute strategies properly, and thereby affect strategy selection. In addition, it was shown that decision makers have a range of implementation times and subjective probabilities associated with each strategy in their repertoires, rather than the specific (point) times and probabilities assumed by the original model (Beach and Mitchell, 1978; Christensen-Szalanski, 1978, 1980). This means that decision makers have more latitude in strategy selection than originally was thought.

The Waller and Mitchell (1984) study focused upon decisions about cost variance investigations in accounting. The independent variables were (1) high and low ambiguity about whether an operating process is out of control, and (2) high and low significance of the decision in terms of how its results will affect the manager's compensation and promotion and how they will affect the financial status of the organization. The dependent variable consisted of five accounting information systems that varied in the amount of analysis required, their accuracy, and their cost.

Sixty-four upper-level accounting majors in a cost accounting course served as participants. They were presented with a case description in which the independent variables were manipulated across participants in a 2×2 between-subjects design.

Results showed that greater ambiguity about the operating process and greater significance of the decision to the decision maker and to the organization resulted in increased selection of analytic strategies (information systems). These results support the strategy selection model.

FORD, SCHMITT, SCHECHTMAN, HULTS, AND DOHERTY (1989)

The experiments discussed above were all designed explicitly to test the strategy selection model. However, there are other studies that bear to one degree or other upon the issues raised by the selection model. Ford *et al.* (1989) reviewed 45 such studies, from 41 published articles, and interpreted the findings in light of the strategy selection model. The criteria for inclusion in the review were (1) that process tracing was part of the methodology, and (2) that one or more information search variables or decision strategies were examined. Process tracing is done in a number of ways, the most common of which is the 'think aloud' method in which the decision maker talks about what he or she is thinking about as the decision is made (Svenson, 1979).

The review showed that decision problem characteristics were the independent variables in most studies, and that decision environment and decision maker characteristics were not investigated. The dependent variable was usually whether the selected strategy was either compensatory or non-compensatory; that is, whether or not the selected strategy permitted positive characteristics of the decision alternative to compensate for negative characteristics.

Results for decision problem characteristics showed that only one of the characteristics listed by Beach and Mitchell (1978), complexity, received extensive examination. The consistent finding is that increased complexity is related to more reliance upon simple, non-compensatory strategies.

Because decision environment characteristics were not manipulated as independent variables, it is difficult to say what effects they may have. However, Ford et al. state:

> Based on the environmental characteristics which typify the process tracing studies, the Beach and Mitchell model predicts that decision makers would tend to use simplifying, noncompensatory strategies. There are few incentives (low task significance, no accountability, no monetary rewards for optimal decision making) in the decision environment to increase the perceived 'benefits' for making a more rigorous analysis so that a more 'correct' or accurate decision could be made. The results of the studies in this review support these predictions as many of the studies found evidence for the use of simplifying strategies. (p. 111)

The process tracing studies reviewed by Ford et al. did not examine the effects of decision maker characteristics on information search or strategy selection. However, Nichols-Hoppe and Beach (in press), replicating Payne (1976), examined the effects of test anxiety on information search. Task variables were high and low performance evaluation pressure; high, medium and low task complexity; and important versus unimportant decisions. It was found that highly anxious decision makers inspected more information, and that more of what they inspected was redundant, than did less anxious decision makers. The amount of information inspected was influenced by all three task variables in addition to anxiety. Task complexity and decision importance, but not evaluation pressure, as well as anxiety influenced the amount of reinspection (redundancy) of information. However, there were no differences between high- and low-anxiety decision makers in the use of compensatory and non-compensatory strategies, so it is not clear exactly what effects high anxiety may have other than to produce inefficient information search. Because this study and Christensen-Szalanski's (1980) study of non-mathematical students are, apparently, the only studies of the effects of decision maker characteristics on information search and strategy selection, it is clear that more research is needed.

SUMMARY

In this chapter we have seen how the profitability test, which is a collection of choice strategies rather than merely one strategy, is related to Beach and Mitchell's (1978) strategy selection model. The model views the selection of a strategy for choosing among multiple survivors of the compatibility test as contingent upon the characteristics of the decision task and environment, and the characteristics of the decision maker. Six experiments were described, the results of which support the model. However, questions about the profitability test remain, in part because it includes the strategies that have been most heavily investigated by behavioral decision research, and their relationship to image theory must be made clear. The following chapter examines these questions.

7 More on Profitability

The strategy selection part of image theory may describe how strategies are selected for making profitability decisions, but it says little about the specific strategies themselves. This raises a number of questions, of which we will address the following:

(1) What strategies are available to decision makers for use in making profitability decisions?
(2) Are complex strategies actually more accurate than simpler strategies for making choices?
(3) Can decision makers use the expected value maximization strategy, and if they can, should they?
(4) Where does all of this leave us in terms of decision aids?

QUESTION 1: WHAT STRATEGIES ARE AVAILABLE TO DECISION MAKERS FOR USE IN MAKING PROFITABILITY DECISIONS?

As was explained in Chapter 6, the choice of strategies available for the decision maker's repertory can be viewed as occupying a continuum that ranges from non-analytic to analytic (forgetting for the present the differentiation between aided-analytic and unaided-analytic strategies). Extremely non-analytic strategies are quick-and-dirty, minimal-effort methods of making a choice among multiple candidates, that require little or no attention to profitability or much of anything else. That is, while the more analytic strategies usually aim to produce improvement (profit) in various dimensions of the decision maker's situation, or at least to prevent deterioration, the extremely non-analytic strategies simply serve to produce a choice (e.g. flip a coin, draw a number out of a hat). These strategies are often applied when the decision maker has minimal knowledge upon which to differentiate among the candidates' potential profitability, or when the candidates are all equally attractive or unattractive. In some cases, social pressure argues for use of these strategies in the name of 'fairness', which means that the decision maker is not allowed to base the decision upon whatever differentiating knowledge he or she may possess about the candidates' relative potential.

As one proceeds along the non-analytic–analytic continuum, successive strategies make increasing use of knowledge about the candidate's potential profitability. Moderately non-analytic strategies involve comparisons between candidates on each dimension of potential profitability, which, of course, implies the existence of underlying dimensions upon which one candidate can be said to be potentially more profitable than (more attractive than, better than, superior to, etc.) the other.

Moderately analytic strategies usually require within-candidate balancing of potential positive profits against potential negative profits (i.e. gains and losses) and some kind of summary of the overall balance. This is followed by comparison of the summaries for each of the various candidates and by choice of the candidate with the greatest positive balance.

Analytic strategies usually require the same kind of within-candidate balancing, often weighted by assessments of the degree of potential for each dimension of profit. Thus, for example, a candidate may have a low potential for resulting in a high positive profit in money, and a high potential for resulting in a high positive profit in future opportunities, but an equally high potential for resulting in a high negative profit, say, in terms of bankruptcy. The summary would require the high and low potentials to be stated as subjective probabilities, the profits to be stated as high and low positive and negative utilities, and would balance them all against each other to result in an overall appraisal of the candidate's perceived worth. The candidate with the largest overall worth is the one that is chosen.

These descriptions are general approximations to the variety of strategies that are available for profitability decisions. They underscore a primary variable that is used by decision researchers to differentiate among strategies; whether the strategy is non-compensatory or compensatory. This is, whether the strategy permits potential gains to balance-out (compensate for) potential losses in the evaluation of the candidates.

Svenson (1979) has provided a convenient list of the various non-compensatory and compensatory decision strategies that have been discussed in the 'serious' decision literature, and that have received at least rudimentary formalization. By 'serious' literature we mean academic journals; strategies such as coin flipping, augury by signs and omens, revelation, or asking your mother are not usually given much space in such journals and, with the possible exception of coin flipping (probability theory), have not been formalized. However, we would contend that, to a large degree, journal coverage is inversely related to the actual frequency with which strategies are used by decision makers in the course of getting through the average day.

The following gives a general idea of what is on Svenson's (1979) list. We have changed some of his terminology to make the descriptions compatible with image theory terminology.

Formalized non-compensatory strategies

The *dominance* strategy: Choose the candidate whose potential is at least as good as that of all other candidates on all dimensions of profitability and better than all others on at least one dimension (Lee, 1971).

The *conjunctive* strategy: Choose the candidate whose potential reaches some critical level on dimension A of profitability *and* on dimension B *and* on dimension C, etc. If more than one candidate meets all the criteria, a different strategy must be used to break the tie in order to reach a final choice (Dawes, 1964).

The *disjunctive* strategy: Choose the candidate whose potential reaches some criterion value on dimension A of profitability *or* on dimension B *or* on dimension C, etc. Again, this may result in more than one alternative meeting the criteria and require application of some other strategy to make the final choice (Dawes, 1964).

The *lexicographic* strategy: Choose the candidate whose potential is best on the most important dimension of profitability. If two or more candidates are equal on that dimension, move to the next most important dimension, etc., each time dropping the least potentially profitable candidates until a single candidate remains (Fishburn, 1974). Tversky's (1969) lexicographic semi-order is a special case of this strategy in which exact equality is not necessary; near equality is sufficient.

The *elimination by aspects* strategy: First select the most important dimension of profitability and eliminate any candidate whose potential on that dimension fails to meet some preset criterion. Repeat the process using the next most important dimension, and the next, and the next until only one candidate remains (Tversky, 1972).

The *number of potentially profitable dimensions* strategy: For two competing candidates, classify one as more profitable than, equal to, or less profitable than the other on each dimension of profitability. Choose the candidate that has the largest number of 'more profitable than' classifications (Svenson, 1979).

The *choice by least potentially profitable dimension* strategy: From a pair of candidates, eliminate the one with the least potential on any of the dimensions of profitability (Svenson, 1979).

The *choice by most potentially profitable dimension* strategy: Choose the candidate whose potential is greatest on some dimension of profitability (Svenson, 1979).

Formalized compensatory strategies

Formal compensatory decision strategies are the stock-in-trade of classical decision theory. As a result there are many formalized strategies, all of which are variations on the following two strategies and all of which define profitability in terms of utility, in the strict utility theory sense.

The *additive difference* strategy: Compute a weighted sum of the signed differences in utility between two candidates on each dimension of utility, where the weights reflect the importance (or some similar differentiation) of each dimension. Choose the candidate for which the sum is positive (Tversky, 1969). A special case of this strategy is merely to sum the utilities (or the weighted utilities) for each candidate and choose the candidate for which the sum is greatest (Tversky, 1969).

The *expected value* strategy: For each of two or more candidates, weight the dollar (market) value of its potential payoff on each dimension of profitability by the probability that choice of that candidate would eventuate in the dollar value accruing to the decision maker. Compute the weighted sum of the dollar values for each candidate and choose the candidate for which the sum is greatest (Edwards, 1954). Three special cases of this strategy are generated by substituting utilities for dollar values and subjective probabilities for 'objective' probabilities. The *expected utility* strategy uses the sum of utilities weighted by objective probabilities, the *subjective expected value* strategy uses the sum of dollar values weighted by subjective probabilities, and the *subjective expected utility* strategy uses the sum of utilities weighted by subjective probabilities (Edwards, 1954). Dollar values are 'objective' valuations of the profit in question (a specific improvement in the decision maker's situation), utilities are the decision maker's subjective valuation of the profit in question, probabilities are the 'objective' potential of a candidate's adoption eventuating in accrual of the profit in question, and subjective probabilities are the decision maker's subjective appraisal of the potential that adopting the candidate will eventuate in the profit accruing to him or her.

QUESTION 2: ARE COMPLEX STRATEGIES MORE ACCURATE THAN SIMPLER STRATEGIES FOR MAKING PROFITABILITY DECISIONS?

The three most thorough studies that address this question use computer simulations to compare the relative accuracy of various strategies. The first, Thorngate (1980), only did the simulation. The second, Payne *et al.* (1988), did the simulation and then followed it up with empirical research using real decision makers. In both cases the criterion for accuracy was a compensatory expected-value strategy that used as much of the available information as efficiently as possible. The third, Paquette and Kida (1988), focused on real decision makers using various strategies and an externally defined criterion for assaying accuracy, and followed this up with a small simulation study using the same accuracy criterion.

Thorngate (1980)

The simulation was performed by constructing a 'candidates × outcomes' matrix in which the cells contained randomly assigned profits and probabilities that were assigned to the outcomes. (In Thorngate's terms, the 'alternatives × outcomes' matrix cells contained randomly assigned payoffs.) Thus it was possible to compute the expected value for each candidate, and this is the criterion for accuracy against which all the other decision strategies were compared. Eighteen hundred such matrices were constructed; 200 for each combination of two, four or eight candidates and two, four or eight outcomes.

Ten decision strategies, including some of those listed by Svenson (1979) as well as variations, were each applied to each matrix. The choice dictated by each strategy for each matrix was compared with the choice dictated by the expected value strategy. A running score was kept for each strategy of the number of times its first choice coincided with the expected-value strategy's first choice, with the expected value strategy's second choice, and so on to the expected value strategy's last choice.

The results showed that, while there were differences among the 10 strategies, virtually all of their first choices coincided with the expected value strategy's first or second choice, and most frequently it was with the expected value strategy's first choice. It is particularly interesting that the two strategies that were especially accurate made either no use, or little use, of probability information. As Thorngate says, this result suggests 'that "good" choices can very often be made with scant regard for the subtleties of accurate probability estimation procedures' (pp. 223–224).

In light of his overall results, Thorngate also points out:

> The goal of maximizing expected value may or may not be important for a decision maker, or may at least be less important than other goals. For example, if a decision maker desired only to avoid the alternatives with the lowest EV, then almost all the [strategies] investigated here could be recommended. (p. 224)

However, there were subtle differences that possibly could make some of the strategies more desirable than others in some circumstances, depending upon what the decision maker wished to accomplish:

Such possibilities illustrate the necessity of understanding a decision maker's motives before prescribing, describing, or explaining the use of various decision [strategies]. (p. 224)

One of the central assumptions of the strategy selection model (Beach and Mitchell, 1978) is that decision makers think that use of more analytic strategies, which also tend to be more complex strategies, tend to produce the most accurate decisions. As we have seen in the research described in the previous chapter, there is evidence that decision makers, in fact, think this way. However, a second assumption of the model is that the more analytic strategies tend to require more time and effort in their execution. This means that decision makers may strive for accuracy, but that they also may be willing to trade off accuracy for reduced effort, particularly when there are severe time constraints. The following experiment examined both the relative accuracy of simple and complex strategies and the issue of trade-offs between accuracy and effort, as well as the effects of time constraints on the trade-offs.

Payne, Bettman, and Johnson (1988)

The first experiment in this research was similar in spirit and in execution to Thorngate's (1980) simulation experiment. In this study the matrix was defined by candidates × outcomes × time constraints. The latter was the amount of time allowed for execution of the strategy, and corresponds to the time constraints previously examined by Christensen-Szalanski (1980) and Smith *et al.* (1982). As in Thorngate's (1980) experiment, probabilities were assigned to the outcomes and the expected value could be computed for each alternative. Two hundred decision problems were generated for each combination of six independent variables, only three of which (two, four or eight candidates; two, four or eight outcomes; four levels of time constraint) are pertinent here. The result was that nine decision strategies were applied to a total of more than 25 000 simulated decision problems.

The question was how often each strategy's choice coincided with the choice of the criterion strategy, which again was the expected value strategy. In addition, using methods devised in earlier research (Johnson and Payne, 1985), the experimenters could calculate the degree of effort required to execute each strategy for each decision. This permitted examination of trade-offs between effort and accuracy for the various strategies.

The ten strategies are all included in Svenson's (1979) list, given above. They were: the expected value strategy (which was also the criterion for accuracy against which the other strategies' choices were compared); the sum of utilities (the special case of the additive difference strategy); elimination by aspects; number of potentially profitable dimensions; lexicographic; lexicographic semi-order; conjunction; and two mixed strategies—(1) a combination of the elimination by aspects strategy and expected value, and (2) the combination of the elimination by aspects strategy and number of potentially profitable dimensions.

The simulation's results showed that when sufficient time allowed for execution of any and all of the strategies:

> [Under the best conditions of the simulation the strategies] can approximate the accuracy of the normative strategy [the expected value] with substantial savings of effort. A decision maker using the [sum of utilities] strategy, for example, can achieve 89% of the relative performance of the normative model, with only about half the effort. (p. 539)

There were systematic effects of the number of candidates and number of outcomes, and they differed for different strategies. However, the most striking finding was the relative robustness of the various strategies under different conditions—although they clearly varied in accuracy from one condition to another.

When time constraints were introduced it was found that the more complex strategies suffered most; they require that all information about the candidates and outcomes be processed, and often there was not sufficient time. Strategies that permitted at least *some* processing of information about *all* candidates, even though processing was not complete, often did a better job because they could be executed in the time allowed. The authors conclude that the simulation's results

> . . . clearly suggest the possibility that a decision maker might maintain a high level of accuracy *and* minimize effort by using a diverse set of [strategies], changing rules as contexts and time pressures change. (p. 541).

Following the simulation, two experiments were performed in which decision makers were presented sets of four gambles. Each gamble was a candidate that offered four possible outcomes (payoffs) ranging from one cent to $9.99. Each outcome had a specified probability, thus permitting computation of each candidate's expected value. Twenty such sets of gambles were presented under high time constraints and 20 were presented under low time constraints. The participant's task was to choose the best gamble of the four in each set.

The dependent variables of interest were particular aspects of the pattern of information search for the various candidates—various sub-patterns were identified that suggested that participants were using one or another general approach to information search (Payne, 1976). The question was whether the observed information search patterns were congruent with the kinds of strategies that were found to be most accurate for the effort in the simulation. The question was whether these patterns suggest that decision makers can maintain high accuracy for low effort by changing rules as the context and time pressure change. The authors summarize the results by saying:

> The experimental results clearly demonstrate a shift in processing strategies with variation in context. People demonstrated an ability to shift processing to take advantage of problem structure so as to reduce processing load while maintaining accuracy. (p. 545)

> . . . people adapted to time pressure by accelerating processing, increasing the selectivity of processing, and moving toward more attribute-based processing. (p. 546)

Attribute-based processing suggests a shift to simpler, perhaps non-compensatory, strategies as time constraints increase, which agrees with the predictions of the strategy selection model (Beach and Mitchell, 1978; Christensen-Szalanski, 1980; Smith *et al.*, 1982).

Indeed, while these studies do not address the question of *how* strategies are selected, Payne *et al.* (1988) note that they are based upon the viewpoint that:

> . . . a decision maker possesses a repertory of well-defined strategies and selects among them when faced with a decision by considering the expected costs and expected benefits of each strategy. This top-down view of strategy selection is consistent with . . . Beach and Mitchell (1978). (p. 550)

Paquette and Kida (1988)

This study was similar in spirit to Payne *et al.*'s (1988) empirical studies. Participants were 48 professionals in accounting, financial analysis, cost accounting or controllership. They each were assigned to one of four conditions which consisted of instruction about, and enforced use of, a specific decision strategy on 21 decision problems. The strategies were (1) weighted sum, (2) additive difference, (3) elimination by aspects, and (4) a mixed elimination by aspects and weighted sum strategy in which the two strategies were applied sequentially. The 21 decision problems were sets of five financial ratios from records about real firms; seven of the 21 problems involved only two firms, seven involved five firms, and seven involved nine firms (this was a manipulation of the complexity of the decision problem by increasing the number of decision alternatives). The participants' task was to process the financial ratios using the decision strategy that they had been assigned, and to choose the firm with the highest bond rating. The correct answer was the firm that actually had had the highest bond rating, and it is indeed possible to use the ratios to predict bond ratings ($R = 0.69$).

Results showed that, while there was considerable differences in the amount of time required to execute each of the different strategies, there was very little difference in accuracy among the strategies. For example, the elimination by aspects strategy was fairly consistently the fastest strategy to execute, but it was not any more, or any *less*, accurate than the other strategies, all of which were about 70% accurate.

In a follow-up simulation, the experimenters carefully applied the weighted sum strategy, which was the most analytic compensatory strategy, and the elimination by aspects strategy, which was the fastest non-compensatory model.

The simulated weighted sum strategy attained 100% accuracy for two alternatives, 100% for five alternatives, and 66% accuracy for nine alternatives. The corresponding accuracies for the real decision makers who had used this strategy were 83%, 76%, and 51%, which is considerably worse than what is afforded by flawless application of the strategy.

The simulated elimination by aspects strategy attained 83% accuracy for two alternatives, 83% for five alternatives, and 66% for nine alternatives; it was less accurate than the weighted sum strategy for two and five alternatives and just as accurate for nine alternatives. Accuracies for the real decision makers who used this strategy were 86%, 82%, and 58%, which is not much different from what is afforded by flawless application of the strategy.

The authors conclude that the difference between the simulation and the real decision makers for the weighted sum strategy and the similarity between the simulation and the real decision makers for the elimination by aspects strategy 'suggests that the decision makers' limited processing abilities may reduce the accuracy that can be realized when a complex [strategy] is utilized' (Paquette and Kida, 1988, p. 139). Overall, the results appear to mean that non-compensatory strategies may permit time efficiency with no particular drop in accuracy, a result that is congruent with Payne *et al.*'s (1988) findings.

One must not draw the conclusion from these studies (Thorngate, 1980; Payne *et al.*, 1988; Paquette and Kida, 1988) that all strategies are equally efficacious. Thorngate (1980) and Payne *et al.* (1988) found clear and significant differences between them under different conditions. Even Paquette and Kida's (1988) results suggest that some strategies are less efficient than others, if only because decision makers find them too demandding to use. On the other hand, it is appropriate to conclude, however tentatively, that simple strategies are more robust than was at first imagined (Klayman, 1985). Moreover, it is particularly clear that decision makers can (and do) change strategies as conditions change in order to maintain a respectable level of accuracy at minimal effort (see also Klein, 1983), which is the central proposition of the strategy selection model (Beach and Mitchell, 1978).

The difficulty with all of this, of course, is that the strategies that have been examined, even the simplest ones, are all pretty analytic—nothing so informal as asking your mother or flipping a coin. As a result, it is not clear that the results generalize to the non-analytic strategies that probably account for the majority of moment-to-moment decision making. Perhaps it will be possible to extend the present research to these non-analytic strategies, but the time is not yet. Until then, Question 2 must be answered with a qualified 'It depends'. That is, complex strategies are not necessarily more accurate than simpler strategies—because decision makers appear to be able to switch between strategies in order to retain accuracy while reducing effort and working within time constraints.

QUESTION 3: CAN DECISION MAKERS USE THE EXPECTED VALUE STRATEGY FOR PROFITABILITY DECISIONS; AND IF THEY CAN, SHOULD THEY?

The research that addresses Question 2 does not address the question of whether decision makers can or do use anything like the expected value strategy for profitability decisions. Neither Thorngate's (1980) nor Payne *et al.*'s (1988) simulations can answer this question because real decision makers were not involved. Payne *et al.*'s empirical work with real decision makers analyzed information search patterns (accuracy is difficult to interpret), which provide only indirect evidence about the strategy that decision makers are using. And, Paquette and Kida (1988) did not use expected value as their accuracy criterion. Therefore, we must turn to other research for an answer to Question 3.

The motivation for research on the descriptive sufficiency of the expected value strategy, and its variants (Edwards, 1954), is the same as the motivation for Thorngate's and Payne *et al.*'s use of the expected value strategy's choice as the criterion for the accuracy of the other strategies' choices. In classical decision theory, expected value maximization is generally considered the prototypic optimal strategy for decision making. As a result, most of the classical studies in behavioral decision research have begun with the assumption that their participants were at least attempting to maximize expected value (more often, subjective expected utility) and then have examined the degree to which the attempt was successful (e.g. Davidson *et al.*, 1957; Galanter, 1962; Mosteller and Nogee, 1951; Preston and Baratta, 1948; Tversky, 1967). In hindsight, the results of these studies are mixed—whether decision makers were applying the expected value strategy or not often seems to depend upon who is interpreting the results. In most cases the behavior is not precisely what the strategy would prescribe, but in many it is not so deviant as to wholly rule out the conclusion that participants were attempting to use the strategy, however imperfect the results of that attempt.

There is one study that stands out, however, because it obtained very clear results (Gray, 1975). Oddly, it is seldom cited, perhaps because its participants were third-grade children. However, there is an unpublished codicil to the study that replicates the children's results with college under-grauates. At any rate, it is worth examining the study in some detail because it clearly answers the first part of Question 3—whether decision makers *can* use the expected value strategy. Following the description we will examine the question of whether they really should use it—at least whether they should do so for all decisions.

Gray (1975)

The purpose of this study was to see if children's willingness to attempt new school tasks could be accounted for by their perceptions of the probability of success and by the payoffs for success. To this end, a large set of third-grade level arithmetic problems was divided into six distinct levels of difficulty. Then the problems were each written on cards and the six levels formed six decks of cards. The participant was asked to try to solve a problem from each deck in order to gauge the various levels of difficulty. Then, for each deck they were asked, 'If you had to do 10 problems from this deck, and they were all pretty much like the one you tried first, how many do you think you could get right out of the 10?' (p. 150). This served as an estimate of the subjective probability of getting a problem right for each deck.

Next, the participants were each told that he or she would be allowed to select 15 problems from the decks to solve. If they got the correct answer to a problem they picked, they would receive a reward that depended upon the deck from which the problem came. The rewards were small red poker chips, and in the first experiment the rewards were an increasing function of the difficulty levels of the decks. That is, correctly solving a problem from the hardest deck, deck 6, earned six chips, a correct problem from deck 5 earned five chips, deck 4 paid four chips, etc., down to one chip for deck 1, which contained the easiest problems. On the other hand, an incorrect solution led to the loss of the number of chips that were assigned to the deck. The participant was given a bankroll of 10 chips to get started.

The participant's subjective probabilities, together with the experimenter's rewards and penalties, permitted computation of the (subjective) expected value for each deck of problems of each participant. The prediction was that the participant would consistently choose problems from the deck that had the maximum expected value. The alternative hypotheses were that participants would select problems solely on the basis of the rewards—consistently selecting high-reward deck 6—or solely on the basis of the probabilities of success—consistently selecting high-probability deck 1.

The data analysis consisted of computing the expected value of each deck for each participant and then seeing, across participants, how many choices corresponded to the high-expected-value decks (which were different decks for different participants). The results are presented in Figure 7.1. This is for the first 15 problems selected by the participants—a second set of 15 followed re-estimation of the probabilities to allow for changes due to experience with the problems. Results for the second set are similar but not quite as clean.

Note (1) that participants' choices were not dictated solely by the value (chips) of the reward, (2) that the choices were not dictated solely by the subjective probabilities, and (3) that the choices apparently *were* dictated by the expected value of the decks. Note also that the difference in the expected value for the second highest deck in the lower bar-graph is, on the average, only 0.1–0.4 of a chip lower than the expected value for the maximal expected value deck. Indeed, it is only the fourth highest deck that differs as much as one full chip from the highest deck. In short, the subjective probabilities tended to create what is called 'a flat maximum', which means that the highest expected value option often tends to be not very much higher than the runner-up and even the second runner-up (von Winterfeldt and Edwards, 1986). (It might be noted that flat maxima are so common that they largely make moot the argument that the expected value strategy is to be preferred because of its analytic precision—often any of the top few candidates are 'good enough'.)

In light of the flat maximum, Gray thought it necessary to produce more evidence before concluding that participants were sensitive to the expected values of the various decks. Therefore, she conducted a second experiment using the same children who had participated in the first experiment. This time she changed around the rewards and penalties for the decks for each individual participant so that a different deck became his or her high-expected value deck. The idea was that if the participants' choices changed to reflect this change in the optimal deck, it would be strong evidence of the descriptive sufficiency of expected value for the children's decision strategies in this setting.

The results for the first 15 problems in the second experiment are shown in Figure 7.2; results for the second 15 problems are virtually identical. Remember, because of the switch in the rewards and penalties, each participant's high-expected-value deck in this experiment is not the same as in the first experiment and not the same as for the other children. The results

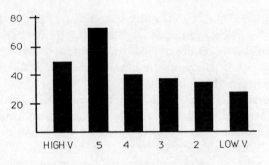

Decks ordered by value

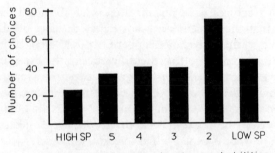

Decks ordered by subjective probabilities

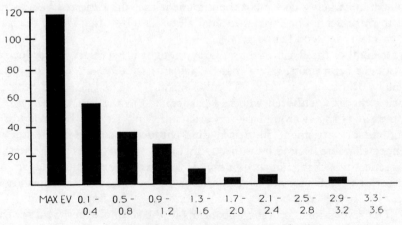

Deviations from maximum expected value

Figure 7.1   Relationship between choices and value, probability, and expected value in experiment 1 by Gray (1975). Adapted by permission of Academic Press and the author

show that the participants switched and consistently chose problems from their new high-expected-value deck, implying that they were using a decision strategy that can be sufficiently described by expected value maximization.

Because data on children failed to impress some critics (among them the Navy, which was supporting our laboratory), Gray's dissertation (1972) included another group that was not included in the published version (1975). These participants were 14 Naval ROTC students who were presented high-level mathematical problems from a mathematics proficiency test. The experiment replicated the first of Gray's experiments; the participants provided subjective probabilities and the experimenter-assigned rewards were negatively correlated with the difficulty of the problems in six decks. Because the problems took so much time to solve, each of the 14 participants only solved 15 problems. Of the $14 \times 15 = 210$ problem selections, 98 were from the participants' high-expected-value decks and 70 were from the second highest deck, for a total of 168 (80%) from one or the other decks. These results are less striking than for the school children. However, close examination revealed a greater variance in ability to solve the problems for the college students than for the grade school students. The mathematics problems were pretty much beyond the ability of some of the college students, while the problems for the school children were specifically for third-graders, most of whom could solve the problems in at least the easiest three decks. Taking this into account, the results for the college students add support to the results for the third-graders; the expected value strategy is a sufficient description of the choice of problems to attempt as a function of subjective probability of success and of the rewards and penalties for success or failure. In short, decision makers *can* use the expected value strategy.

But should they?

Having provided evidence that decision makers *can* use the expected value strategy for profitability decisions, even children, we turn to the question of whether they *should*. The issue is complicated and the answer arrived at depends very much upon where one starts. In what follows, we will be looking at things from the viewpoint of expected value as a strategy for making decisions, not as a coherent mathematical or logical system independent of human ability or interest in its practical application. This means that those who enjoy axiomatic systems for their own sake, or even those who are convinced that in the best of all possible worlds prudent decision makers would use the strategy, may continue to do business as usual. For those of us who are trapped by mundane reality, such soaring and lofty thoughts must yield precedence to more practical considerations.

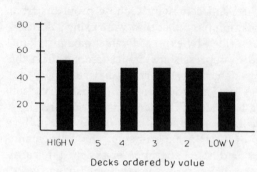

Decks ordered by value

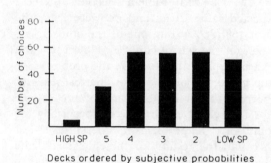

Decks ordered by subjective probabilities

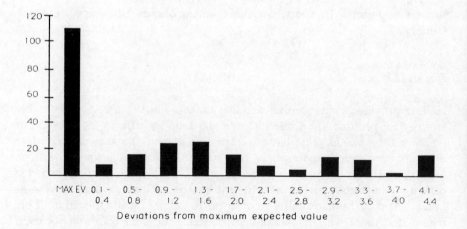

Deviations from maximum expected value

Figure 7.2 Relationship between choices and value, probability, and expected value in experiment 2 by Gray (1975). Adapted by permission of Academic Press and the author

The following are the practical considerations.

While there are numerous critiques of the logical and descriptive adequacy of the expected value strategy, what follows is based in large part upon Shafer (1986). Before outlining the pertinent parts of Shafer's argument, let us observe that much of the discourse on expected value and related models of decision making makes extensive use of 'thought experiments' in which the author sets up small examples and then describes what a rational decision maker supposedly would do. We are struck by the fact that nearly all of these thought experiments are, in fact, behavioral experiments with a sample size of two; the author and the reader. Invariably, of course, the results of these experiments support the point being made and further the discussion towards its preordained conclusion. This is an accepted and familiar mode of argument in theory presentation, but for a behavioral scientist it falls short—we expect a next step consisting of a real experiment using more than just two people who are already in cahoots.

When real experiments are done on the examples that are used to bolster expected value as a decision strategy, quite often the results do not come out the way the thought experiments did. Indeed, as Fishburn (1986) points out, the large number of empirical studies done by Edwards, Coombs, Luce, Lichtenstein, Slovic, Tversky, Kahneman, Einhorn, and MacCrimmon, among others, simply do not support the notion that ordinary people reach the same conclusions that theorists do. The issue is, what do these results mean for the prescriptive status of the expected value strategy?

Shafer (1986) directs his analysis at Savage's (1954) conclusion that it is optimal to make choices that maximize subjective expected utility (i.e. the version of the expected value strategy that uses subjective probabilities and utilities), and that to do otherwise is to behave irrationally. Savage's argument begins with a set of postulates about preferences among actions that, if satisfied by the decision maker's preferences, imply that the decision maker's preferences are congruent with ranking by subjective expected utility. Of course, from a decision strategy viewpoint, if the decision maker already had preferences there would be no need for a decision. The whole point of employing a strategy is to explore the issues involved in the decision and to figure out what one's preferences are.

The vehicle used by Savage (1954) to examine the congruence between preferences and expected value is the gamble. That is, decisions under uncertainty are regarded as gambles and the analysis of the decisions follows the analysis that would be appropriate for gambles. Shafer contends that:

> The analysis of a decision problem by subjective expected utility is merely an argument by analogy. It draws an analogy between that decision problem and the problem of a gambler who must decide how to bet in a pure game of chance. Sometimes such arguments are cogent; sometimes they are not.

Sometimes other kinds of arguments provide a better basis for choosing among acts. Thus subjective expected utility is just one of several possible tools for constructing a decision. (p. 463)

Shafer (1986) goes on to point out that Savage's postulates have two interpretations. One is empirical, in which one can see if decision makers' preferences actually obey the postulates and are congruent with a ranking by subjective expected utility. The other is normative, in which the postulates are a standard of rationality; the issue is not whether real people's preferences obey the postulates, it is only that they should. Shafer contends that these two interpretations are not independent—that the normative interpretation, unless the argument is to become wholly academic, must take into account the results of examining the empirical interpretation. And that examination shows that real people's preferences do not agree with the postulates.

Three courses of action

This non-agreement argues for one of the three courses of action. One is exemplified by Pratt's (1986) response to Shafer's analysis:

If your procedures or decisions or feelings are intransitive or otherwise discordant with subjective expected utility, they are incoherent, 'irrational', or whatever you want to call it, and trying to justify them as coherent or find other rationalities is a waste of time. (p. 498)

This view saves the theory and rejects the behavior. If one enjoys the expected value logic for its own, normative, sake, such a view is not wholly unreasonable, but it fails to be of much interest to the rest of us.

The second course of action is to retain the expected value logic but modify it in light of the experimental results. This is the motivation for behavioral economics, as exemplified by Machina's (1982) work on modifying independence assumptions, Bell's (1982) and Loomis and Sugden's (1982) work on regret, and Kahneman and Tversky's (1979) prospect theory. We have commented elsewhere (Beach and Mitchell, 1990) that, while this course follows a time-honored tradition in science, modifying theory in light of evidence, it also runs the risk of simply propping up a bankrupt, but attractive, theory whose day is done. If history provides examples of theories being improved by modification in light of evidence, it also provides examples of theories that were retained too long. Recall that epicycles were modifications in light of evidence that permitted the overlong retention of the Ptolemaic theory of the solar system.

The third course of action is to step back and look at the various ways in which people make decisions and to try to see what seems to work for them. Such observations might serve to make the analysis of decision making more flexible and realistic, and to suggest new models that go beyond the expected value view to broaden our conception of how decisions can and should be approached. One of the first things that such observations would reveal is that subjective probabilities and utilities seldom conform to the independence postulate of subjective expected utility. This is as empirically true (Slovic, 1966) as it is intuitively reasonable—'The process of formulating and adopting goals creates a dependence of value on belief, simply because goals are more attractive when they are feasible' (Shafer, 1986, p. 479).

One of the next things that observations of actual decision behavior would reveal is that the analogy between risky (von Neumann and Morgenstern, 1947) or uncertain (Savage, 1954) decisions and gambles is seldom apt. When the analogy is not apt, much of the power goes out of the arguments for the prescriptivity of expected value (Shafer, 1986). Observations of managerial decision making by Selznick (1957), Mintzberg et al., (1976), and Isenberg (1984), among others, makes it quite clear that decision makers do not view decisions as gambles. In large part, this is true because, unlike the expected value view of decision making, real decision makers usually exert control over subsequent events in order to make favored outcomes happen—when you can control outcomes the gambling analogy no longer applies.

The gambling analogy

This analogy was adopted in the first place because it makes the differentiation between probabilities and outcomes so very clear. And, in experiments like Gray's (1975), in which the probabilities and outcomes are made clear and independent, the analogy holds and to one degree or other the expected value strategy accounts for choices. On the other hand, few real-life decisions provide such clear differentiation between probabilities and outcomes.

The gambling analogy is in trouble for other reasons, too. First of all, a good argument can be made that it does not apply to unique decisions. Lopes (1981) makes this argument, in the course of which she includes a telling quotation from a paper by the celebrated economist Paul Samuelson (1963). Samuelson recounts offering to bet his colleagues $200 to $100 that the side of a coin they specified would not appear at the first toss. One colleague replied:

> I won't bet because I would feel the $100 loss more than the $200 gain. But I'll take you on if you promise to let me make 100 such bets. . . . One toss is

not enough to make it reasonably sure that the law of averages will turn out in my favor. But in a hundred tosses of a coin, the law of large numbers will make it a darn good bet. I am, so to speak, virtually sure to come out ahead in such a sequence, and that is why I accept the sequence while rejecting the single toss. (p. 109)

According to Lopes, Samuelson is interested in this answer because he considers it 'irrational'.

Samuelson's point is that the expected value of the single bet favors the colleague 2 : 1. Therefore the rational decision maker should be willing to accept the bet. By expressing an unwillingness to do so, Samuelson's colleague had shown himself to be irrational. Moreover, Samuelson goes on to prove that in these circumstances anyone who wants to maximize expected utility cannot accept a sequence of bets if each of the single bets is unacceptable. Samuelson must conclude, therefore, that his colleague did not want to maximize expected utility—which seems to us very likely to have been the case. Whether that actually makes the colleague irrational, as Samuelson claimed, we leave to the reader to decide.

Lopes' (1981) arguments were countered in a subsequent paper by Tversky and Bar-Hillel (1983), which is surprising considering Tversky's role in casting doubt on the descriptive adequacy of expected value (e.g. Kahneman and Tversky, 1979). However, as Keren and Wagenaar (1987) point out, the disagreement between Lopes and Tversky and Bar-Hillel resulted from treating the question from different viewpoints. Lopes examined the adequacy of expected value for unique decisions from a descriptive viewpoint, and Tversky and Bar-Hillel examined it from a normative viewpoint—their counter-arguments focused mainly on differences in interpretation of the examples in Lopes' paper. Keren and Wagenaar took Lopes' descriptive analysis one more step, obtaining empirical evidence that she was correct about the descriptive inadequacy of expected value. They presented pairs of gambles to participants and asked them to choose the one they would prefer to play. In one condition the gambles were unique in that the chosen gamble would be played only once. In the other condition the gambles were repeated in that the chosen gamble would be played 10 times. The gambles were designed so that the one with the highest expected value had the lower probability of winning. If the participants were operating like Samuelson's colleague, they should prefer the lower-expected-value gamble (which had a higher probability of winning) when the gamble is to be played only once, but they should prefer the higher-expected-value gamble (which had a lower probability of winning) when it is to be played repeatedly. The results were precisely as predicted: when the gamble was unique, 68% of the participants preferred the lower-expected-value gamble; but, when the gamble was to be played repeatedly, 67% preferred the high-expected-value gamble.

If decision makers regard the majority of their decisions as unique, which may well be the case (Beach *et al.*, 1988b), Lopes' (1981) arguments and Keren and Wagenaar's (1987) results suggest that they would be disinclined to use the expected value strategy to make the decision, even in an explicit gambling situation. The extreme test of this statement lies in how real gamblers view gambling. That is, if gamblers do not conceive of gambles in terms that parallel the components of expected value, then it does not make much sense to suppose that ordinary decision makers conceive of their risky and uncertain decisions as gambles to be dealt with using the expected value strategy.

In a study in which gamblers were interviewed about various aspects of gambling (Keren and Wagenaar, 1985; Wagenaar *et al.*, 1984), it was found that gamblers attend to a third variable that is not part of expected value—luck. Someone who is lucky will win irrespective of the probabilities involved. In lotteries, for example, the odds are low for any single player, but there is no statistical law preventing that player from winning: *someone* will win and that someone is the person who is lucky. Players do not appear to believe that they can influence the outcome of gambles, but luck influences their choice of what to bet on, and if their luck is running this choice will be the correct one. That is, the gamble favors no one, but luck favors some. As Wagenaar and Keren (1988) point out, this concept of luck does not run counter to a purely physical explanation of randomness for roulette wheels, dice, cards, etc.; it merely makes such an explanation irrelevant to the behavior of the gambler. In short, gamblers' conceptions of gambles do not much resemble the expected value conception (see also Wagenaar *et al.*, 1988).

Wagenaar and Keren (1988) followed up their observations of real gamblers with an experiment that used 400 college students. Two hundred participants were asked to write a short description of an event that happened in their own lives—100 were asked for an example of something that happened by chance and 100 were asked for an example of a lucky event. These stories were then sorted and pairs of chance events and lucky events that were similar in content were selected. This resulted in 40 stories of each kind that were presented to the second 200 students. These students rated each story on a 12-point scale, running from 'not applicable' to 'totally applicable', for each of 12 dimensions: important consequences, luck, escape from negative consequences, fun, social contact, level of accomplishment, emotions, prolonged consequences, probability, chance, coincidence, and surprise.

A discriminant analysis was conducted using the ratings as the independent variables and the original classifications of the stories as luck (+) or chance (–) as the dependent variable. It was found that two dimensions described the data—luck and escape from negative consequences accounted for high positive weights in the function, meaning that they were diagnostic of the

luck category; and surprise, chance, and coincidence accounted for the high
negative weights, meaning that they were diagnostic of the chance category.
The weight for probability was –0.04, meaning that it was not diagnostic of
either category.

In summary, it appears that when conditions are exactly right, as in Gray's
(1975) experiment, decision makers *can* use the expected value strategy, but
it is highly questionable whether these conditions occur very often outside
the laboratory. And outside the laboratory the evidence for its use simply
does not exist. As a result, those of us who are interested in descriptive
decision theory find ourselves losing interest in expected value as the
prepotent strategy. As much as one may admire the mathematical aesthetics
of expected value, and aesthetics is sufficient reason for some researchers to
maintain their theoretical allegiance, the argument for its normative
superiority requires one to step into the small circle of its logic—if one
refuses to take that step, or if one demands that the circle include conditions
that might reasonably characterize real decisions, then expected value ceases
to be of much importance. It simply becomes one strategy from among
many that is available for decision makers to make profitability decisions—
one that they apparently can use but that they seldom use. As Thorngate
and Payne *et al.* have shown, other strategies produce nearly the same results
as the expected value strategy in many conditions—which alone demonstrates that its prescriptions are not unique. All in all, the performance of
the expected value strategy, after having been given ample opportunity to
demonstrate its descriptive sufficiency and a considerable amount of good
will on the part of researchers, simply does not turn out to be all that one
might expect of a supposedly optimal strategy. In reference to the subjective
expected utility (SEU) strategy, and by implication expected value strategies
in general, Fischhoff *et al.* (1983) sum things up very well:

> The story of behavioral decision theory has been the growing realization that
> SEU often does not describe the decision-making process either as it is
> designed or executed. The dramatic tension has been provided by SEU's
> remarkable ability to hang on despite mounting doubts about its descriptive
> competence. (p. 317)

QUESTION 4: WHERE DOES THIS LEAVE US IN TERMS OF DECISION AIDS?

In April of 1988, an international conference was held at the University of
Leiden, The Netherlands, at which the status of classical decision theory in
behavioral decision research was examined in some detail (Beach *et al.*,

1988b). The conclusions reached there were not too different from the conclusions stated above, except perhaps that they were stated a little less bluntly. However, after all was said and done, many conferees felt a great deal of uneasiness about ending the reign of classical theory, particularly subjective expected utility. Part of this we attribute to distress about abandoning the status quo of behavioral theory and research—indeed, many participants clearly had no intention of abandoning anything. And part of the uneasiness could be a attributed to a practical concern about the future of decision aiding as an applied technology. After all, decision aids are the most visible product of behavioral research's affair with classical decision theory—perhaps the most impressive product of all these years of work. Is it all to go by the boards simply because we are no longer confident that its underlying logic is applicable?

Some opinions

If what was said in the answer to Question 3 distressed anyone, what is about to be said should be worse. It is, however, our opinion—based upon our experience with applications of decision aiding schemes to real decision problems. It is our observation that, in spite of a stated allegiance to classical theory, most applications of decision aids are astonishingly cavalier and pragmatic. Rarely are the underlying assumptions of probability theory and utility theory met to any but a minor degree. Probabilities are obtained from clients as easily and as quickly as possible and, other than seeing that they sum to 1.00, coherence is seldom checked. Similarly, utility assessments are only cursorily checked to see if they conform to utility theory—scaling assumptions are seldom met and nobody seems to worry about it. Morevoer, some variant of the expected value strategy is simply imposed on this odd collection of numbers, and the results come out looking solidly prescriptive. If the saying 'Garbage in, garbage out' is true, one cannot help wondering about those results.

Now, please do not misunderstand; this does not necessarily mean that decision analyses are fraudulent. It merely means that whatever good they do is not necessarily attributable to their being solidly grounded in classical decision theory. Rather, these analyses are useful because they help the client figure out what the alternatives are, what he or she wants from the decision, and whether one or the other of the alternatives will supply what is wanted. In short, they require the client to impose order and some degree of comprehensiveness on his or her thinking, and that may well be the major benefit and the driving force behind their contribution to the decision.

Some lessons learned

Over the last 15 years my colleagues and I have examined a broad range of real-life decisions that were extremely important to the participants in our studies. These include decisions about whether to have a child (Beach *et al.*, 1976; Beach *et al.*, 1979), whether to be assertive in the face of unreasonable social demands (Fiedler and Beach, 1978), whether to commute to work by bus or by car (Beach *et al.*, 1981), whether to commit a crime (Cimler and Beach, 1981), whether to be surgically sterilized (Beach *et al.*, 1982), in which of an array of sports to participate (Fiedler and Beach, 1982), which options for public parks development should be pursued (Barnes *et al.*, 1983), whether and when to retire (Prothero and Beach, 1984), whether to have corrective jaw surgery (Kiyak and Beach, 1983), whether to commit suicide (Coolidge *et al.*, 1985), and whether to get an annual influenza vaccination (Carter *et al.*, 1986).

One of the first things we learned while doing these studies is that probabilities mean little to decision makers and have surprisingly little impact on their decisions (Beach, 1983). Moreover even if they did, decision makers' probabilities bear little relationship to decision theorists' probabilities (see also Teigen, 1988). Risk is a factor, yes, but it is viewed as a global, negative aspect of the candidate rather than as a weight on each of the candidate's potential outcomes. Probability is of little concern because decision makers assume that their efforts to implement their decisions will be aimed, in large part, at *making* things happen. This assumption makes probability, in any random sense, irrelevant. Controlling the future is what decision making really is about (Bazerman and Mannix, 1989; March and Shapira, 1987; Phillips, 1985, 1986).

The second thing we learned is that most important decisions are compatibility decisions. They involve only one candidate, a single alternative to the status quo. In these decisions, the status quo is seldom viewed as a competing alternative—it is the baseline against which possible change is evaluated (see Chapter 3).

The third thing we learned is that even compatibility decisions can be forced into an expected values analysis—or, as was the case in most of our studies, multi-attribute utility analysis (von Winterfeldt and Edwards, 1986). Although it was inappropriate, imposing this structure on the decisions often proved enlightening both to our participants and to us because it made them do the main thing that decision aiding ought to do: it made them think in a systematic way about the various ramifications of the decision and how they felt about them. Decision makers seldom come to the decision task with a clear preference. Decisions are decisions because it is not immediately apparent what to do. Decisions makers are usually looking for arguments, from themselves and from other people, that will help them construct a preference. So, even when we force compatibility decisions into expected value or multi-attribute utility frameworks, which are designed for profitability decisions, decision makers benefit from the exercise. Empirically, we make prediction errors as a result of the inappropriateness of our scheme (we consistently overpredict decisions to abandon the status quo), but the fact that the errors are small attests to the robustness (or elasticity) of the analysis schemes. However, even though use of an inappropriate scheme proves beneficial, it is not the best way to go about things.

It is our opinion that decision analysis schemes are in need of overhaul. They could do with a dose of honesty—admission that they are more pragmatic than theoretically pure; admission that they treat subjective probabilities and utilities in a most cavalier manner; and admission that they force every decision into the same framework or a minor variation on that framework. It is time to develop aids that are appropriate and congenial to the kinds of decisions that decision makers actually face. These aids should be congruent with the ways that decision makers think about their decisions— with special emphasis on screening and compatibility, for a start, and greater flexibility in the selection of a choice strategy rather than single-minded imposition of expected value (especially for unique decisions). If for no other reason, appropriate, congenial, congruent aids would promote greater user understanding of the underlying logic and greater confidence in the results.

A major feature of this new generation of decision aids ought to be ways of explicitly helping the clients to systematically consider the implications of decisions for their principles, their existing goals, and their ongoing plans. As things often are now, emphasis upon the potential profits of decisions, particularly short-term profits, easily diverts attention from other important considerations. That is, the logic of most decision analyses stresses that 'more is better', where more usually is in terms of money. This focus makes it easy to overlook, or at least to relegate to a subordinate position, the other implications of adopting the candidate, particularly subtle ethical implications. We are not issuing a call to moral reawakening or any other such evangelical prescription; We are saying merely that the explicit inclusion of principles, goals, and plans in the analysis would better serve clients' broader interests.

Another feature of the new generation of decision aids, a corollary of not imposing the expected value strategy on any and all decisions, is the jettisoning of the logic of gamble equivalencies and the entire technology that follows from it. Clients do not subscribe to the gambling metaphor without a great deal of training, if then. Therefore, basing the central measurement technique upon the logic of this metaphor cannot help but distort the process. Certainly the technology impresses the client and its rationality impresses the decision analyst, and it bears the scent of science;

nonetheless it is inappropriate. Small wonder that Isenberg (1984) found that even decision makers who have been trained to use decision analytic schemes seldom do so—and that they distrust the results of such schemes if those results run counter to their intuitions.

Of course, from the image theory perspective, the major change that must be made in the new decision aids is that they must include both steps of the decision process, rather than just the second step. That is, present schemes assume the first step, screening, and only consider the second step, choice. However, our experience and that of other researchers is that most important decisions involve only single alternatives to the status quo. And the status quo is not regarded as a competing alternative—it is the anchor against which change is evaluated (see also Kahneman and Tversky, 1979). This means that a thorough decision analysis or any similar aid ought to provide for two steps, using the first step to screen candidates and the second to choose the best candidate where there are multiple survivors of the first step. But there should be greater flexibility in selecting the choice strategy to be used, perhaps even through consultation with the client about what it should be.

The major point to be made here is that, no matter how aesthetically pleasing they may be, it is foolish to hold on to decision aiding schemes that are based on classical theory if (1) the theory may not even be demonstrably the best way to make choice decisions (see Questions 2 and 3), let alone screening decisions, (2) the schemes impose an arcane, narrowly focused, and probably inappropriate logic on the client's decision deliberations, and (3) if the schemes ignore the very important role of screening and single alternatives in decision making.

In contrast, new decision schemes should play down the role of probability, subjective and otherwise; should provide structure for the client to consider both screening and choice; and should include compatibility as a major factor in decision making. (One possibility is to expand and adapt 'the Battelle method' of constructing strategic planning scenarios, which uses 'compatibility matrices' to find clusters of variables that tell coherent stories about possible futures (Brauers and Weber, 1988).) In addition, if the van Zee et al. (1989) results are found to be general, the new schemes must help clients understand that information used for screening is not necessarily 'used up', and that it should be carried forward for use in choice among the survivors of the compatibility test.

8 Implementation and Progress

Adopting a plan to achieve a goal tends, in itself, to set the plan in motion. Thereafter, implementation must be monitored to make sure progress toward the goal is maintained.

It is surprising how little research has been done on decision implementation and the assessment of its progress. Behavioral decision research, like classical decision theory, seems to wash its hands of decisions once they are made. This is another unfortunate result of characterizing decisions as gambles. For a gambler the decision is the end of the line—you place your bet and passively wait to see if you won or lost. In contrast, when decisions are characterized as the adoption of goals and plans, the decision itself is only the beginning. The real work lies in implementation, which is an active effort to achieve the goal by following a flexible plan.

The plan is flexible because at the time it is adopted it is quite abstract—even its tactics exist only in the imagination of the decision maker. As implementation proceeds, however, those imagined tactics must be converted into concrete acts in a concrete world. And that world is dynamic. It is seldom exactly as was anticipated when the plan was adopted and, of course, it changes as a result of implementation—not always in the way it was supposed to. All of this requires the plan to be revisable in light of the successes and failures of tactics, either of which may open unforeseen opportunities. In addition, failures often require renewed effort or new tactics, and they sometimes call for either withdrawal or end-runs that look like even more failure, but that may eventuate in progress toward the goal.

Probably no plan can be successful in its original form. In retrospect, even a plan that has resulted in success will have been revised and adjusted in light of feedback—patched and made to work, coaxed by the decision maker into doing the job it was adopted to do almost in spite of itself.

CONTROL

Implementation and monitoring is far more than merely executing a decided-upon course of action. Indeed, the analogy between action and scripts or between action and computer programs is deceptive. Implementation and monitoring are best described as *control* of the environment. The striking thing about them is not so much that they change the environment, although they do so, but that they maintain the course set down by the plan in spite of unanticipated changes and events in the environment. This, of course, is the true function of feedback in control theory (Powers, 1973); it permits the system to compensate for environmental fluctuations and maintain its preordained course.

This is how a thermostat works, and it is how the cruise control in an automobile works. One difference between these servomechanisms and decision implementation is that the preordained course for servomechanisms is a single point, a target temperature or speed, whereas implementation's preordained course is a complex plan.

A second difference is that, while both the servomechanism and implementation monitor their environments and use feedback to maintain adherence to their courses, implementation also uses that feedback to change its own course. That is, when servomechanisms cannot produce homeostasis, they either keep trying and keep failing, or they break down, perhaps going out of control with unpredictable results. In contrast, if failure persists in spite of increased effort or revisions of tactics, implementation modifies the plan while maintaining the goal of the plan. Moreover, if this still does not produce progress toward the goal, implementation rejects the goal rather than plodding blindly onward or going out of control.

Even policies are flexible. A plan that worked in the past cannot be blindly re-implemented. Marken (1988) illustrates the absurdity that would result:

> Imagine replaying into your muscles, with perfect precision, the same motor impulses that were present yesterday when you drove to work. Would you be willing to drive the car to work today under these conditions? Of course not! Even if the muscles were so precise that their sensitivity to neural impulses were the same today as yesterday, small changes in the prevailing environmental conditions (tire pressure, road condition, traffic, etc.) would quickly turn the results of yesterday's muscle forces into today's catastrophe. . . . When analyzed carefully it will be found that any consistent behavior is . . . always different. It will also be found that these variations . . . are absolutely *necessary* to compensate for changes in the environment that would otherwise prevent repetition of the behavior. (pp. 200–201)

In short, action is not the 'output' of a rigid, computer-like cognitive system. Action is very much keyed to its environment, and this fact is central to understanding it. Cognitive psychology frequently overlooks this simple truth, as Marken (1988) observes:

> The illusion of output has had a profound influence on models in cognitive psychology. The cognitive revolution gave mental concepts like 'intention'

renewed respectability. But there is a tendency to skip over the fact that intended results (or goals) are produced by the actions of the organism and environment combined. By ignoring the contribution of environmental disturbances it has been possible to imagine that achieving a goal (reference state) is just a computational (programming) problem. The term 'intention' has come to refer to an internal trigger for carrying out one or another preprogrammed sequence of actions that produce the goal (Brand, 1984; Norman, 1981). In this context the term *control* refers to the process of carrying out the program implemented to achieve the goal. (p. 203)

Indeed, use of the emasculated definition of *control* wholly misses the point of the concept; control means that a system stays on course in the face of events that would otherwise divert it.

PROGRESS DECISIONS

Recall that progress decisions serve two functions. Both are about plans and both are made in the same way. The first is decisions about whether a candidate plan holds sufficient potential to permit it to be adopted for the strategic image. The second is whether an adopted plan is making sufficient progress toward its goal to permit its retention on the strategic image. The second function is of primary interest here, but let us take a moment to review the first function, the role of progress decisions in adoption of new plans.

CANDIDATE PLANS

When a plan is being considered for adoption, those aspects of it that are well defined (see Figure 2.2) provide initial values for the variables that make up the decision maker's mental model of the situation. These initial values constitute a scenario that, when the model is run, generates a forecast. If the forecast includes the goal for which the plan is being considered, without foreseeable interference with other plans or goals, and without apparent violation of the decision maker's principles, it is adopted.

However, if the plan is incompatible with the goal or with the various images, it must be rejected and another candidate considered in its place. Formally this means that a wholly new candidate must go through the same process the first one did. In practice, however, it usually means that the first plan can be tinkered with, altered in view of the part of the causal mental model that caused it to miss its mark, the goal. The altered plan is then treated like a new one and run through the mental model. Indeed, the planning process consists in large part of tinkering with, altering candidate plans to see if the resulting forecast can be made to include the goal, or to see if some incompatibility with an image can be made to go away. Tinkering consists of using plan components from the decision maker's repertory to alter the plan (the do-it-yourself metaphor in Chapter 2).

If tinkering is to no effect, the decision maker may have to begin at the beginning, seeking a new plan from someone, looking for an analogy between the present context and some previous context for which a policy exists (the not-quite-right policy can be tinkered with to make it fit), or trying to build a new plan from his or her repertory of plan components.

EXISTING PLANS

Candidate plans are often rather vague, causing their forecasts to be highly conjectural. Indeed, depending upon the circumstances, decision makers may be overly optimistic about how well a candidate plan will work out, or overly pessimistic, because the vagueness permits a great deal of latitude in setting the initial values for the mental model.

Existing plans, on the other hand, are in the midst of being implemented. This means that feedback about their success is available—at least on the tactical level if not on the strategic level. This reduces the decision maker's latitude for biasing the forecast, and it means that the evaluation is more stringent. The result is that plans adopted in a mood of hopefulness may turn out to be the ones most quickly rejected after implementation begins, and plans rejected in a mood of downheartedness may be unappreciated gems that are lost forever.

The reason for periodically re-examining existing plans is to permit them to be retained or replaced in light of their progress, or lack of it, toward their goals. In addition, their continued compatibility with the other images must be maintained or they must be rejected. The process itself is much the same as for plan adoption. It merely is better informed because of feedback resulting from implementation. Here the plan is entered into the mental model, but the mental model also reflects knowledge about changes in the environment, if any. The scenario generates a forecast that is evaluated for compatibility with the images, including the goal on the trajectory image. If this compatibility test is passed, the plan is retained in its existing form and is implementation continues.

If the plan does not pass the compatibility test, it must be removed from the strategic image and be replaced by another plan that can pass the test. In fact, as is the case for candidate plans, this new plan is usually a tinkered-with version of the first plan. It is in this way, through a series of progress decisions, that plans get revised to fit changes in the environment as well as to reflect unforeseen complications or opportunities that may arise in the course of pursuing the goal. In short, as implementation goes on, plans are usually adapted to feedback about their progress by replacing them with modified versions of themselves.

Sometimes tinkering does not work. Sometimes no variation on a plan will result in an acceptable forecast. Here again the decision maker must seek a plan, either from asking for advice or adapting an existing policy, or build a new plan from scratch using parts from his or her repertory.

If still no plan can be found that will pass the compatibility test, the goal must be re-examined. A goal that cannot be attained is no goal at all, it is merely an unfulfilled desire—of pyschological interest, no doubt, but not part of our present concern. Goal replacement is a good deal like plan replacement. That is, formally a potential replacement is a wholly new candidate, but in practice the new candidate is an altered version of the first goal. The alteration is whatever is necessary to make it attainable by one of the plans that has been considered and found incompatible with everything but goal attainment, and not missing that by much. That is, the decision maker compromises on the goal, makes it more attainable, thus permitting the plan that looks as though it can attain it to be adopted. Remember, however, the compromise goal is now a new candidate that must first be submitted to the compatibility test before its compromise plan can be resubmitted to the compatibility test. If they both pass, they are added to their respective images and life goes on. If one or the other fails the test, the whole process begins again.

If every compromise for the goal makes it incompatible with one or another images, then no plan can be adopted and the goal must be rejected. If the goal came into being in the first place because of internal necessity deriving from principle imperatives, or if the goal owes its being to external necessity deriving from some problem that requires solution, it cannot be neglected, so the search for an adoptable plan must continue.

For the most part, progress decisions do not constantly monitor implementation; they are only made from time to time. As long as things do not go drastically awry, the decision maker will continue to implement existing plans in pursuit of existing goals. If, however, trouble arises, feedback about failure of a tactic or aggregation of tactics will trigger re-evaluation of the plan through the progress decision process. If no failure is detected, which may be merely the absence of feedback (no news is no news, but it may be treated as good news), the decision maker may plunge on. However, from time to time even non-drastic events will trigger re-evaluation of even apparently successful ongoing plans. For example, a birthday may prompt reflection on how one's career is progressing, or a conversation with a friend may prompt re-examination of progress in some other areas of one's life. Incidentally, decision makers' faith in the progress of their existing plans toward their existing goals in the absence of clear feedback to the contrary is but another facet of the specialness of the status quo and the resulting tendency to continue with business as usual.

To put all of this informally, when deciding how to achieve a goal, people tell themselves stories about what they will have to do. If the stories are plausible and do not appear to interfere with other goals or plans, or to require anything immoral, unethical, or improper, the plan that is embodied in the story will be accepted and implemented. If the story is not quite right, it can be changed until it seems plausible, or the goal can be changed a bit so that it is the logical end-point of the story. As the plan is implemented, difficulties prompt review and revision of the story and these changes consititute changes in the plan. In this way the plan, in effect, 'feels its way along' toward its goal (Beach and Wise, 1980). Moreover, as it feels its way along, it requires compromise in its goal. This means that as things progress and the plan and its story evolve to fit the feedback, the goal also evolves along with them. The result is that when one finally arrives, it may work out that neither the plan nor the goal are precisely what they started out to be. Like the sportsman who started out to shoot a duck and returned having caught a fish instead, decision makers often end up having accomplished things they never really set out to accomplish, things which, nonetheless, are satisfactory because they are compatible with their principles, their other goals, and their other plans.

IMPLEMENTATION AND MONITORING RESEARCH

Although behavioral decision research generally has ignored implementation and monitoring, there are three sources of information that, while they are very different, each cast light upon it. The first of these is the formal programs that help people implement personal decisions such as giving up drinking, quitting smoking, or losing weight. The second is a series of complex, interactive simulations in which decision makers had to implement their plans and then deal with the ongoing effects of implementation in the course of pursuing specific goals. The third is observation of the implementation of strategic decisions by businesses, government agencies, and similar organizations. We will discuss each in turn.

PERSONAL DECISIONS

In Chapter 4 we noted that, as part of the compatibility test, decision makers frequently ask 'Is it worth it?'. The first 'it' in the question refers to the goal, and the second refers to the plan. We said that this question arises when an imperfect plan, one that is not wholly compatible with the decision maker's principles, goals and plans, appears to be the only way of achieving the goal. If the goal is highly desirable (i.e. if equation 4.1 is near zero), the flawed plan will be adopted. This might seem like a special and infrequent case, but it is not. In fact, most plans require effort, time, and money and are considerably less pleasant than the goals they are designed to yield. After all, a job may put food on the table but it nonetheless is work.

The conflict between means and ends is most clear when people decide to reform, to turn over a new leaf, to stop doing something that is bad for them. The goal is desirable because it offers health and happiness, both of which are treasured principles. The plan ordinarily is undesirable because it requires abstinence from something that the decision maker enjoys, perhaps even craves, or it may require actively doing something unpleasant. Examples, in addition to quitting smoking or drinking and losing weight, are exercising regularly, taking medications, or replacing junk food with a proper diet. In each case, many of the pleasant features of the goal lie in the future but almost all of the plan's aversive features are immediate.

Resolutions to reform are noteworthy for their failure. Most New Year's resolutions have been broken by the end of January. Most smokers will tell you that they have quit, repeatedly. Lost weight usually is found again. In short, attempts to realize these good intentions are seldom successful, in large part because the only way to achieve them is so unpleasant. Sad to say, the road to good intentions is paved with hell.

In answer to the need, numerous formal programs have come into being to help decision makers keep from backsliding. They are all roughly based on the first such program, Alcoholics Anonymous. Examples are Weight Watchers, Overeaters Anonymous, Gamblers Anonymous, post-cardiac exercise programs, stress reduction programs, and other self-help programs that require members' continued participation. These all have a common core of methods for helping their members implement their plans in order to reach their goals, and for monitoring progress toward those goals. Beach (1985) described the common core of these programs as follows.

(1) *Externalized monitoring*

Weight Watchers, for example, has its members 'weigh-in' at group meetings, and each loss or gain is publicly noted. Exercise classes urge members to go at their own pace, but progress and regress is noted and large doses of encouragement are administered when motivation flags.

(2) *Instruction about tactics*

Concrete rules to follow, such as 'Don't shop for groceries when your're hungry', 'Make new friends and stay away from old drinking buddies', as well as specific instructions about such things as how to prepare low-calorie meals or how to replace cravings with exercise, provide specific, proven tactics for implementation. For example, Alcoholics Anonymous warns that hunger, anger, loneliness, and tiredness promote relapse (the mnemonic HALT helps identify these danger conditions) and provides tactics for coping with them that prevent drinking. Marlatt and Gordon (1985) have developed 'Relapse Prevention Therapy' which teaches people to use mental imagery to rehearse coping with tempting situations that could disrupt implementation. For example, people who are trying to control their intake of alcohol or food are taught to stop before entering a situation in which drink or food are freely available and to use mental imagery to focus on the goal and to rehearse what they will do in the situation to keep from relapsing. This 'mental inoculation' training is much like Meichenbaum's (1977) 'stress inoculation' training.

(3) *Goal-centered thinking*

Regular attendance at meetings and participation in the group's activities helps members to keep their goal foremost in mind. In some cases the details, and the denial, involved in day-to-day implementation are so salient that implementation can become an end in itself and the goal is lost sight of. Once the goal is out of mind it is easy to make subtle changes in the plan that make it a non-aversive, empty ritual.

(4) *Social support*

Knowing that one is not alone, and knowing that help is available if things get rough, help strengthen resolution and prevent relapse. The positive encouragement of the other members of the program when progress is made, and their (albeit supportive) negative reactions when it is not, motivates members to persist in their efforts. Indeed, social facilitation, merely knowing that others are watching one's progress, is often sufficient in itself.

(5) *Testimonials*

Success stories about graduates and testimonials from long-time members of the group set an example and provide credibility for the program as a way of achieving the goal. In contrast, reminders about the awful consequences of failure and about how bad things were before the goal was adopted provide motivation and renewed resolve to attain the goal.

It would appear that some decision makers 'naturally' possess the ability to use these five or similar methods to assure successful implementation of their plans, while others do not. We suspect that the people who are frequently identified as 'good decision makers' are those whose decisions are followed by action and goal attainment. Decisions are easy, they can be made and unmade in a moment. Implementation is quite another matter. It demands that the decision maker take charge and make the right things happen so the goal can be attained. However, even the best decision maker lacks the ability to carry through on some intentions and the programs discussed above give help in the following areas.

First, the programs help the decision maker generate and clarify plans. In addition, they provide guidelines and good advice about which plans are most suitable in various circumstances. Many decision makers appear to be deficient in these skills—they know what they want to achieve, but they do not know how to go about achieving it. In many cases they rely on advice from persons of equal inability in selecting plans and arraying their tactics, and the results are no better than if they had relied on their own poor skills.

Second, the programs provide instruction about concrete tactics that work, particularly in times of stress.

Third, they provide instruction about how to measure progress and how to tell when lack of progress is merely temporary and when it is a sign of backsliding or stagnation. As part of this they help the decision maker recognize successful goal attainment and provide guidance in how to maintain it.

Fourth, the programs help decision makers modify existing plans and tactics when things start to go awry. When modification is not enough, they actively help with the generation of new plans and tactics.

Fifth, they help the decision maker keep tactics subordinate to progress toward the goal. Success of a tactic that does not aid progress is a hollow victory. Consider an analogy to a long-distance swimmer. When the swimmer's head is in the water the focus is on execution of the appropriate swimming stroke, but from time to time she must lift her head to see if all the exertion is resulting in progress toward the finish line.

Finally, the programs help decision makers detect conditions in the environment that make the plan and its tactics obsolete. Obsolescence may result from major unforeseen changes in the environment or from errors in evaluation of the environment or the attractiveness of the goal at the time the decision was made.

SIMULATION DECISIONS

Now we turn to the results of a series of simulation studies reported by Reither and Stäudel (1985). The simulations were of hypothetical countries and towns for which the participants role-played officials who had to make decisions and implement plans to reach various goals. For example, one simulation was of a third-world country that was inhabited by 300 nomads and their cattle. The people had a high birth rate, poor living conditions, and a short life expectancy. Their cattle were in poor physical condition, lacked good pasture, and provided only a subsistence-level existence for the human population. The participants' task was to improve living conditions and to increase both the human and the cattle populations while avoiding extreme population growth for either species. They could influence the human population size by introducing birth control and medical care. They could influence the cattle population size by controlling tsetse flies. They could improve irrigation and they could arrange for markets for native products. Their task was to decide what to do and then to do it. The computer simulation covered 20 years of development and provided feedback about the effects of the decision makers' actions.

Across a number of such simulations, Reither and Stäudel examined the features of the participants' implementations. They found that successful implementation required dealing with many hidden interrelationships among variables that define the environment that supports (or fails to support) implementation. Monitoring progress toward a goal was, therefore, especially difficult when the decision maker was ignorant about how execution of one tactic influenced the applicability and success of other tactics. In short, tactics may help each other or hinder each other for reasons that the decision maker can only guess and for reasons that he or she could not foresee. In such circumstances, the decision maker was often reduced to sheer trial and error until understanding of causal relationships could be gained to guide subsequent implementation or to guide plan revision. The authors observed that successful decision makers asked specific questions in an effort to understand the larger picture—the general structure of the decision environment.

When ignorance abounds, monitoring of progress is particularly difficult because feedback about progress may not be very informative. This lack can be complicated even further if the goal itself is not clearly defined. Reither and Stäudel observed a tendency for unsuccessful decision makers to leave their goals rather vague and ill defined, but, with experience, the successful decision makers clarified and defined their goals. By the same token, successful decision makers sought information about the task that was more abstract than that sought by unsuccessful decision makers—information relevant to the success of tactics *vis-à-vis* the goal, not just tactical success for its own sake.

Reither and Stäudel also found that decision makers often focused on dealing with one feature of complex implementations, ignoring the others. This, of course, is like letting tactics become autonomous and ignoring the larger picture. In addition, many decision makers were content to wait for crises and then react to only that specific problem. Often the interventions 'overdosed' because decision makers could not anticipate the extent of the impacts of their actions. Also, when failure was experienced, some decision makers forced a solution. In some cases, force was also used when progress was too slow for the decision maker's taste.

The characterization of a successful decision maker that emerged from these studies was one of a self-confident, orderly, thoughtful 'winner'. Experience with the task, coupled with some experience with failure, led these decision makers to reflect upon what they were doing and to modify it in light of what they learned. This sort of reflection led to concrete formulation of the goal, crisper delineation of the plan and its tactics, and greater flexibility in discarding or adopting plans and tactics. These decision makers appear to have felt in control and proficient to do the task. They worked efficiently, with purpose, and they persevered. They appear to have had broad vision. They executed orderly, well-structured tactics, and they did not get lost in detail. Most of all, they took measured risks and profited from experience, reflecting upon what they were doing and how they could improve.

In contrast, unsuccessful decision makers appeared to lack confidence. They kept things vague, they approached both the decision and its implementation in a diffuse manner, and they jumped about in a way that Reither and Stäudel describe as 'thematic vagabonding'.

ORGANIZATIONAL DECISIONS

Decision implementation in organizations is somewhat different from implementation by a single decision maker, although there are similar themes. For organizations in which strategic decision making takes place at the top, implementation may consist of disseminating the plan to key people in the organization and inducing them to follow it in making decisions in their own bailiwicks, decisions that support and advance the larger plan. While this top-down arrangement has its critics (e.g. Hayes, 1985), it probably is fairly descriptive of how most business and public sector organizations work (Steinbruner, 1974). In what follows we will refer to leaders and followers instead of top management and employees in order to make the discussion a bit more general.

To ask followers to accept a plan is to ask them to accept organizational change. In image theory terms, acceptance of the plan requires followers to give up the status quo. As we discussed in Chapter 3, there generally is resistance to giving up the status quo, and this is precisely what is observed when leaders attempt to implement organizational change.

Kotter and Schlesinger (1979) identified four common reasons why people resist change. The first is parochial self-interest that is greater than interest in the greater good of the organization. Often this is due to a perception that whatever may be lost as a result of change constitutes an unfair violation of an implicit contract with the organization. Resistance is frequently in the form of political behavior, behind-the-scenes scheming, and power struggles.

The second reason for resisting change is misunderstanding and lack of trust. Kotter and Schlesinger note that few organizations have a high level of trust between followers and leaders, expecially when the former are employees and the latter are management. Consequently, misunderstandings develop easily when change is introduced.

The third reason is that differences in information available to leaders and followers often leads logically to different conclusions. The conclusions reached by followers may or may not be more accurate than those reached by the leadership, but leaders often fail to recognize that a legitimate difference in views can exist. The result is a tendency to regard the resulting resistance as merely wrongheadedness.

The fourth reason for resistance is fear—fear that the plan will fail, fear that skills will be insufficient, fear that the organization is becoming something undesirable. As Hayes (1985) points out, the objectives of change for leaders are often too abstract for followers. That is, leaders think about the grand scheme while followers think about getting their jobs done correctly, meeting delivery schedules, having an acceptable working environment, and job satisfaction. If the proposed change threatens these day-to-day considerations, seldom noted in the leaders' grand schemes, resistance is bound to be generated.

Kotter and Schlesinger propose a number of ways of dealing with resistance, all of which Nutt (1987) found to be used by managers (see also Sproull and Hofmeister, 1986). Nutt studied 68 service organizations (hospitals, charities, professional societies, governmental agencies) that had implemented strategic plans in areas such as mergers, physical plant expansion, major equipment purchases, marketing programs, service development, organizational restructuring, space renovation, and the like. Key people in each organization were interviewed about what had happened in the course of implementation, and their descriptions were checked with other people in order to verify the details. Then the different cases were sorted according to their similarities.

Nutt found four methods of implementation that were used with different frequencies across the various cases. The most common (48% of the cases) consisted of demonstrating the value of the plan in attaining the goal, usually with the help of an in-house expert. The second most common method (21%) consisted of creating a need for change in the minds of key people by demonstrating that things were not working well, identifying plausible causes in current practices, and suggesting improvements (the plan) that could overcome the problems.

The first (16%) of the two least-common methods consisted of the leaders announcing the plan and prescribing how it is to be implemented. Kotter and Schlesinger (1979) note that this 'implementation by edict' often required selective use of information, the manipulation of events, implicit and explicit coercion, and co-opting potential resistors by giving them a desirable role in the implementation program. The potential for problems from such manipulativeness was, of course, very high.

The second (15%) of the two least-common methods consisted of the readers identifying strategic needs and delegating plan development to a group of representative followers who had the authority to make decisions without top management veto, as long as they stayed within the area that was identified. Sometimes the result was that the other followers subscribed to the plan because their interests appear to have been represented in its formulation.

Resistance is but one barrier to successful implementation of organizational plans, albeit an important one. Even when subordinates accept the plan and tailor their own decisions to it in an effort to make it work, other difficulties may arise to prevent achievement of the goal. Alexander (1985) surveyed 93 company presidents about the implementation problems that they had encountered. Ten problems were mentioned by more than 50% of the interviewees. These were: more time required than anticipated; unanticipated problems; ineffective coordination; diversion of attention to competing activities and crises; inadequate employee skill; inadequate employee training; uncontrollable environmental factors; inadequate leadership and direction at departmental levels; inadequate definition of key tasks; and inadequate monitoring systems.

One last thought: Hayes (1985) notes that most organizations, especially businesses, tend to focus on short-term successes. The result is that their long-term survival and prosperity is jeopardized because no care is taken to build the resources that will be needed in the future. One result of this is that followers have difficulty keeping track of why they are doing whatever it is that is currently being asked of them, they have no sense of continuity and permanence, and they become resistant to participating in and facilitating even more change lest it compound what they already perceive as a threatening situation. It may well be true that similar observations could be made for short-term personal decision making and for short-term decision making in very small groups, such as families.

It is curious that in all of the foregoing there is no reference to what seems to be a major prerequisite for successful implementation of strategic plans: that is, the clear specification of the compatibility between the plan, the goal, and the organization's value image—its principles. Apparently, only three studies have focused on the communication of such compatibility, and all three examined the effects of changes in principles on the success of attempts to change followers' goals and plans and their implementation of those plans.

Beck (1987) described the well-programed introduction of changes in the principles governing BankAmerica, and how the changes in principles led to changes in the behavior of bank employees. Old principles such as risk avoidance and self-protection gave way to 'smart' risk taking and a premium on innovation. According to Beck, the effects were profound, once subordinates were clear about what the new principles were and had accepted them. Clear definition of the new principles increased cooperativeness, innovativeness, appraised performance, and subordinates' sense of direction. And it reduced the self-protective 'analysis paralysis' that had slowed decision making in the past.

Bjork (1985) described a program aimed at changing the organizational value image of the University of New Mexico from that of a teaching institution to that of a research and graduate institution. The change was brought about over the years from 1967 to 1978, and involved getting key stakeholders to accept the new view of the university and its mission, thus 'legitimizing' the organization's new value image. The result was that, as the new image was adopted by decision makers throughout the university, their decisions reflected the change and contributed to attainment of the goals that the university had adopted as part of that new image.

In summary, there are commonalities in implementation of personal decisions, implementation of simulation decisions, and implementation of organizational decisions. In order for people to work toward successful implementation, they have to believe that the goal has value and that it is in their best interests to pursue it. They must know how to implement the plan for achieving the goal—vagueness leaves too many opportunities for failure. They must be able to monitor implementation and know when progress is or is not taking place. Finally, they must be able to keep the long-range goal in mind so they do not get so caught up in the tactics that they never reach the goal.

A MODEL FOR IMPLEMENTATION MONITORING

COMPONENTS OF MONITORING

The research discussed above provides a background for thinking about implementation monitoring. Therefore, the remaining pages of this chapter will present some tentative ideas about the factors that influence how decision makers monitor progress in the course of implementing a particular plan in pursuit of a particular goal. Because this model is brand new, there has been no opportunity to test it. As a result, it must be emphasized that it is highly tentative.

Every decision implementation is different. Even for similar goals and plans, environmental conditions change over time, as do the decision maker's knowledge and skills. Therefore it is difficult, and perhaps not very valuable, to formulate a general model of implementation *per se*. However, there is one thing that is common to all implementations—progress monitoring. Because monitoring, and the progress decisions that are at its core, is central to image theory, it is the focus of the present model.

The basic assumption of the model is that the chances of a successful conclusion to implementation (either attainment of the original goal or attainment of a substitute goal that emerges in the course of implementation) is enhanced by rigorous monitoring. Rigorous monitoring permits faltering plans to be remedied or replaced and goals to be more sharply defined, revised, or replaced as conditions dictate. In short, monitoring provides the opportunity to use feedback to control progress in the manner discussed at the beginning of this chapter.

Thoroughness

Monitoring can be described in terms of thoroughness and frequency. Thoroughness means that more than just the most salient features of the strategic image's forecast are checked for compatibility with the relevant principles, goals, and plans in order to assess progress. Thoroughness requires the decision maker to step back mentally from the details of implementation and to view things in a broader framework defined by the relevant constituents of the images (Mitchell and Beach, in press). This means that the price of thoroughness is expenditure of energy, time, and (sometimes) money.

Frequency

Recall the analogy used earlier about the long-distance swimmer who must occasionally interrupt the routine of swimming to look up and take bearings in order to gauge progress toward the goal. Increased frequency of checking progress assures greater accuracy because it permits timely correction of deviations from the most efficient path, but it exacts the price of interrupting the flow of swimming (implementation).

Effort

Monitoring of an implementation's progress has its advantages in that it increases the likelihood of a desirable conclusion, but it has its price in that it requires diversion of effort from the task at hand. We define monitoring effort as the expenditure of energy, time, and (sometimes) money.

Within limits, it is reasonable to trade off between thoroughness and frequency of monitoring. This is because infrequent but thorough monitoring can detect small or obscure signs of impending implementation difficulties and corrective steps can be taken by the decision maker before anything dire occurs. On the other hand, frequent but less thorough monitoring can detect glaring difficulties almost as soon as they arise and can instigate remedial action. Therefore, while there obviously are exceptions, especially at the margin, we assume that thoroughness and frequency can be traded off for any given level of effort.

Figure 8.1 contains hypothetical trade-off functions that illustrate this assumption; the functions are straight lines because we do not yet know what their actual shape may be. Thus, each point on each function represents a unique combination of thoroughness and frequency of monitoring. All points on a particular function represent a given level of effort. For a given level of effort, a particular function, a point near the upper end of the function is a combination of more thorough and less frequent monitoring. A point near the lower end of the same function is a combination of less thorough and more frequent monitoring. Note that for the function at the bottom left, both thoroughness and frequency are narrowly restricted—implementation had better be easily monitored or its success better be fairly unimportant, because not much effort is going to be devoted to monitoring its progress. In contrast, functions on the right of the graph represent investment of a great deal of effort in terms of both thoroughness and frequency.

The purpose of the present model is to identify the contingencies that

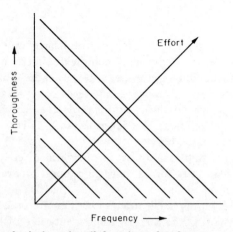

Figure 8.1 Hypothetical trade-off functions for frequency and thoroughness of implementation monitoring for increasing levels of effort.

determine (1) the level of effort, and (2) the combination of thoroughness and frequency that will be devoted to monitoring a particular implementation.

EFFORT

It is reasonable to think that the level of effort invested in monitoring an implementation is dictated by the value to the decision maker of the goal of the plan that is being implemented. Recall from Chapter 2 that the value of a goal, the motivation for pursuing it, is determined by the degree to which it complies with and promotes the decision maker's principles.

CONTINGENCIES

Thoroughness and frequency of monitoring are shaped by the decision maker's perceptions of three sets of contingencies. The first set is defined by the characteristics of the plan that is being implemented. The second set is defined by the characteristics of the environment within which the implementation is taking place. The third set is defined by the characteristics of the decision maker who is doing the implementation. Some of these characteristics can be gleaned from the literature discussed above and from further thinking about the subject, but no doubt there are others that are not yet on the list.

Characteristics of the plan

Decision makers perceive plans to differ in their clarity and complexity, and in intrinsic pleasantness. Clarity and complexity were examined in the discussion that accompanied Figure 2.2, and the reader is invited to review what was said there. In addition, recall that plans change throughout implementation, so perceived clarity and complexity also change. It is their perceived status at the moment that is important—as is the case for all of the variables to be discussed here.

The pleasantness (or unpleasantness) of plans was discussed earlier in the present chapter in relation to formal implementation programs. The biggest problem with aversive plans, of course, is the risk that they will be abandoned, thus precluding goal attainment. On the other hand, pleasant plans can also present problems. If implementation of a plan is itself extremely pleasurable, it is possible for the decision maker to get so caught up in doing it that he or she neglects to monitor progress toward its goal. If the goal changes or ceases to exist, so that the plan is no longer necessary, intrinsic pleasure may make the implementation autonomous and even counter-productive (e.g. tranquilizers taken to reduce stress may become the end in themselves and addiction may develop).

Characteristics of the environment

The three major characteristics of the implementation environment are its perceived predictability, the perceived quality of the feedback it provides, and the perceived degree to which it supports the implementation.

Predictability was discussed in Chapter 2 and need not be expanded upon here.

Perceived feedback quality refers to whether the decision maker thinks that he or she is able to discern the effects of implementation upon the environment. In some cases the results of executing a tactic may not be known until some time in the future. Or, the effects may be minor at the moment but be cumulative over time. In other cases, the decision maker may not have a method of measuring the effects and as a result may remain uncertain about what the implementation actually is doing.

Inability to discern (measure) feedback is a major problem for businesses and other organizations. Alexander (1985) found that about half of the executives in a sample of 93 firms reported difficulties arising from inadequate information systems for monitoring the impact of implementation. This is also a major problem in the public sector—plans often involve such diverse groups and interests that it is often not at all clear what to look at to gauge progress. Anyone who has attempted to conduct a program evaluation for a social service program, for example, can attest to the difficulty of even identifying the important indicants of progress, let alone measuring them. The decision maker who anticipates such problems must be especially careful during implementation because, in large part, he or she is operating in a state of ignorance and high uncertainty.

Feedback quality can be a problem even when supposedly hard numbers exist. Grades in school are supposed to measure attainment of knowledge, but no thoughtful student or teacher believes it; partly because there is no independent, agreed upon, definition of knowledge or of when it is attained. Job performance evaluations are similarly flawed; an employee would be ill-advised to rely upon them as the sole source of feedback about progress on the job even though they may appear to be quite straightforward. Similar examples abound, and feedback that appears clear to an outsider may be regarded as useless to the better informed. The legislator who thinks that the ratio of degrees granted to the total cost of running a state university is clear feedback about educational effectiveness may be stunned by the reception he or she receives from the faculty. Again, the decision maker who must rely upon such feedback had best be wary.

Perceived environmental support refers to the perceived availability of means for advancing the implementation. Some support is physical—for you to be willing to walk across the room, the floor must be perceived to be capable of supporting your progress. Other support comes from instrumental agents—people or systems who can be depended upon to provide information, opportunities, or labor. In some cases the decision maker relinquishes part of the implementation to such agents, as when a consultant is hired, part of a task is contracted out, or when a friend does a favor that advances your interests. To the degree that the decision maker perceives these agents as competent and reliable, he or she can be personally less involved in the implementation.

As we saw earlier in this chapter, when implementation requires that other people (often subordinates, but also spouses and colleagues) adopt the plan and tailor their decisions to it, the decision maker often encounters difficulty in the form of resistance. We also saw that the most common (48%) method used by decision makers for getting cooperation was to persuade the necessary people that the candidate plan could attain mutually desired goals (Nutt, 1987). The second most common (21%) method was to demonstrate to such people that a problem exists (thus defining the goal) and that the candidate plan can remedy it.

Both methods make an appeal to the people who must be relied upon as implementing agents to adopt the candidate plan. Image theory suggests that the appeal will be most effective when it can demonstrate the compatibility of the plan with mutually held principles, goals, and plans. That is, the candidate plan is more likely to be adopted by the agents if they can be shown that it is capable of attaining a recognized organizational goal without violating the organization's recognized principles or interfering with the agent's ongoing plans in pursuit of other organizational goals. Sometimes compatibility will be readily apparent and no resistance will be encountered. Sometimes successful demonstration will eliminate resistance. Sometimes the decision maker's best efforts at demonstrating compatibility will meet with failure, but that failure can be informative. It may mean that the plan actually is flawed (feasibility). It may mean that the agent's views about the organization's principles (ethics), goals (legitimacy), or plans (conflicts) are different from the decision maker's. Or it simply may mean that the demonstration failed to address the issues correctly. In any case, resistance means that more thought and, perhaps, more careful development of the plan and definition of its goal may be called for if the decision maker is to rely upon the help of others in advancing the implementation.

Characteristics of the decision maker

The major characteristics of the decision maker's self-perception in relation to implementation are perspective, control, and proficiency.

Perspective involves the perceived ability to avoid getting lost in the implementation. This includes the ability to separate short-range and long-range considerations and to keep the former subordinate to the latter, to keep the goal in mind while executing the tactics that make up the plan, to discriminate between important setbacks and minor ones, to invest energy and resources in only what is important, and to avoid getting side-tracked by trivial issues or diverted into dealing with the wrong problems.

Perspective derives from being on top of things; from having a clear view of why the organization is doing what it is doing (principles), what it actually is doing (goals), and how it is doing it (plans). However, the more that is going on, the more difficult it is for the decision maker to remain convinced that he or she has a comprehensive view of everything. When the decision maker's personal life is complex, it is difficult to keep any one implementation in perspective, and the more difficult it is to monitor any single implementation thoroughly because there are other demands on his or her attention. Similarly, the more multifacited an organization is, the more difficult it is for any single decision maker or group of decision makers to. give each implementation much attention. The result is that decision makers often perceive themselves as having too little perspective on any single implementation.

Perceived control involves the perceived ability to execute tactics with timing and precision. In some sense, promptness tells the decision maker that monitoring need not be frequent because a remedy can be quickly applied when difficulties arise. On the other hand, it also tells him or her that monitoring must follow every execution closely, if only to avoid the 'overdosing' that was observed in Reither and Stäudel's (1985) simulations. When execution is extended in time, there is often an opportunity to produce a graded, fine-tuned effect that will advance the plan smoothly and efficiently toward the goal.

To a large degree, control is part of the environment in the sense that other people and outside events must cooperate if the decision maker is to exert control. Remember, however, that all of the variables in this model are defined in terms of the decision maker's perception of them, and those perceptions may or may not be correct. Thus, it may well be that the environment would support control, but if the decision maker does not recognize that fact, from his or her viewpoint controllability is low. Or, the decision maker may perceive high controllability when actually it is low, with the result that he or she assumes that implementation orders are being carried out by agents when they are not. This happens in private life as well as in large organizations, as any parent can attest, and it may mean that the implementation may go awry because of the decision maker's false sense of security.

Another part of perceived control is the decision maker's knowledge that he or she possesses a varied repertory of tactics for use in implementations. In the course of performing implementations, the decision maker learns how to do the many small tasks that are common to numerous plans—knowing who to call to get this or that accomplished, knowing the forms that have to be submitted, knowing how to make a machine (or a bureaucracy) work to one's advantage. As this repertory expands through experience, the decision maker's sense of control (self-efficacy) increases and an implementation that earlier on would have been difficult and would have required careful attention becomes easy and almost casual.

Perceived proficiency involves the perceived ability to be sensitive to the subtleties of the implementation and to react to them appropriately. It includes the perceived ability to recognize signs of progress or failure when monitoring takes place. Moreover, it involves recognition that tactical failure is not necessarily regress because, in addition to providing information about what will not work, it often provides suggestions about what might work. Trial tactics are a way of diagnosing the environment—if nothing bad occurs it may mean that the direction taken by the tactic provides an opening for further progress. In this way the implementation, the plan, can 'feel its way along' through unknown territory until the goal is attained, or at least until more familiar ground is encountered. The decision maker who recognizes the value of failed tactics can approach implementation more confidently. However, this use of tactics requires close attention or their lessons are lost.

Perceived proficiency also involves the perceived ability to make the entire implementation process conceptually clearer so that everyone who is party to the implementation knows what is to be done when the time comes and can gauge progress for themselves.

In short, of interest to the model is the degree to which the decision maker perceives himself or herself to have the necessary perspective, control, and proficiency to implement the plan and achieve the goal.

PREDICTING EFFORT, THOROUGHNESS, AND FREQUENCY

Now we return to the hypothetical trade-off functions in Figure 8.1. Recall that from left to right the various functions represent increasing amounts of effort invested in monitoring and that each point on a function represents a combination of thoroughness and frequency of monitoring.

The basic assumption

All else being equal, increased investment of effort in monitoring results in increased chances of successful implementation.

Effort

The degree of effort invested in monitoring is an increasing function of the goal's value to the decision maker *relative* to the other goals that are being pursued at the time.

Thoroughness and frequency

The mix of thoroughness and frequency of monitoring of implementation is determined by the decision maker's perception of the contingencies imposed by the plan, the environment, and his or her own abilities. Because the amount of allocated monitoring effort is fixed for any given goal, it is seldom possible to invest in both very frequent and very thorough monitoring. The question is what combination of the two is best given the circumstances.

Until data are available to provide grounds for a better guess, the hypothesis is that, for a given level of effort, (1) the *less* clear, simple, and pleasant the plan is perceived to be, (2) the *less* predictable and supportive the environment is perceived to be and the *lower* the perceived quality of the feedback it presents, and (3) the *less* the decision maker perceives himself

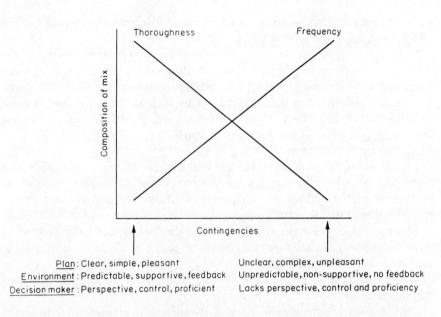

Figure 8.2 Hypothetical mixes of thoroughness and frequency of implementation monitoring for various combinations of contingencies imposed by the characteristics of the plan, of the environment, and of the decision maker.

or herself to have a clear perspective, be in control, and to be proficient, the greater the pressure for thorough monitoring, which requires diversion of effort from frequency. Conversely, when the contingencies are at the opposite extreme, the decision maker will focus upon more-frequent, less-thorough monitoring.

Figure 8.2 lists the two sets of extreme contingencies. Less-extreme contingencies, and combinations of contingencies, produce different combinations of thoroughness and frequency, as indicated by the hypothetical functions in the figure.

A major implication of all of this is that, in theory at least, the mix of thoroughness and frequency of monitoring is independent of the level of effort. That is, if the decision maker is presently using a mix that he or she deems appropriate, an increase in effort should not change the mix. Instead the increase in effort should be apportioned between thoroughness and frequency in a manner that maintains the existing mix.

Of course, in reality it may be that the whole reason for increasing the effort may be because the present mix is not deemed appropriate. This implies that there is an ideal mix, dictated by the variables listed in Figure 8.2, that cannot be attained with the present level of effort. Under these circumstances the increase in effort will indeed be accompanied by a change in the thoroughness–frequency mix, but merely because the mix was artificially constrained in the first place.

Consider a hypothetical example. Imagine the problem faced by the director of a new state program (plan) to eliminate unemployment in some depressed local industry (goal). Let us call the program the EUP, for short. The state legislature has many worthy goals such as the EUP, and it must fund each of them as best it can. Unfortunately, the EUP does not have a very high priority, so its funding is considerably lower than the level requested by the director.

The level of funding sets the maximum that the director's office can undertake (i.e. the resources dictate the overall level of effort that can be put into the EUP). Moreover, that level of effort must support implementation of the EUP and monitoring of the progress of the implementation.

The portion of the *requested* funding the director would have devoted to monitoring identifies the *ideal* function in Figure 8.1. The mix of thoroughness and frequency of monitoring on that function is determined by the director's perceptions of the variables in Figure 8.2. Together, these factors determine an *ideal point* in Figure 8.1.

The portion of the *actual* funding the director devotes to monitoring identifies the *actual* function in Figure 8.1, and the variables in Figure 8.2 determine the mix. This defines an *actual point* in Figure 8.1.

Underfunding makes the director's ideal and actual points quite different. However, if the actual point does not lie on an excessively restrictive effort function (not enough money to do much of anything), the thoroughness–frequency mixes represented by the ideal and actual points should be the same. On the other hand, if the actual point lies on an effort function that is excessively restrictive, the mix will not be the same as the mix for the ideal point. If the legislature supplemented the EUP budget so that the monitoring effort could be increased, the new actual mix would move closer to the ideal mix.

This simple example contains a number of important points. First, of course, is the disparity between ideal and actual levels of effort and the implications (or lack of them) for the mix of thoroughness and frequency of monitoring. The second is that external forces often determine the level of effort the decision maker can invest. Sometimes this is through funding, sometimes it is through social pressure to be more or be less aggressive in pursuing some goal, and sometimes it is through making other demands upon the decision maker's resources—time, energy, money, support personnel, etc. The third point is that, of the overall level of effort available, part must be allocated to monitoring. The present model is concerned only with what happens with the part that is allocated to monitoring, for that is the effort level that is represented in Figure 8.1; the model does not address the split between implementation and monitoring. However, the split clearly is important. All too often, especially when resources are very limited, there is considerable pressure to invest most of the resources in implementation and little or none in monitoring. Often, if the decision maker yields to these pressures, the result is that the implementation plunges blindly onward—no feedback about progress is available until or unless a crisis occurs. Moveover, when the crisis occurs, the absence of the information that monitoring could have provided often means that the decision maker has no idea about how to remedy things. Even if danger signals exist all around, they are wasted if there is no provision for monitoring them.

Three cautionary notes: First, as an implementation progresses, plans and their goals change (e.g. Mintzberg, 1978, 1987). This means that there will be corresponding changes in effort and in the mix of thoroughness and frequency of monitoring. Similarly, the environment and the decision maker change over time, both because of the effects of the implementation itself, unrelated changes in the environment, and because the decision maker gains experience. This means that frequency and thoroughness will change as well.

Second, the model is designed for the case in which the decision maker has the freedom to monitor at will. Often, however, this freedom is constrained by unavailability of the opportunity to monitor. For example, grades are only available after exams and at the end of term, so monitoring that relies upon them can only be done at those times. Information for use in monitoring for organizations may be compiled only on a monthly or quarterly basis, thus restricting monitoring to those times.

Third, the decision maker usually has more than one implementation going on at a time. As a result, rather than being constant, as implied by Figure 8.1, effort may vary over time—if the decision maker is tired, all implementations will get less effort. If some implementations go especially well, effort may be freed to be invested in other implementations. Crises may divert effort from some implementations to others. In short, although the model assumes a constant level of effort over time, reality is otherwise.

SUMMARY

In this chapter we examined decision implementation and progress monitoring as control processes; the similarities and differences. Then we discussed progress decisions in detail before reviewing three areas of research. The first area involved the implementation and monitoring techniques that have evolved in groups like Alcoholics Anonymous and Weight Watchers. The second involved simulations in which decision makers see the results of implementing their decisions and have to deal with those results as part of an ongoing interaction with a simulated world. The third area involved the implementation of decisions in organizations and the resistance that is commonly encountered.

Out of this was developed a model of implementation monitoring in which a given amount of effort is allocated to an implementation, depending upon the relative importance of its goal. This fixed amount of effort is then apportioned between thoroughness of monitoring and frequency of monitoring. The mix of thoroughness and frequency is predicted to be determined by the characteristics of the plan that is being implemented, the characteristics of the environment in which the implementation is being carried out, and the characteristics of the decision maker who is carrying out the implementation.

9 Image Theory Applied

This final chapter contains three essays in which image theory is used in the examination of specific examples of three kinds of decisions: business, personal, and political. The business decision essay is a revised version of an article by Beach and Frederickson (1989). Image theory is proposed as an alternative both to classical decision theory and to heuristics and biases as a framework for the behavioral accounting analysis of financial auditing decisions.

The personal decision essay is a much revised and extended version of an article by Beach and Morrison (1989). Image theory is proposed as an alternative both to cost–benefit and to expectancy value models that lately have been dominant in the study of dyadic decision making in general and childbearing decision making in particular (Brinberg and Jaccard, 1988).

The political decision essay was written for this book, and developed in parallel with work by our colleague Emily van Zee on the function of questions in decision deliberation. Image theory is used to examine transcripts of two meetings held in the White House on 16 October 1962, at the beginning of the Cuban Missile Crisis. The purpose is to demonstrate the descriptive usefulness of image theory for a real, exceptionally important, political decision. In addition, in this essay image theory is applied to a group decision.

AN IMAGE THEORY ANALYSIS OF AUDITING DECISIONS

In 1984, Waller and Felix proposed a new model for describing how financial auditing decisions are made. Their thesis was that the auditor reaches an opinion about the absence of material error in a set of financial statements through a series of revisions and modifications of his or her knowledge structure. These revisions and modifications are made in light of audit evidence about account balances and about the procedures used by the client to collect and store accounting information. The auditor's knowledge structure both guides the search for and the interpretation of the evidence that modifies it, and the structure's modified form represents the current state of that evidence *vis-à-vis* the requirements that the client's data and procedures must meet.

The Waller and Felix (1984) analysis was quite bold, especially because behavioral accounting has enthusiastically adopted the concepts provided by classical decision theory and the heuristics and biases research (e.g. Ashton, 1982). Their analysis was a profound departure from the established view, but because it rejected the classical view it lacked a decision model to which it could be tied. Since then, image theory has been developed. What follows is an extension of Waller and Felix's thinking using image theory.

Waller and Felix divide the audit process into four steps:

(1) deciding to perform the audit, (2) gaining an understanding of the client . . . and a preliminary evaluation of internal accounting controls . . ., (3) planning and execution of audit activities . . . and, (4) forming an opinion. (p. 37)

Step 1 involves deciding about the 'auditability' of the potential client. Step 2 involves obtaining information about how the client's accounting information system actually transforms economic activity into accounting numbers. What is learned here sets the criteria that must be met by evidence obtained during the execution of the audit. Step 3 involves planning and execution of the audit. Step 4 involves assessing the implications of what is learned in the implementation of the audit (step 3) in regard to presence or absence of material error in the client's financial statements. Apparent presence of error warrants continued audit work or a recommendation that the client adjust the financial statements. If neither of these courses of action produces appropriate results, then a qualified opinion must be issued.

THE IMAGE THEORY ANALYSIS

The image theory analysis is done from the point of view of the member of an accounting firm who is primarily responsible for the audit. This auditor's decisions are (1) whether to accept or retain a client, and (2) whether the client's financial statements are without material error. In this we adopt Schandl's (1978) view that 'the purpose of the audit is to see if events conform to some desired state of affairs [where] the norms used are the image or images of the desired state of affairs' (p. 69).

The images

The auditor shares with others in the auditing firm an idea of what constitutes the firm's *value image*—its principles, including business principles (e.g. profits, clientele), acceptable accounting principles, and acceptable auditing standards and techniques (appropriate compliance and substantive tests). The latter two, which are part of the frame that defines the focal activity as an audit, will be called the firm's *audit principles*.

The *audit trajectory image* consists of multiple, but similar, goals: a correct audit for each of the auditor's clients. The goal in the present frame is a correct audit for this particular client, where a correct audit is defined as whether the audit process supports issuing an unqualified opinion (i.e. lack of material error in the client's financial statements). For convenience we shall call this a 'successful' audit; an 'unsuccessful' audit is one in which an unqualified opinion is not supported by the audit.

The *audit strategic image* consists of the audit plans for examining the auditor's different clients' financial statements in order to render an opinion. The frame for the present client includes the plan that is unique to that client's particular circumstances. The plan consists of major tactics, individual audit steps, that are aimed at producing satisfactory progress toward the larger goal of a successful audit. The plan's minor tactics are more or less assumed; ascertaining where information is filed, footing columns of numbers, making phone calls, and the rest of the day-to-day activities that make a plan work but that are not necessarily thought out at the time the plan is formulated.

The plans on the audit strategic image generate forecasts that are used to assess the audit's progress. That is, as the plan is implemented through execution of its component tactics, its forecasted results are tested for their compatibility with the criteria for a successful audit. Forecasted success leaves the plan in place. Forecasted failure results in adjustments to the tactics, such as revising the audit steps or increasing the extent of substantive testing. If adjusting the tactics does not reduce anticipated failure, the plan itself must be revised. If plan revision provides no remedy, the goal must be rejected. Goal rejection means that the auditing firm cannot affirm without qualification that the client's financial statements are free from material error.

Types of decisions

Let us examine the auditor's decisions within this framework. First, the auditor must decide whether to accept a potential new client for his or her firm (or to retain a present client). That is, the first decision is an adoption decision—whether or not to adopt the candidate client, which is the same as adopting the goal of a successful audit for that client. This adoption decision depends upon the compatibility of the client's attributes with the firm's audit principles. Do the client's attributes violate any of the firm's relevant principles? Information about these attributes is drawn from records, from inquiries made of previous auditors, from governmental agencies, etc. (Waller and Felix, 1984). If the information indicates that the client's 'auditability' is *not* low, and that the audit is *not* an inappropriate undertaking for the firm in other regards (e.g. it does not impede the firm's business goals), the client will be adopted or retained. Once adopted, the client and its successful audit become a constituent of the firm's audit trajectory image, with its location on the trajectory being determined by the deadline for completion of the audit.

The second decision is the error decision; whether the audit evidence supports an unqualified opinion about the lack of material error in the client's financial statements. As outlined by Waller and Felix, the first step in making the error decision is a preliminary evaluation of the client's internal accounting controls. Here again the firm's audit principles are brought to bear, except that this time they are used to set the criteria that must be met before the goal can be regarded as having been achieved. Poor internal controls prompt more stringent criteria in terms of the timing and extent of substantive tests. Moreover, it is during this step that the major tactics of the plan begin to take shape. The general form of the plan is fairly clear from the beginning—it is dictated by generally accepted auditing standards and by prototypic audit plans developed by the audit firm. However, the prototypic audit plan is modified in light of the preliminary evaluation of internal controls and the resulting criteria for each client. It is during this step in the auditing process that the task requirements begin to become clear and that the process begins to be crafted to fit the unique characteristics of the particular client and the environment in which the client operates.

The second step toward the error decision is the implementation of the audit plan. Each tactical activity is aimed at seeing whether the information that it examines advances the audit toward achievement of the various criteria for goal accomplishment. When a criterion is met, tactical activity related to it stops. If prolonged activity does not produce progress toward meeting a criterion, the tactic is reviewed and changed if some alternative seems more promising. If the new tactic produces no progress and no alternative to it appears promising, the plan itself must be reviewed. If the plan does not appear to be faulty or if no alternative can be adopted to replace it (perhaps there simply is no way to obtain necessary information or the client refuses to cooperate in some important way), the goal must be rejected.

Goal rejection means that the error decision is negative; the firm must propose adjustments to the client's financial statements or, lacking client support for adjustments, it must attach qualifications to its report on those statements. Usually, a negative error decision is negative because the plan could not produce events that met the criteria. In most cases the plan's lack of progress accurately reflects the gap between the client's financial statements and the supporting evidence. Thus the plan's default leads to rejection of the goal of a successful audit and to the conclusion that the client's financial statements are not materially correct. Criteria that are unmet indicate where qualification is required.

Setting criteria

Criteria for a particular audit are addressed by the substantive and compliance tests that are the major tactics comprising the audit plan. If the tests yield results that meet all of the criteria, the goal of a successful audit is regarded as having been achieved and the auditor can issue an unqualified opinion. The question is what is meant by criteria and how they are set.

Criteria addressed by substantive tests are the amounts reported in the client's financial statement. Criteria addressed by compliance tests are dictated by the firm's audit principles—its image of appropriate accounting procedures and internal controls. As described by Waller and Felix, meeting substantive criteria is of primary importance; meeting compliance criteria merely allows the auditor to rely upon the client's internal controls, thereby allowing a reduction in the extent and/or timing of substantive testing.

Theoretically, decisions about whether criteria have been met often are described as Bayesian, sometimes short-circuited by judgemental heuristics. Practically, such decisions often appear to rest on tests of the null hypothesis that the amounts adduced from the audit evidence are not significantly different from the financial statements. Probably neither of these accurately reflects how the decisions actually are made. The process of setting criteria and making decisions about whether criteria have been met cannot properly be described using statistical concepts because both are influenced by variables that have no counterparts in statistics. Although a parallel exists between these activities and what statisticians do, the resemblance is superficial and can be misleading.

In answer to Question 3 in Chapter 5 (How close is close enough?) we discussed the idea of the equivalence interval (EI). It will be recalled that the EI is the maximum difference that can exist between some reference point and a derived point that still permits the two to be regarded as essentially the same—which is also the definition of materiality in auditing. From an image theory viewpoint, a criterion is the specific, precise reference point on some dimension related to the audit, and the EI indicates the precision with which the audit evidence must match that precise point in order for the criterion to be regarded as having been met. The preliminary evaluation of the client's internal controls sets EIs for criteria on each of the dimensions relevant to the audit—both compliance criteria and, through them, substantive criteria. Of course, these EIs can be revised throughout the audit process as additional information is gathered.

The point is, audit evidence is not used in a strictly Bayesian manner, or even in a heuristic manner, nor are statistical tests really very germane to the error decision. In fact, the auditor's judgments of what constitutes 'close enough', materially correct, are determined by many non-statistical variables. On the other hand, these judgments govern the decision about when a criterion has been met and when there has been progress toward achieving the goal, so they are important to the understanding of audit decisions.

SOME RESEARCH QUESTIONS

The foregoing analysis raises interesting research questions, the answers to which could be of service in the further development of both behavioral accounting research and image theory. The questions fall into two categories, those involving images and those involving the implementation of the audit and the decisions that result from the audit.

Questions about images

The first question is about the auditing firm's value image. What are the constituent principles and how do they differ from one kind of firm to another? It has been found that for both persons (Brown *et al.*, 1987) and organizations (Beach *et al.*, 1988a) it is possible to discover constituent principles. Moreover, it has been found in both cases that it is possible to use knowledge of these principles to predict subsequent decisions. Auditing firms present an especially interesting setting for such research because, while each firm is unique, they nonetheless are quite similar in many ways. That is, some of their principles are unique to the business environment in which each of them operates, but other principles are similar across firms because of the strong norms and guidelines for the auditing profession. To be credible, research findings must reflect this diversity and similarity.

A second question concerns the degree to which ethical principles pervade the various spheres of the firms' and the individual auditors' activities. That is, are ethical principles applied more directly in the evaluations of clients than in the determination of the firm's own activities? Do firms' ethical principles (and one assumes, their practices) reflect the instruction, or lack of it, received in the programs in which the partners got their training? How are ethical principles, as well as the other constituent principles, transmitted to newcomers to the firm—how does acculturation take place?

A third question involves the image of the 'successful' audit and its role in audit decisions. Even though a correct opinion is the abstract goal, if an unqualified opinion is the concrete goal toward which the audit is oriented, what sort of biases does this introduce? It is widely accepted that anchor points have an effect on subsequent decision making, although the effect to be expected is not always clear. In the present case, the audit is seen as having to marshal evidence in order to achieve the goal of a successful audit. In this view the thrust is from doubt and ignorance toward affirmation, which according to the anchoring and adjustment hypothesis (Tversky and Kahneman, 1974) might induce a bias against goal attainment. On the other hand, one could construct a case for the effects of the thrust, the striving toward the goal, producing the opposite bias. It really is not at all clear which bias, if any, is to be expected, and that is why research is needed.

A fourth question involves how forecasts are created. This is a general question for image theory, but auditing is a particularly appropriate arena in which to investigate it. The forecast is the anticipated results of the audit at any moment during the audit. The concept assumes a mechanism for bridging the gap between that moment and the future so that progress can be assessed. The question is how bridging takes place. Is it accomplished, for example, merely by extrapolating the present in some simplistic linear fashion? Probably not. Is it accomplished, as was suggested in Chapter 2, by constructing a story about how events might unfold to form a path from here to there? Perhaps in some cases, but in auditing this description may be more elaborate than what is needed or what actually happens. Clearly, research is called for.

Questions about implementation

The first question about implementation is actually about the prior issue of how clients are adopted or retained. Because clients are usually considered one by one (it is seldom a question of this client *or* that one), their adoption or retention is a decision about optional change. Recall that optional change decisions are those in which the auditor has the option of doing nothing at all and staying with the status quo. In this case staying with the status quo means either not taking on the new client or retaining the old client. Research shows that in optional change decisions the status quo tends to be favoured over change (e.g. Samuelson and Zeckhauser, 1988). This suggests that, business concerns aside, auditors may tend to be biased against accepting slightly incompatible new clients, while at the same time being equally biased toward retaining slightly incompatible old clients. The possible paradox is that, all else being equal, a firm might retain a client that it would not adopt were it a new candidate, and it might reject a new candidate that it might retain were it an old client. A corollary of this may be that, because progress decisions are optional decisions, there may be a bias toward staying with an 'unsuccessful' audit (the status quo) longer than an outside observer would recommend, perhaps pouring even more resources into it in an effort to make it work (e.g. Staw, 1981).

The second question about implementation involves how evaluations of the client's internal controls influence both the EIs for criteria and the structure of the audit plan. Clearly, the course of the entire audit is conditional upon the quality of the client's internal controls. During preliminary evaluation the apparent quality sets preliminary EIs, thus determining the major tactics of the audit plan. As the audit proceeds and compliance tests are performed, if the preliminary evaluations of the controls are revised there must be a complementary revision in the EIs and in the tactics that comprise the plan. It is tempting to couch these revisions in Bayesian terms, but as explained above, this will not do. There are too many non-statistical considerations operating in these revisions, from hard data to gossip. Perhaps a better starting place would be the attitude change literature. While EIs may not be attitudes in the strict sense, they are not very different. They have an evaluative aspect and they have strong implications for behavior in that they influence both the formulation (and reformulation) of plans as well as the criteria that those plans strive to meet. Hence, attitude change may be an appropriate perspective for thinking about EI revision.

The final research question about implementation involves how implementation results in decisions. Ignoring the complications implied by the questions raised above, the adoption/retention decision about clients is more straightforward than the materiality decision. It is customary to think of it as a routine business decision dominated by financial considerations. However, this may reflect an inaccurate stereotype about how business is done. Certainly the firm's profit is a large factor in the decision, and a firm that needs business may let this factor dominate. But principles other than solvency may also play a large role in adoption/retention decisions, and it is important to examine their contributions.

Of course, the decision about material error is our primary interest. The image theory description of how this decision is made is quite different from the usual cost–benefit, expected utility description. In the present analysis the decision actually is a decision about progress toward the goal, rather than about the goal itself. Insofar as costs, benefits, probabilities, or utilities are involved at all, they influence the breadth of the EIs for the criteria rather than being properties of or outcomes of the goal. No doubt some readers will regard this description as distressingly unparsimonious. However, a parsimonious description of unparsimonious events may be a Pyrrhic victory of style over substance.

Of course, because of its importance, all of the research questions outlined here have implications for the error decision. However, additional questions involve the criteria that comprise the goal, the manner in which tactics are designed to address these criteria, whether some criteria are primary to the goal and others are secondary or whether all are of equal status. Finally, there is the question of how compliance tests contribute to the goal; is the contribution direct or is it through influencing the criteria that must be met by the substantive tests?

SUMMARY

We have presented an image theory interpretation of audit decisions based upon an analysis of auditing by Waller and Felix (1984; Felix and Kinney, 1982). The purpose has been to provide the reader with an elaborated example of the application of the image theory view to a specific business decision environment. The analysis is quite different from that provided by the conventional application of classical decision theory, the view that presently dominates behavioral accounting research. It is our opinion that because of the explicitness of the process and because of the importance of the task, auditing provides a potentially valuable arena for investigation of decision making in general and image theory in particular.

AN IMAGE THEORY ANALYSIS OF CHILDBEARING DECISIONS

In 1973, Hoffman and Hoffman issued a call for the study of the psychological costs and benefits that influence decisions about childbearing. This call prescribed an alternative to the then dominant demographic viewpoint that featured the social correlates of childbearing. The alternative featured the assumption that the positive (benefits) and negative (costs) consequences of childbearing for individual couples dictated the decisions that they made. The Hoffman and Hoffman call was readily answered (Newman and Thompson, 1976), and among the answers was a large-scale, longitudinal study by Beach et al. (1979). The results of this study appeared to support the descriptive sufficiency of the cost–benefit model for childbearing decisions.

However, closer examination of the data revealed that an alternative model was needed to describe the decisions accurately.

BEACH, CAMPBELL, AND TOWNES (1979)

The participants in the study were 165 married couples who were considering whether or not to have a (or another) child within the following two years; all were currently using contraception. Forty-seven couples had no previous children, 40 had one child, 46 had two children, and 32 had three or more children. Each of the two people in each couple separately filled out an extensive questionnaire that elicited their views on the potential costs and benefits of having the child. From the answers to this questionnaire, the net cost or net benefit was calculated for each person, and a composite net value was calculated for the couple as a unit. Two years later the couples were contacted to see what their decision had been. If the couple had stopped using contraceptives, if they were actively trying to conceive, if the wife was pregnant, or if a child had been born (or adopted), they were regarded as having made a positive decision. If none of these obtained, or if either person had been sterilized electively or if the wife had become pregnant and had elected abortion for other than medical reasons, the couple was regarded as having made a negative decision.

Predictive accuracy

Overall predictive accuracy was 72%, suggesting that the cost–benefit model was moderately predictive. However, closer analysis showed that things were far more complicated than suggested by the model.

Although the model predicted rather well for couples who had not yet attained their desired family size (DFS), it did not do well for those who had. This was because very few (five out of 68) of the couples who had attained their DFS decided to have another child. This was true even for the 19 couples in this group for whom the perceived benefits associated with having the child exceeded the perceived costs; only two of the 19 couples decided to have a child. It was as though having achieved the prior goal of a specific number of children made considering another child an irrelevant exercise, even though the other considerations favoured having the child.

Even in the case of the 97 couples who had not yet attained their DFS, the errors in prediction were systematic and could not be accounted for solely in terms of cost–benefit. Negative decisions were correctly predicted but positive decisions were not, an error pattern found in other expectancy theory studies (Davidson and Beach, 1981). That is, of the 21 couples who were predicted to decide *not* to have a child, 18 (86%) in fact decided not to and only three (14%) decided to do so. In contrast, of the 76 couples who were predicted to decide to have a child, only 53 (70%) did so while 23 (30%) did not. As discussed by Davidson and Beach (1981), this result reflects an unwillingness to leave the status quo unless the attractiveness of the alternative (having the child) is extremely attractive. Beach *et al.* (1982) report similar results for sterilization decisions.

Examination of the consequence that had a large effect on couples' childbearing decisions showed that they were different from those that had a small effect. In general, the decisions turned on consequences such as the possible impact of a (or another) child on the parents' achievement of educational or career goals, on their growth and maturity, on their relationship, or on the well-being of the family (Townes *et al.*, 1980). These consequences can be cast as profit or loss, benefits or costs, but doing so requires considerable contortion. A more straightforward interpretation is that the contributing consequences were those involving the child's compatibility with the couple's existing principles, goals and plans. Thus, compatibility, the 'fit' of a (or another) child with the rest of the couple's life and their vision of their future, rather than maximization of return, appeared to influence most heavily the childbearing decision.

THE DECISION AID

A secondary purpose of the study by Beach *et al.* (1979) was to produce a decision aid for family planning counseling. The aid, the Optional Parenthood Questionnaire, the OPQ (Beach *et al.*, 1978), was designed to help couples think through and evaluate the consequences of having a child. The OPQ has been widely used in counseling; over 2000 copies 'have been distributed, most of which have been photocopied many times. However, a follow-up survey of counselors revealed that they did not use the OPQ in the way intended by the researchers who created it. They seldom had their clients numerically evaluate the costs and benefits of the various consequences. Even when they did, they seldom performed the cumbersome calculations that were necessary to precisely weight and balance the evaluations. On the rare occasions that they did the calculations, they did not use the results to prescribe the 'correct' decision to their clients. Instead, they used the OPQ as a consciousness raising device. That is, the counselors used it to lead their clients through a thorough but informal (non-numerical) survey of their own feelings about the implications of having the child. In short, the counselors used the OPQ to educate intuition rather than to help their clients perform a precise analytical examination of the costs and benefits of having the child.

Instead of berating the counselors' lack of progressiveness or bemoaning their failure to appreciate the decision aid's lovely prescriptive logic, we must recognize that the education of intuition is a quite legitimate enterprise. Certainly from the point of view of image theory it is fundamental. Educated intuition is better able to assess compatibility. Because childbearing decisions are usually optional decisions, having a child is a single alternative to the viable status quo, assessment of compatibility is often the sole basis for the decision and anything that facilitates its assessment is of value.

Facilitation of compatibility assessment raises an interesting research question that must be part of the work on future decision aids. It has become axiomatic in psychology that the human mind is a limited information processor. However, the data that demonstrate this apparent truth refer almost exclusively to conscious capacity. We have little or no idea about non-conscious or unconscious capacity, especially when the process in question involves something as simple as merely tallying violations. Thus, an important prior question for decision aiding and the education of intuition involves finding out just what such aids are in aid of. That is, if there are cognitive limits on the thoroughness of compatibility assessment, how severe are they and what are their ramifications for decision making? Until this has been assessed, attempts to design decision aids may be premature. This is because, if current aids are any example, the logic of aiding strives to make all evaluations conscious, apparently on the assumption that conscious evaluation is necessarily 'better' than non-conscious or unconscious evaluation. Do not misunderstand, we do not advocate murkiness over clarity. However, imposition of clarity on that which is inherently murky may either hinder or help. It behooves those who champion clarity to know which result they are effecting.

CONFLICT COUPLES

In the Beach et al. (1979) study, and in related work on voluntary sterilization (Beach et al., 1982), it was found that couples decided to stay with the status quo unless the alternative was extremely attractive. In the course of examining these data further, it was found that there were two ways in which a couple could end up staying with the status quo. One way was for neither partner to strongly favor the alternative (having a child in the one study, being sterilized in the other study). The other way was for one partner to favor the alternative and the other not favor it, thus leaving them stalemated (although for both childbearing and sterilization the woman's view counted for more than the man's). Stalemated couples were labeled 'conflict couples'. Of the 97 couples in the childbearing study who had not already attained their desired family size, 25 were conflict couples. Of the 150 couples in the sterilization study, another 25 were conflict couples.

Examination of the individual conflict couples' results showed that there were major differences in what was determining the two partners' disparate viewpoints, and that these differences were often about consequences that, in image theory terms, could be described as principles and goals. Indeed, the overall impression was that these conflicting partners held distinctly different views and that often they did not recognize how much their views differed from their respective partner's. In related work, Wood *et al.* (1977) describe individual couples for which such differences were encountered in the course of family planning counseling using the OPQ. They suggest that these differences could be used as a way of diagnosing the stability of the couples' relationships. Subsequent anecdotal reports by other counselors who have used the OPQ in their practices indicate that such differences frequently are encountered and that counseling often revolves around them.

While conflict couples constituted a minority of the couples in these two studies, they were still a sizable minority (50/247 = 20%). Moreover, as pointed out by Wood *et al.*, conflict in an area as basic to a relationship as family building may be symptomatic of a relationship that is unstable and in danger of dissolution. It is to this issue of conflict in couple (dyadic) decision making to which we now turn.

The 'We' frame

It is easy to assert that conflict implies that a relationship is in difficulty. However, beyond the inherent reasonableness of such an assertion, the study by Beach *et al.* (1988a), reported in Chapter 4, provides evidence, albeit oblique, for the assertion. Recall that the study showed that executives in a stable firm showed a high degree of agreement about the compatibility of various plans their firm might use to accomplish a given goal; the executives in a moderately stable firm showed a moderate degree of agreement; the executives in an unstable firm showed a fairly low degree of agreement. The image theory interpretation of the results was that, when an organization is in flux, the members of the organization do not share a common view of the organization's value image, its principles, and therefore cannot agree about the suitability of competing plans for adoption by the organization.

Now, extend this same line of thought to two-person groups, married couples. That is, couples can be thought of as dyadic organizations that each have their own culture, their own set of principles ('What *we* believe, strive for, etc.'). Just as the stability of the untroubled firm was reflected in its executives' shared views about how it ought to behave, the partners in a stable personal relationship might be expected to exhibit similarly shared views. Just as the instability of the troubled firm was reflected in the absence of agreement among its executives, so too might couples in an unstable relationship fail to agree, especially about something as central to the relationship as childbearing.

To go even further, it may well be that the partners in a stable relationship share highly similar 'We' frames for various contexts, and that their respective private 'I' frames are to a large degree similar to them. In contrast, the partners in an unstable relationship, conflict couples, may not have highly similar 'We' frames, and this dissimilarity may result from their incorrect assumptions that 'We' are more like 'I' than is justified.

There are several lines of research in the literature on marital conflict and interpersonal attribution that, to one degree or other, support what is being suggested here. One such line has focused on the congruence between individuals' self-concepts and their partners' concepts of them. People tend to form relationships with individuals who see them as they see themselves (Swann, 1983) and are happier in such relationships (Laing et al., 1966; Swann and Predmore, 1985). Dymond (1954) found that the partners in happy marriages were significantly more accurate in predicting each other's self-descriptions than were the partners in unhappy marriages. In addition, the partners in happy marriages gave more similar self-descriptions than the partners in unhappy marriages. Moreover, the partners in unhappy marriages were more· likely to predict similarity where none existed, suggesting that they underestimated the differences between themselves and their partners. These results were the same for both husbands and wives and were not influenced by the length of time the couples had been married.

Research on self-disclosure and perspective-taking in close relationships has focused on individuals' attempts to explain their points of view to their partners and to understand conflicts from their partners' viewpoints. Higher rates of self-disclosure are associated with greater happiness in close relationships (Burke et al., 1976). Franzoi et al. (1985) found that greater perspective-taking skill was related to greater satisfaction in relationships, satisfaction over and above the effects of self-disclosure.

Attribution theory, too, has been extended to the study of close relationships. Stillars (1985) distinguishes between attributions (naive constructions of the partner's intentions and feelings) and metaperspectives (understanding from the partner's perspective). He notes that familarity, though generally assumed to lead to greater understanding, may also be misleading and cause people to overestimate how much they know about their partners. This can result in entrenchment of existing impressions such that partners fail to notice, acknowledge, or adapt to changes in the other person.

Knudson (1985) comes closest to the concept of a 'We' frame. In his view, marital compatibility is a function of 'the degree to which, at any given point in time, the parties . . . have achieved and can sustain a shared construction of reality' (p. 233). The concept of a shared construction of reality emphasizes the partners' shared views of themselves *vis-à-vis* some sphere of their lives, as opposed to their views of themselves as separate units. In the same vein, Berger and Kellner (1984) suggest that couples are motivated to construct a joint reality both through their relationship generally and through conversation with each other, resulting in a strengthened relationship and a stable 'common objectivated reality'.

In short, ideas similar to those being advanced here already exist, although in a somewhat fragmented form, in the literature; which is comforting. However, while the research resulting from them may bear on the issue, they do not speak directly to the question of childbearing decisions and the stability of couples' relationships, two issues that are closely linked if the child is to have a stable home. Moreover, they do not have a common theoretical core, as provided by image theory, with which to address these issues.

Clearly, an important part of helping couples make decisions about whether to have a child involves the prior question of whether their relationship is stable enough to support that child. It would seem, therefore, that in addition to the education of intuition, decision aiding should include a diagnosis of the degree to which the partners hold a 'We' frame for the decision. If research were to show that a strongly overlapping 'We' frame is related to a strong relationship and a weaker, less overlapping 'We' frame is related to a weak relationship, counseling should address the question of marital stability before turning to the childbearing decision. It is not uncommon to observe couples who decide to have a child in an attempt to strengthen their marriage—which may or may not work. However, given the plight of children in modern society, this solution seems particularly ill-advised. Indeed, such a solution is backwards; the stability of the relationship should be the precondition for childbearing, not the other way round. Informal observations made during the Beach *et al.* (1979) study suggested that many conflict couples may have been aware of their conflict, and perhaps were aware of underlying problems with their relationships. However, they were addressing the childbearing decision instead of the conflict, in part because they could more easily focus on the concreteness of the childbearing decision. In family counseling however, the job of the decision aid, and of the counselor, must be to change the priorities—to resolve the conflict issue before, or instead of, considering the childbearing decision.

SUMMARY

In this essay we have reviewed some of the results of a large study that attempted to impose a cost–benefit model on couples' decision making about whether to have a (or another) child. The difficulties encountered in doing this, as well as the failure of the data to wholly support such a goal, are in large part responsible for the evolution of image theory. Moreover, experience with the decision aid that was a by-product of the study made it clear that decision aiding is probably best invested in the education of intuition rather than in complex mathematical schemes that receive little sympathy from those for whom they are designed. Finally, examination of the results for couples who had conflicting views about whether to have a child led to speculations about the existence of a 'We' frame, a set of principles held in common by the partners in a marriage. This led to further speculation about the relationship between the 'We' frame and the stability of a couple's relationship.

AN IMAGE ANALYSIS OF THE CUBAN MISSILE CRISIS

Perhaps there have been other times of which the world is not aware, but the Cuban Missile Crisis of 1962 is generally regarded as the closest that the superpowers have ever come to nuclear war. It was occasioned by the surreptitious installation of nuclear missiles in Cuba by the Soviet Union. Routine photo reconnaissance flights by the Americans revealed the existence of the missiles. Photo technology was not sufficient to tell if the missiles were already armed with nuclear warheads—but because they were less than 150 miles from the United States it was clear that the missiles posed an unacceptable threat.

President John F. Kennedy convened a series of meetings in which he and his advisors considered the various candidate plans for dealing with the threat. This began with two off-the-record meetings held in the White House on the morning and in the evening of 16 October 1962. A secret tape-recording system in the room recorded the proceedings of both meetings. These recordings subsequently were transcribed and filed at the John F. Kennedy Library in Boston. Although detailed minutes of some of the later meetings were made public rather early on, the word-for-word transcripts of these first two off-the-record meetings were not released until 1985. The transcripts have been 'sanitized', which means that personal conversations between the president and his family (his children for instance), and sensitive military information, have been removed. Moreover, because the recording system was not very sophisticated, parts of what was said are unintelligible (a technical flaw shared with the Watergate tapes). However, on the whole it is easy to follow the discussion, and when a speaker was permitted to proceed without interruption the transcript is quite complete.

The crisis has been studied by many researchers in many disciplines. Most pertinent to our interests, however, is the work of Anderson (1983) who examined the decision processes in the minutes of the fifth through eighth meetings, which were all that were available in 1983. Anderson provided both quantitative analyses and examples of how the discussions proceeded and how decisions were reached. As we shall see, the conclusions reached in his study are particularly cogent to image theory.

What follows is fairly straightforward: We will outline the course of the two 16 October meetings in which the groundwork was laid for all subsequent meetings. In doing this we will rely upon image theory as a conceptual framework. Then we will turn to the Anderson (1983) research, citing the parallels between his findings for the later meetings, what we have observed for the 16 October meetings, and how these findings relate to image theory.

A technical note: In quotations from the transcripts, [x x x] indicates the transcriber's conjectures about unintelligible words on the tapes, an ellipsis (three periods) indicates an unfinished sentence or skipped material, and {x x x} indicates our comments.

THE WHITE HOUSE 16 OCTOBER 1962, 11:50 a.m.

Participants: President John F. Kennedy, Attorney General Robert Kennedy, Secretary of State Dean Rusk, Special Assistant to the President for National Security Affairs McGeorge Bundy, Secretary of Defense Robert McNamara, Secretary of the Treasury Douglas Dillon, Vice President Lyndon B. Johnson, Chairman of the Joint Chiefs of Staff Maxwell Taylor, and others. The president is the center of the discussion, although he does little more than ask short questions and summarize options. Everyone addresses comments, information, and suggestions to him; he clearly is in charge and will make the final decisions.

Framing the context

The discussion opens with the president being shown the photographs of the missile installations and identification of their locations. He then turns to how many, what kinds, and the potential ranges of the missiles, and whether they are operational. Other participants ask questions and McNamara emphasizes the link between the operational readiness of the missiles and the time available for 'forming our plans'. More recent photographs are being prepared and will be available later in the day.

Adoption of the goal

However vaguely, the participants had been briefed before the meeting and had had time to think. Apparently they had all adopted the same goal, because there is no discussion of it—Secretary of State Rusk merely states: '. . . we have to set in motion a chain of events that will eliminate this base. I don't think we [can] sit still.'

Identifying candidate plans

Without pausing, Rusk goes on to state what are to become the two candidate plans that dominate this and future meetings about the crisis: 'The question becomes whether {plan number one} we do it by sudden, unannounced strike of some sort, or we {plan number two}, uh, build up the crisis to the point where the other side has to consider very seriously about giving in, or, or even the Cubans themselves, uh, take some, take some action on this. . . . Uhm, so I think we, we have to think very hard about two major, uh, courses of action as alternatives. One is the quick strike {whereupon he very briefly explores what that might entail—eliminating the base alone, or eliminating all of Cuba}. The other would be . . . that we, uh, stimulate the [Organization of American States] procedure immediately for prompt action to make it quite clear that the entire hemisphere considers that the Rio Pact has been violated. . . . The OAS could, I suppose . . . insist to the Cubans that an OAS inspection, uh, team be permitted to come and, itself, look directly at these sites, provide assurance to the hemisphere. That will undoubtedly be turned down, but it will be another step in building up . . . a position. I think also that we ought to consider getting some word to Castro . . . privately and tell him that, uh, this is no longer support for Cuba, that Cuba is being victimized here, and that, uh, the Soviets are preparing Cuba for destruction or betrayal. . . . And I think there are certain military, uhm, uh, actions that we . . . might well want to take straight away. First, to uh, to call up, uh, highly selective units. . . . Unless we feel that it's better, more desirable to go to a general national emergency so that we have complete freedom of action. . . . We announce that, uh, we are conducting a surveillance of Cuba, over Cuba, and we will enforce our right to do so. . . . We, we reinforce our forces in Guantanamo. We reinforce our forces in the southeastern part of the United States— whatever is necessary from the military point of view to be able to give, to deliver an overwhelming strike at any of these installations, including the SAM sites. . . . I also think that we need a few days, uhm, to alert our other allies, for consultation with NATO. I'll assume that we can move on this line at the same time to interrupt all air traffic from the free world countries going to Cuba, insist to the Mexicans, the Dutch, that they stop their planes from coming in. Tell the British, who, and anyone else who's involved at this point, that, uh, if they're interested in peace, they've *got* to stop their ships from Cuban trade at this point. Uh, in other words, isolate Cuba completely without, at this particular moment, a, uh, a forceful blockade.'

Rusk continues: 'But I think that, by and large, there are, there are these two broad alternatives: one, the quick strike; the other, to alert our allies *and* Mr Khrushchev that there is utterly serious crisis in the making here. . . . I think we'll be facing a situation that could well lead to general war; that we have an obligation to do what has to be done but do it in a way that gives, uh, everybody a chance to, uh, put the [word unintelligible] down before it gets too hard. These are my, my reactions of this morning, Mr President.'

Rusk having stated the candidate plans and outlined in some detail the non-military plan, Secretary of Defense McNamara takes the floor to expand upon the military alternative. McNamara again stresses the unknown time constraints imposed by whether the missiles' nuclear warheads are in place or soon will be: 'Because, if they become operational before the air strike, I do not believe we can state we can knock them out before they can be launched; and if they're launched there is almost certain to be, uh, chaos in part of the east coast {of the United States} or the area, uh, in a radius of six hundred to a thousand miles from Cuba.'

Reviewing violations

McNamara continues: 'Uh, secondly, I, I would submit the proposition that any air strike must be directed not solely against the missile sites, but against the missile sites plus the airfields plus the aircraft which may not be on the airfields but hidden by that time plus all potential nuclear storage sites. Now, this is a fairly extensive air strike. It is not just a strike against the missile sites; and there would be associated with it potential casualties of Cubans, not of US citizens, but potential casualties of Cubans in, at least in the hundreds, more likely in the low thousands, say two or three thousand.' He follows this with a sketch of what a strike would require and the fact that invasion would have to follow, and what mobilization for doing these things would involve.

At this point, General Taylor states that a strike would have to be totally successful if it were to be successful at all—no missiles can remain to be fired at the United States. He also briefly raises the question of a naval blockade to prevent movement of more missiles into Cuba.

After some fragmented discussion of various topics, McNamara states his opposition to an air attack because the possible failure to get all the missiles would constitute a danger to the United States. This is followed by a complete change of topic—conjectures about the Russians' motives for installing the missiles. The presence of American missiles in Turkey are seen as one possible motive—and the fact that the Russian missiles are inaccurate and must be close to their targets in order to hit them. Bargaining Berlin for Cuba is another possibility, but in general all participants seem baffled about why the Russians have changed the status quo.

At this point Secretary of the Treasury Dillon raises violations associated with plan number two—the diplomatic initiative: the difficulties of consulting with NATO allies and that revealing to the public what is happening '. . . would appear to me to have the danger of, uh, getting us [right] out in the open and forcing the Russians to, uh, Soviets to take a, a position if anything was done, uh, they would, uh, have to retaliate. . . . I think that the chance of getting through this thing without a Russian reaction is greater under a quick, uh, strike than, building the whole thing up to a, a climax . . .' Bundy replies: 'The difficulties—I, I share the Secretary of the Treasury's feeling a little bit—the difficulties of organizing the OAS and NATO; the amount of noise we would get from our allies saying that, uh, they can live with Soviet MRBMs, why can't we; uh, the division in the alliance; the certainty that the Germans would feel that we *were* jeopardizing Berlin because of our concern over Cuba. The prospect of that pattern is not an appetizing one . . .'

Then Rusk points out violations associated with plan number one, an air strike: 'And if we go with the quick strike, the, in fact, they *do* back it up, then you've exposed all of your allies [word unintelligible] ourselves to all these great dangers without . . . without, uh, the slightest consultation, or, or warning or preparation'. To which Taylor adds: 'It'll never be a 100 percent, Mr President, we know. Uh, we hope to take out a vast majority in the first strike, but this is not just one thing, one, one strike, one day, but continuous air attack for whenever necessary, whenever we . . . discover a target.' And Bundy adds: 'They're now talking about taking out the air force as well . . .'

This line of the discussion continues with the various problems of an air strike discussed, as well as the difficulties of keeping such a plan secret. Vice President Johnson's opinion is solicited: 'I think the question with the base is whether we take it out or whether we talk about it, and, uh, both, either alternative is a very distressing one, but of the two, I would take it out.' He then goes on to state his negative view about consulting with the OAS: 'I think this organization is fine, but I don't think, I don't rely on 'em much for any strength in anything like this.' Nor is he sanguine about the NATO allies. He then turns to internal politics: '. . . the *fact* is the country's blood pressure *is* up and they are fearful, and they're insecure, and were getting divided . . . take this little *State Department Bulletin* that you sent out to all the congressmen. One, one of the points you make—that any time the build-up endangers or threatens our security in any way, we're going to do whatever must be done immediately to protect our own security. And when you say that, why they give unanimous support. People are really concerned about this, in my opinion . . . [I'm] not much for circularizing it over the Hill or our allies, even though I realize it's a breach of faith. . . . We're not going to get much help out of them.'

Focusing upon plan number one

At this point the president clarifies the air strike plan: 'What you're really talking about are two or three different, ah, [potential?] operations. One is the strike just on this, these three bases. One. The second is the broader one that Secretary McNamara was talking about, which is on the airfields and on the SAM sites and on anything else connected with, uh, missiles. Third is doing both of these things and also at the same time launching a blockade, which . . . is a larger step. And then, as I take it, the fourth question is the, uh, degree of consultation.'

To which Robert Kennedy adds: 'We have the fifth one, really, which is the invasion. I would say that, uh, you're dropping bombs all over Cuba if you do the second, uh, air, the airports, knocking out their planes, dropping it on all their missiles. You're covering most of Cuba. You're going to kill an awful lot of people, and, uh, we're going to take an awful lot of heat on it . . . and, uh, and then, uh, you know, the heat, you're going to announce the reason that you're doing it is because, uh, they're sending in these kind of missiles. Well, I would think it's almost incumbent upon the Russians, then, to say, Well we're going to send them in again, and if you do it again, we're going to do, we're going to do the same thing to Turkey, or We're going to do the same thing to Iran.' Robert Kennedy's comments are followed by a 'sanitized' section of the transcript, so it is impossible to gauge the reaction to this speech. Note, however, that not 'taking heat' is a principle, perhaps not a very moral one considering that the heat would result from having killed a large number of innocent Cubans; but it reflects a principle for political self-preservation and a dislike for looking bad.

The discussion continues in much the same vein. The major topics concern the side-effects of invading Cuba and having to deal with the Cuban populace, the possibility of using Berlin as a diversion for mobilizing troops, time constraints, details of mobilizing an attack and forecasts of its effectiveness, the need for better estimates of how long it would take to mobilize, and the possible effects of letting the Soviets know that strike preparations were being made. At the end of this the president suggests another meeting that evening and summarizes his views up to that point: 'We're certainly going to do number one: we're going to take out these, uh, missiles {the goal}. Uh, the questions will be whether, which, what I would describe as number two, which would be a general air strike. That we're not ready to say, but we should be in preparation for it. The third is the . . . general invasion. At least we're going to do number one . . .'

Plan number two re-emerges

As the meeting begins to draw to a close, it appears that only candidate plan number one, an air strike, has survived and that the question merely is what its specific tactics will be. However, after the president's comments, Bundy says: 'You want to be clear, Mr President, whether we have *definitely* decided *against* a political track. I, myself, think we ought . . . to work out a contingency on that.' This brings plan number two back into the running, but in spite of Bundy's attempts to promote discussion of it, it is dropped for the moment as the meeting draws to a close.

The meeting closes

As things wind down, McNamara lays out the agenda for the evening meeting: 'First, should we surface our surveillance? . . . A second question is should we precede the military action with political action? If so, on what, uh, timing. I would think the answer's almost certainly yes. And I wouldn't, I would think particularly of the contacts with Khrushchev. . . . And, thirdly, we should be prepared to answer . . . questions regarding the, the effect of these strikes and the time required to carry them off.' This leads to questions about the amounts and kinds of information they will need for the evening meeting and thereafter. Then the meeting degenerates into a discussion of who is to go to lunch in whose car, and who can or cannot attend the evening meeting.

SOME OBSERVATIONS

The goal

Note that the goal, removal of the missiles, tacitly was agreed upon when the meeting began; Rusk merely stated what the others already seem to have accepted. In fact, it is unlikely that any other goal would have been possible given the American political climate and the way in which members of the administration conceived of their jobs. Americans already detested Russian intrusion in 'our hemisphere', and they would find the existence of Cuban-based missiles aimed at American territory to be intolerable. The goal of removing the missiles was wholly compatible with the electorate's and the decision makers' values and with political expediency.

The plans

The two candidate plans for achieving the goal emerged quite quickly. The remainder of the discussion, except for digressions about Russian motives and the need for more information, focused on them, especially on their flaws. But it is interesting to note that never were the two plans compared critically. Instead, they were considered intermittently and serially; first one, and then the other, and the one again, and so on. However, the first candidate plan, an air attack, received by far the most attention, in part perhaps because the military always is an option for the president, and when you have a hammer, problems tend to look like nails. However, the second candidate plan received a little attention, primarily in terms of OAS ineffectiveness, possible negative reactions of NATO allies, and the effects of making the crisis public.

Violations

For both plans, the discussion tended to focus upon flaws (i.e. violations). In addition, for the air strike much of what was said focused upon variations on the plan as the discussants searched for its precise formulation. The president twice summarized the variants of air strike, focusing on three but at one point there were five. As the discussion proceeded, candidate number two almost got lost. Although it was brought back at the end, it clearly had less status than candidate number one.

And so the stage is set for the evening meeting.

THE WHITE HOUSE: 16 OCTOBER 1962, 6:30 p.m.

Participants: President Kennedy, General Marshall Carter, Undersecretary of State McGeorge Bundy, Secretary of State Dean Rusk, Secretary of Defense Robert McNamara, State Department Officer Edwin Martin,

General Maxwell Taylor, Secretary of the Treasury Douglas Dillon, Under-secretary of State George Ball, Vice President Lyndon Johnson, and others.

Plan number two explored

The meeting opens with an examination of more recent photographs of the missile sites and more conjectures about when the missiles might become operational. McNamara announces that additional reconnaissance flights have been ordered. Then the discussion turns to a State Department suggestion that Castro be apprised of the deadly jeopardy in which the Russians have placed Cuba. The idea is that Castro might therefore want to break with Moscow. The suggestion is presented in the form of a scenario by Edwin Martin, of the State Department: 'This would be an oral note, message through a third party. Uh, first, uh, describing just what we know about what exists in the missile sites, so that he knows that we are informed about what's going on. Uh, second, to point out that the issues this raises as far as the US security is concerned, it's a breach of two of the points that you {the president} have made public. Uh, first, the ground-to-ground missile, and second, obviously, it's a Soviet-operated base in Cuba. Uh, thirdly, this raises the greatest problems for Castro, as we see it. In the first place, uh, by this action the Soviets have, uh, threatened him with attack from the United States, and uh, therefore the overthrow of his regime; used his territory to, uh, make this, uh, to put him in this jeopardy. And, secondly, the Soviets are talking to other people about the possibility of bargaining this support and these missiles, uh, against concessions in Berlin and elsewhere, and therefore are threatening to, to bargain him away. Uh, in these circumstances, we wonder he, uh, realizes the, the position that, uh, he's been put in and the way the Soviets are using him.'

Martin continues: 'Then go on to say that, uh, we will have to inform our people of the threat that exists here, and we mean to take action about it in the next day or so. And we'll have to do this unless we receive word from *him* that *he* is prepared to take action to get the Soviets out of the site. Uh, he will have to show us that not only by statements, privately or publicly, but, uh, by action; that we intend to, uh, keep close surveillance by overflights of the site to make su-, to know what *is* being done. . . . {If} Castro feels that an attempt by *him* to take the kind of action that we're suggesting to him, uh, would result in serious difficulties for him within Cuba . . . we might have sympathy and help for him in case he ran into trouble trying to throw the old-line communists and the Soviets out.'

The flaws in this scenario begin with the rather obvious 'disinformation' about the Soviets' bargaining of Cuba for Berlin, of which there had been no hint at all. Moreover, although the State Department could not know it at the time, Castro was as much in favor of the missiles as the Soviets were. When Martin finishes, Rusk immediately points out that notifying Castro in the way being proposed would allow him to place mobile anti-aircraft guns around the missile sites, making the missiles even harder to destroy if the air strike plan were implemented.

Back to plan number one

Having made his criticism, Rusk swings the discussion away from this variant on plan number two and returns to the flaws in plan number one, the air strike. The first is the possibility of increased activity by communists throughout Latin America, which could overthrow six or more friendly governments. Rusk continues: 'The other is the NATO problem. Um, we, uh, we would estimate that the Soviets, uh, would almost certainly take, uh, some kind of action somewhere. Um, for us to, to take an action of this sort without letting, uh, our closer allies know of a matter which could subject them to very great, uh, danger {principle}, uh, is a very, uh, far-reaching decision to make. And, uh, we could find ourselves, uh, isolated {principle} and the alliance crumbling {principle?}, very much as it did for a period during the Suez affair, but at a moment of much greater danger over an issue of much greater danger than the Suez affair, for the alliance.'

McNamara then discusses military matters that have been removed from the transcript, but which we can assume refer to the air strike plan. Taylor reiterates that an air strike probably could not destroy all of the missiles and that the strike would invite reprisal. The military clearly would like to stall for time until more information about the site locations is available.

Three plans

At this point, McNamara interrupts to ask the president's permission to state what he sees as the *three* courses open to them: 'The first is what I would call the political course of action, in which we, uh, follow some of the possibilities that Secretary Rusk mentioned this morning by approaching Castro, by approaching Khrushchev, by discussing with our allies. An overt and open approach politically to the problem [in order?] to solve it. This seems to me likely to lead to no satisfactory result, and it almost *stops* subsequent military action.'

'A second course of action we haven't discussed but lies in between the military course we began discussing a moment ago and the political course of action is a course of action that would involve declaration of open surveillance; a statement that we would immediately impose an, uh, a blockade against *offensive* weapons entering Cuba in the future; and an indication that with our open-surveillance reconnaissance which we would plan to maintain indefinitely for the future {the rest of the sentence has been 'sanitized'}.'

'But the third course of action is any one of these variants of military action directed against Cuba, starting with an air attack against the missiles.' McNamara then outlines some of the tactics necessary for this plan— airborne alert, mobilization, etc., and the possibility that an attack would trigger a Cuban uprising, which would force the Americans' hand and result in an all-out invasion.

Plan number two develops

Rusk picks up on McNamara's summary and stresses that there is no such thing as a non-political course of action, and that political issues must be considered for even an air strike or any other military action. The president considers this and goes on to state that the State Department's scenario for Castro is not a good idea, and drops it. However, he renews the idea of communicating with Khrushchev, and wonders how the latter could have so greatly mispredicted the American reaction to the missiles given all of the public statements that he, the president, had made about under what conditions the United States would and would not react: 'He's initiated the danger really, hasn't he? He's the one that's playing [God], not us.'

This leads Rusk to say: 'I would not think that they would use a nuclear weapon unless they're prepared to [join?] a nuclear war, I don't think. I just don't . . . see that possibility. . . . That would mean that, uh, we could be just utterly wrong, but, uh, we've never *really* believed that, that Khrushchev would take on a general nuclear war over Cuba.'

This confession, as it were, leads to a discussion of the impact of the missiles on the balance of power. The bottom line is provided by Robert Kennedy who points out that the missiles permit Cuba and the Russians to blackmail the United States, especially in terms of political intervention in South America. In short, the existence of the missiles constitutes an unacceptable psychological factor. Moreover, having stated that the United States would not tolerate such a move, and the move having been made by the Russians and Cubans, doing nothing is viewed as a humiliation. Nonetheless, the president points out that these missiles are not much when compared with the overall Soviet capability to blow up the United States: 'What difference does it make? They've got enough to blow us up now anyway. . . . After all this is a political struggle as much as military.'

This leads the president to suggest that they merely tell everyone that they know about the missiles and let them draw whatever conclusions they want to. The flaws in this proposal are considered—primary of which is that it would put the Soviets and Cubans on their guard. Then the idea of striking and then issuing a statement is discussed, with Bundy pointing out that this fails to notify our allies and the Congress of what is happening, about which he says: 'I can't . . . I think that's just not, not right.' This institutes a new round of comments about variations on the air strike plan, much of which has been 'sanitized', so it is difficult to tell if anything new is brought up.

A turning point

Here McNamara initiates a discussion of what a post-strike world might look like: 'Mr President, we need to do two things, it seems to me. First, *we* need to develop a specific strike plan limited to the missiles and the nuclear storage sites, which we have not done. . . . The second thing we ought to do, it seems to me as a government, is to consider the consequences. I don't believe we have considered the consequences of any of these actions satisfactorily, and because we haven't considered the consequences, I'm not sure we're taking all the action we ought to take now to minimize those. I, I don't know quite what kind of a world we live in after we've struck Cuba, and we, we've started it. . . . How do we stop at that point?'

McNamara's question prompts a subtle, but important change in the direction of the discussion. Clearly, the possibility of a spreading war is frightening. Then Rusk says: 'In that regard, Mr President, there is a combination of the plans which might be considered, namely the limited strike and *then* the messages, or simultaneously the messages to Khrushchev and Castro, which would indicate to them that this *was* none other than simply the, fulfilling the statements we've made all along.' Suddenly the tide turns. General Taylor argues against invasion because it would tie us up as we are tied up in Berlin. Martin says that an air strike would not result in a popular uprising against the Cuban government—'People would just stay home and try to keep out of trouble.' The cost of an air strike apparently is brought up, but the transcript is 'sanitized'. Robert Kennedy points out that an air strike might knock out the present missiles, but unless something is done the Soviets and Cubans will replace them. McNamara argues that 'You have to put a blockade in following any limited action', and Robert Kennedy says: 'Then we're gonna have to sink Russian ships. Then we're gonna have to sink Russian submarines.' Robert Kennedy then concludes that if Khrushchev '. . . wants to get into war over *this*, uh. . . . Hell, if it's war that's gonna come on this thing, or if he sticks those kinds of missiles in, it's after the warning, and he's gonna, and he's gonna get into a war for, six months from now or a year from now, so . . . ' This leads to yet another discussion of Khrushchev's possible motives.

As things proceed, Bundy returns to McNamara's point about the future: 'Our principal problem is to try and imaginatively to think what the world would be like if we do this, and what it will be like if we don't, {and} if we fail if we do {it}.' McNamara seconds this with: 'We ought to work on that tonight', but nothing comes of it as the discussion turns to the plight of the prisoners on the Isle of Pines.

The president makes a move to wind up the meeting and to schedule for the next day, but in the course of doing so remarks that he is soon to meet with the Russian representative, Andrei Gromyko. Kennedy wonders whether they ought to do something through Gromyko; whether to say anything to him or to try to give him an indirect ultimatum. Kennedy states that Gromyko had said to American officials that '. . . they were not going to put these weapons there. Now either he's lying or doesn't know.' Bundy remarks: 'My, I wouldn't bet a *cookie* that Dobrynin {Russian ambassador} doesn't know a bean about this.' All of this opens a possibility that has not yet been discussed, a warning to Soviet officials aimed at getting them to back down and either disarm or remove the missiles. In the ensuing excitement, the transcripts are quite confusing, with speakers interrupting each other and getting cut off before they express a complete thought. Eventually things settle down and the discussion turns upon the public statements the Soviets have or have not made about their intentions in Cuba. The question is whether making photographs of the missiles public would cause the Soviets embarrassment in light of their own public statements. At about this point the tide begins to go against a purely military solution, plan one, and more attention is given to a political solution, plan two. Clearly the negative aspects of an air strike, especially the possibility of escalation, are beginning to add up. On the other hand, the newly considered political offensive begins to look workable, particularly if coupled with a military threat or with limited military action—and the military threat always remains as a backup if the political plan does not produce progress.

In the closing moments of the meeting, McNamara brings together many of the threads of what has been said, some of which argue against a military strike and some of which argue for a political initiative, although he does not explicitly pit the two alternatives against each other; they both clearly remain candidates. Most important, his remarks redefine the goal—getting the missiles out of Cuba is replaced by making their use unthinkable.

Harkening back to the discussion about what the missiles mean to the balance of power, which in practical terms is very little, McNamara says: 'I, I, I'll be quite frank. I don't think there *is* a military problem here . . . and therefore, I've gone through this today, and I asked myself, Well, what is it then if it isn't a military problem? . . . This is a domestic political problem. The announcement—we didn't say we'd go in and . . . kill them, we said we'd *act*. Well, how will we act? Well, we want to act to prevent their use. . . . We carry out open surveillance, so we know what they're doing. All times. Twenty-four hours a day from now and forever, in a sense indefinitely. What else do we do? We prevent any further offensive weapons coming in. In other words we blockade offense weapons. . . . We search every ship. . . . I call it an ultimatum associated with two actions. . . . {It} is a statement to the world, particularly to Khrushchev, that we have located these offensive weapons; we're maintaining a constant surveillance over them; if there is ever any indication that they're to be launched against this country, we will respond not only against Cuba, but we will respond directly against the Soviet Union with, with a full nuclear strike. Now this alternative doesn't seem to be a very acceptable one, but wait until you work on the others.'

Later he amplifies: 'Oh, well, it's really the, yes, it isn't the surveillance, it's the ultimatum that is the key part in this. . . . Because, as I suggested, I don't believe it's primarily a military problem. It's primarily a, a domestic, political problem.' Ball responds: 'Yeah, well, as far as the American people are concerned, action means military action, period.' To which McNamara replies: 'Well, we have a blockade. Search and, uh, removal of, of offensive weapons entering Cuba.' Ball again: 'Now, one of the things we look at is whether any, the actual operation of a blockade doesn't, isn't a greater involvement almost than a . . .' McNamara: 'It's, it's a search, not a, not an embargo, uh . . .'

At this point, Ball expresses anxiety over the fragmentary nature of this plan and McNamara backs off and begins re-examining the flaws in the military plan, presenting a series of questions about the post-strike world—would there be a popular uprising in Cuba? What would Castro do? How will the Soviets react? Could Khrushchev afford not to react? What happens when we mobilize—How does it affect our allies' support in terms of Berlin? What happens to other trouble spots throughout the world? And then the discussion peters out, and planning begins for a meeting the next morning. So, things are left hanging until the morning, and the final sounds on the tape are made by the cleaning man as he straightens up the room.

Ultimately, of course, these plans and everything related to them would be debated again and again in future meetings. But it is instructive to note that almost everything that was to be brought up in the future was first brought up in these first two meeting, and most of it was brought up in the first meeting.

ANDERSON'S (1983) ANALYSIS

Anderson's findings, as well as his conclusions, are remarkably compatible with our analysis and with the ideas advanced in image theory, although the language he uses is slightly different from ours. For example, he uses the word 'goal' for both the objectives of tactics and the objectives of plans, while we reserve it for the objectives of plans. He uses the word 'decision' both for the steps in making a set of tactics into a plan and for choosing among alternative plans, while we reserve it for adoption or rejection of candidate goals and plans. However, once these differences are straightened out, the parallels between Anderson's conclusions and image theory are striking.

Anderson's motivation was to study decision processes in the context of a real social setting. His thesis was that the traditional description of decision making is inaccurate—that alternatives are not necessarily compared as competing options, that tactical objectives (which he refers to as discovered goals, in contrast to global goals) emerge as decisions are considered rather than being clear beforehand, and that decision makers are not always trying to find a maximally effective solution to a clearly defined decision problem, that they often adopt courses of action that offer only to not make things worse.

The quantitative results

Anderson's quantitative data derived from coding individual sentences from the minutes of the four meetings for which he could obtain records. Coding was accomplished by submitting each sentence to a sequence of yes–no questions. The path through the resulting binary tree resulted in each sentence being assigned to one of 12 categories that described functional parts of the discussion. As one might expect, the results showed that the largest number of classifiable sentences pertained to the various candidate plans and the next largest number pertained to possible tactics, and tactical objectives, for those plans.

The global goal was not discussed much, but then as we saw above, this goal was tacitly accepted by everyone from the beginning and thus required no discussion. However, when tactical objectives and the global goal are considered alone, 58% of the comments pertained to the global goal, usually in terms of general characteristics of an acceptable resolution of the crisis, and 42% pertained to plausible tactical objectives within the alternative plans.

The qualitative results

Anderson's qualitative analysis revealed: First,

> . . . that decision making during the missile crisis involved sequential choices over arrays of compatible, noncompeting courses of action more frequently that it did choices among competing alternatives. (p. 208)

Second,

> . . . conflict and disagreement with respect to courses of action did not occur as a result of advocacy of competing alternatives but as a result of objections to pursuing a particular course of action. (p. 209)

Third, tactics that would only contribute to goal attainment, but that were themselves not sufficient, tended to be adopted if they would not make matters worse; that is, if the risk of their failure was sufficiently low.

Fourth, and finally, principles were the ultimate criteria. For example, at one point Robert Kennedy pointed out that the United States would undermine its moral position at home and abroad if it were to launch a surprise attack on a small nation like Cuba. This Pearl-Harbor-in-reverse analogy caused Secretary Dillon to change his position about plan number one, the air strike; Americans ought to be true to themselves and a surprise attack was not in the American tradition (i.e. violated Dillon's belief in American fairness).

Anderson concludes that:

> Goals {tactical objectives} are discovered through a social process involving argumentation and debate in a setting where justification and legitimacy play important roles. Not just any sort of goal {tactical objective} will be discovered; it will be one that is consistent with shared organizational goals {goals}. (p. 214)

Out of all of this, Anderson evolved a loose picture of decision making, which he called Decision Making by Objection. In this picture, a global goal is identified, a course of action is proposed along with positive arguments (that mostly serve to define it), objections are raised to it, and if the objections are telling it is revised or a new course if action is considered. When an action is agreed upon, it is adopted. The parallels with image theory are clear: the goal, a candidate plan that is evaluated in terms of violations. If violations disqualify the plan it is rejected or revised, otherwise it is accepted.

HOW IT ALL TURNED OUT

Finally, let us provide closure for those readers who may not be familiar with the details of the crisis and how it was resolved. The United States pursued multiple courses, all of which constituted a fairly concerted plan to put pressure on the Soviets and Cubans to neutralize or withdraw the missiles. The plan's tactics, most of which had been discussed in the 16 October meetings, consisted of pressure through the United Nations and the OAS, public disclosure of the photographs of the missile sites, a selective blockade of Cuba, continued surveillance flights, and the continued threat of military action. Between the sixth and seventh meetings, Khruschev made conciliatory overtures, but followed them with a hard-line proposal to trade American missiles in Turkey for those in Cuba. Ultimately, the Soviets decided to withdraw the Cuban missiles, which were then dismantled and shipped back to Russia.

P.S.

A postscript was added in February of 1989, when senior Soviet, Cuban, and American officials who had participated in the respective crisis decisions met in Moscow to discuss what had happened. Robert McNamara (1989) reports that all the participants were shocked by the degree of misinforma-tion and misjudgment on both sides. The Soviets introduced the missiles because they thought the United States intended to invade Cuba, which was untrue. The Americans believed that the Soviets would not place missiles outside their own territory, which they did. The Soviets believed they could maintain secrecy, which they could not. The Americans believed that there were 10 000 Soviet troops in Cuba to repulse an invasion, but there were 40 000 in addition to 270 000 well-armed Cuban troops. McNamara (1989) sums up:

> The proximate cause of the crisis was the introduction into Cuba of nuclear-capable missiles, targeted on U.S. cities. More fundamentally, it was a function of the cold war: of the gross misperceptions and the deep-seated mistrust that has existed between East and West for four decades. These must be removed. . . . Together, the United States and the Soviet Union need a vision of a world free of that enmity. . . . If we dare to break out of the mind-sets {frame} of the past four decades we can help shape relations among nations in ways that will lead to a far more peaceful world {goal dictated by principles}, and a far more prosperous one {goal dictated by principles}. (p. 47)

References

Abbott, V. and Black, J. B. (1986). Goal-related inferences in comprehension. In J. A. Galambos, R. P. Abelson and J. B. Black (eds.), *Knowledge Structures*. Hillsdale, NJ: Erlbaum.

Abelson, R. P. (1976). Script processing in attitude formation and decision-making. In J. S. Carroll and J. W. Payne (eds.), *Cognition and Social Behavior*. Hillsdale, NJ: Erlbaum.

Alexander, L. D. (1985). Successfully implementing strategic decisions. *Long Range Planning*, **18**, 91–97.

Allais, M. (1953). Le comportment de l'homme rationnel devant le risque: Critique des postulats et axioms de l'écol américaine. *Econometrica*, **21**, 503–546.

Anderson, B. F., Deane, D. H., Hammond, K. R., McClelland, G. H. and Shanteau, J. (1981). *Concepts in Judgment and Decision Research*. New York: Praeger.

Anderson, P. A. (1983). Decision making by objection and the Cuban Missile Crisis. *Administrative Science Quarterly*, **28**, 201–222.

Anderson, R. C. and Pichert, J. W. (1978). Recall of previously unrecallable information following a shift in perspective. *Journal of Verbal Learning and Verbal Behavior*, **17**, 1–12.

Ashton, A. H. (1982). The descriptive validity of normative decision theory in auditing contexts. *Journal of Accounting Research*, **20**, 415–428.

Axelrod, R. (1973). Bureaucratic decision making in the Military Assistance Program: Some empirical findings. In M. H. Halperin and A. Kanter (eds.), *Readings in American Foreign Policy: A Bureaucratic Perspective*. Boston: Little, Brown.

Bandura, A. (1986). *Social Foundations of Thought and Action: A Social Cognitive Theory*. Englewood Cliffs, NJ: Prentice-Hall.

Barclay, S., Beach, L. R. and Braithwaite, W. P. (1971). Normative models in the study of cognition. *Organizational Behavior and Human Performance*, **6**, 389–413.

Bar-Hillel, M. (1980). The base-rate fallacy in probability judgments. *Acta Psychologica*, **44**, 211–233.

Barnard, C. I. (1938). *The Functions of the Executive*. Cambridge, MA: Harvard University Press.

Barnes, V. E. (1984). The quality of human judgment: An alternative perspective. Unpublished doctoral dissertation, University of Washington, Seattle.

Barnes, V. E., Beach, L. R. and Fiedler, F. (1983). *Parks Preference Survey: Report to the Citizen's Committee on Parks, Recreation, and Open Spaces*. Seattle: University of Washington, Department of Psychology, Organizational Psychology Laboratory.

Bartlett, F. C. (1932). *Remembering: A Study in Experimental and Social Psychology*. Cambridge: Cambridge University Press.

Bateson, G. (1972). *Steps to an Ecology of Mind*. San Francisco: Chandler.

Bazerman, M. H. (1984). The relevance of Kahneman and Tversky's concept of framing to organizational behavior. *Journal of Management*, **10**, 333–343.

Bazerman, M. H. and Mannix, E. A. (1989). Review of 'Rational choice in an uncertain world'. *Journal of Behavioral Decision Making*, **2**, 63–64.

Bazerman, M. H., Mannix, E. A. and Thompson, L. L. (1988). Groups as mixed-motive negotiations. *Advances in Group Processes*, **5**, 195–216.

Bazerman, M. H. and Neale, M. A. (1983). Heuristics in negotiation. In M. H. Bazerman and R. J. Lewicki (eds.), *Negotiating in Organizations*. Beverly Hills, CA: Sage.

Beach, L. R. (1964). Recognition, assimilation, and identification of objects. *Psychological Monographs*, **78**, 22–37.

Beach, L. R. (1983). Muddling through: A response to Yates and Goldstein. *Organizational Behavior and Human Performance*, **31**, 47–53.

Beach, L. R. (1985). Action: Decision–implementation strategies and tactics. In M. Frese and J. Sabini (eds.), *Goal Directed Behavior: The Concept of Action in Psychology*. Hillsdale, NJ: Erlbaum.

Beach, L. R., Barnes, V. E. and Christensen-Szalanski, J. J. J. (1986). Beyond heuristics and biases: A contingency model of judgmental forecasting. *Journal of Forecasting*, **5**, 143–157.

Beach, L. R., Beach, B. H., Carter, W. B. and Barclay, S. (1974). Five studies of subjective equivalence. *Organizational Behavior and Human Performance*, **12**, 351–371.

Beach, L. R., Campbell, F. L. and Townes, B. D. (1979). Subjective expected utility and the prediction of birth planning decisions. *Organizational Behavior and Human Performance*, **24**, 18–28.

Beach, L. R., Christensen-Szalanski, J. J. J. and Barnes, V. E. (1987). Assessing human judgment: Has it been done, can it be done, should it be done? In G. Wright and P. Ayton (eds.), *Judgmental Forecasting*. London: John Wiley.

Beach, L. R. and Frederickson, J. R. (1989). Image theory: An alternative description of audit decisions. *Accounting, Organizations and Society*, **14**, 101–112.

Beach, L. R., Hope, A., Townes, B. D. and Campbell, F. (1982). The expectation-threshold model of reproductive decision making. *Population and Environment*, **5**, 95–108.

Beach, L. R., Mai-Dalton, R., Marshall, M. and Beach, B. H. (1981). The METRO study: A closer look at mispredicted decisions. *Organizational Behavior and Human Performance*, **28**, 50–61.

Beach, L. R. and Mitchell, T. R. (1978). A contingency model for the selection of decision strategies. *Academy of Management Review*, **3**, 439–449.

Beach, L. R. and Mitchell, T. R. (1985, October). *Emotional concomitants of decision making*. Paper presented at the meeting of the Society for Organizational Behavior, Pittsburgh, PA.

Beach, L. R. and Mitchell, T. R. (1986, August). *The self in decision making and decision implementation*. Paper presented at the meeting of the American Psychological Association, Washington DC.

Beach, L. R. and Mitchell, T. R. (1987). Image theory: Principles, goals, and plans in decision making. *Acta Psychologica*, **66**, 201–220.

Beach, L. R. and Mitchell, T. R. (1990). Image theory: A behavioral theory of decisions in organizations. In B. M. Staw and L. L. Cummings (eds.), *Research in Organizational Behavior* (Vol. 12). Greenwich, CT: JAI Press.

Beach, L. R., Mitchell, T. R., Paluchowski, T. F. and Van Zee, E. H. (in press). Image theory: Decision framing and decision deliberation. In F. Heller (ed.), *Leadership and Decision Making*. Cambridge: Cambridge University Press.

Beach, L. R. and Morrison, D. (1989). Expectancy theory and image theory in the description of decisions about childbearing. In D. Brinberg and J. Jaccard (eds.), *Dyadic Decision Making*. New York: Springer-Verlag.

Beach, L. R. and Scopp, T. S. (1968). Intuitive statistical inferences about variances. *Organizational Behavior and Human Performance*, **3**, 109–123.

Beach, L. R., Smith, B., Lundell, J. and Mitchell, T. R. (1988a). Image theory: Descriptive sufficiency of a simple rule for the compatibility test. *Journal of Behavioral Decision Making*, **1**, 17–28.

Beach, L. R. and Solak, F. (1969). Subjective judgments of acceptable error. *Organizational Behavior and Human Performance*, **4**, 242–251.

Beach, L. R. and Strom, E. (1989). A toadstool among the mushrooms: Screening decisions and image theory's compatibility test. *Acta Psychologica*, **72**, 1–12.

Beach, L. R., Townes, B. D. and Campbell, F. L. (1978). *The Optional Parenthood Questionnaire*. Baltimore, MD: National Alliance for Optional Parenthood.

Beach, L. R., Townes, B. D., Campbell, F. L. and Keating, G. W. (1976). Developing and testing a decision aid for birth planning decisions. *Organizational Behavior and Human Performance*, **15**, 99–116.

Beach, L. R., Vlek, C. and Wagenaar, W. A. (1988b). *Models and Methods for Unique Versus Repeated Decision Making* (Leiden Psychological Reports: Experimental Psychology, EP04-88). Leiden, The Netherlands: Leiden University, Psychology Department.

Beach, L. R. and Wise, J. A. (1980). Decision emergence: A Lewinian perspective. *Acta Psychologica*, **45**, 343–356.

Beck, R. N. (1987, February). Visions, values, and strategies: Changing attitudes and culture. *Academy of Management Executive*, **1**, 33–41.

Behn, R. D. and Vaupel, J. W. (1982). *Quick Analysis for Busy Decision Makers*. New York: Basic Books.

Bell, D. (1982). Regret in decision making under uncertainty. *Operations Research*, **30**, 961–981.

Ben Zur, H. and Breznitz, S. J. (1981). The effects of time pressure on risky choice behavior. *Acta Psychologica*, **47**, 89–104.

Berger, P. and Kellner, H. (1984). Marriage and the construction of reality. *Diogenes*, **46**, 1–24.

Bettenhausen, E. and Murnighan, J. K. (1985). The emergence of norms in competitive decision-making groups. *Administrative Science Quarterly*, **30**, 350–372.

Beyer, J. M. (1981). Ideologies, values, and decision making in organizations. In P. C. Nystrom and W. H. Starbuck (eds.), *Handbook of Organizational Design* (Vol. 2). New York: Oxford University Press.

Bjork, L. G. (1985). The function of cognitive images in facilitating organizational change. *Journal of Human Behavior and Learning*, **2**, 44–54.

Black, C. (1987). *It Will Never Happen To Me!* New York: Ballantine.

Boulding, K. E. (1956). *The Image*. Ann Arbor: University of Michigan Press.

Bourgeois, L. J. (1980). Performance and consensus. *Strategic Management Journal*, **1**, 227–248.

Bourgeois, L. J. (1985). Strategic goals, perceived uncertainty, and economic performance in volatile environments. *Academy of Management Journal*, **28**, 548–573.

Bouwman, M. J., Frishkoff, P. A. and Frishkoff, P. (1987). How do financial analysts make decisions? A process model of the investment screening decision. *Accounting, Organizations and Society*, **12**, 1–29.

Brand, M. (1984). *Intending and Acting: Toward a Naturalized Action Theory*. Cambridge, MA: MIT Press.

Brauers, J. and Weber, M. (1988). A new method of scenario analysis for strategic planning. *Journal of Forecasting*, **7**, 31–47.

Brinberg, D. and Jaccard, J. (eds.) (1988). *Dyadic Decision Making*. New York: Springer-Verlag.

Brown, F., Mitchell, T. R. and Beach, L. R. (1987). *Images and Decision Making: The Dynamics of Personal Choice* (Technical Report No. 87-1). Seattle, WA: University of Washington, Department of Psychology.

Burke, P. J. and Reitzes, D. C. (1981). The link between identity and role performance. *Social Psychology Quarterly*, 44, 83–92.

Burke, R. J., Weir, T. and Harrison, D. (1976). Disclosure of problems and tensions experienced by marital partners. *Psychological Reports*, 38, 531–542.

Carter W. B., Beach, L. R. and Inui, T. S. (1986). The Flu Shot Study: Using multiattribute utility theory to design a vaccination intervention. *Organizational Behavior and Human Decision Processes*, 38, 378–391.

Casey, J. T., Gettys, C. F., Pliske, R. M. and Mehle, T. (1984). A partition of small group predecision performance into informational and social components. *Organizational Behavior and Human Performance*, 34, 112–139.

Chapman, L. J. and Chapman, J. P. (1967). Illusory correlation as an obstacle to the use of valid psychodiagnostic signs. *Journal of Abnormal Psychology*, 74, 271–280.

Christensen-Szalanski, J. J. J. (1978). Problem-solving strategies: A selection mechanism, some implications, and some data. *Organizational Behavior and Human Performance*, 22, 307–323.

Christensen-Szalanski, J. J. J. (1980). A further examination of the selection of problem-solving strategies: The effects of deadlines and analytic aptitudes. *Organizational Behavior and Human Performance*, 25, 107–122.

Christensen-Szalanski, J. J. J. and Beach, L. R. (1982). Experience and the base-rate fallacy. *Organizational Behavior and Human Performance*, 29, 270–278.

Christensen-Szalanski, J. J. J. and Beach, L. R. (1984). The citation bias: Fad and fashion in the judgement and decision literature. *American Psychologist*, 39, 75–78.

Cimler, E. and Beach, L. R. (1981). Factors involved in juveniles' decisions about crimes. *Criminal Justice and Behavior*, 8, 275–286.

Cohen, M. D., March, J. G. and Olsen, J. P. (1972). A garbage can model of organizational choice. *Administrative Science Quarterly*, 17, 1–25.

Cohen, P. and Perrault, C. R. (1979). Elements of a plan-based theory of speech acts. *Cognitive Science*, 3, 177–212.

Connolly, T. (1980). Uncertainty, action and competence: Some alternatives to omniscience in complex problem-solving. In S. Fiddle (ed.), *Uncertainty: Social and Behavioral Dimensions*. New York: Praeger.

Connolly, T. and Wolf, G. (1981, August). *Deciding on decision strategies: Toward and enriched contingency model*. Paper presented at the meeting of the Academy of Management, San Diego, CA.

Coolidge, T., Beach, L. R. and Linehan, M. (1985). *Thinking about suicide questionnaire*. Unpublished questionnaire, University of Washington, Department of Psychology, Seattle.

Crocker, J. (1981). Judgment of covariation by social perceivers. *Psychological Bulletin*, 90, 272–292.

Crocker, O. L. K., Mitchell, T. R. and Beach, L. R. (1978). A further examination of equivalence intervals. *Organizational Behavior and Human Performance*, 22, 253–261.

Csikszentmihalyi, M. and Csikszentmihalyi, I. S. (1988). *Optimal Experience: Psychological Studies of Flow in Consciousness*. New York: Cambridge University Press.

Cyert, R. M. and MacCrimmon, K. B. (1968). Organizations. In E. Aronson and G. Lindsey (eds.), *The Handbook of Social Psychology* (2nd edn). Reading, MA: Addison-Wesley.

Cyert, R. M. and March, J. G. (1963). *A Behavioral Theory of the Firm*. Englewood Cliffs, NJ: Prentice-Hall.

Czapinski, J. (1987, September). *Informational aspects of positive–negative asymmetry in evaluations*. Paper presented at the Small Group Meeting on Social Cognition, Jena, East Germany.

Davidson, A. R. and Beach, L. R. (1981). Error patterns in the prediction of fertility behavior. *Journal of Applied Social Psychology*, **11**, 475–488.

Davidson, D., Suppes, P. and Siegel, S. (1957). *Decision-Making: An Experimental Approach*. Stanford, CA: Stanford University Press.

Dawes, R. (1964). Social selection based on multidimensional criteria. *Journal of Abnormal and Social Psychology*, **68**, 104–109.

Dearborn, D. C. and Simon, H. A. (1958). Selective perception: A note on the departmental identification of executives. *Sociometry*, **21**, 140–144.

Dinsmore, J. (1987). Mental spaces from a functional perspective. *Cognitive Science*, **11**, 1–21.

Dufty, N. F. and Taylor, P. M. (1962). The implementation of a decision. *Administrative Science Quarterly*, **7**, 110–119.

Dymond, R. (1954). Interpersonal perception and marital happiness. *Canadian Journal of Psychology*, **8**, 164–171.

Edwards, W. (1954). The theory of decision making. *Psychological Bulletin*, **51**, 380–417.

Einhorn, H. J. (1970). Use of nonlinear, noncompensatory models in decision making. *Psychological Bulletin*, **73**, 221–230.

Einhorn, H. J. and Hogarth, R. M. (1982). Prediction, diagnosis, and causal thinking in forecasting. *Journal of Forecasting*, **1**, 23–36.

Einhorn, H. J. and Hogarth, R. M. (1986). Judging probable cause. *Psychological Bulletin*, **99**, 3–19.

Einhorn, H. J. and Hogarth, R. M. (1987, January/February). Decision making: Going forward in reverse. *Harvard Business Review*, 66–70.

Ellis, A. (1963). *Reason and Emotion in Psychotherapy*. New York: Stuart.

Ellsberg, D. (1961). Risk, ambiguity, and the Savage axioms. *Quarterly Journal of Economics*, **75**, 643–669.

Englander, T., Farago, K., Slovic, P. and Fischhoff, B. (1986). A comparative analysis of risk perception in Hungary and the United States. *Social Behavior*, **1**, 55–66.

Erez, M. and Zidon, I. (1984). The role of goal acceptance in goal setting and task performance. *Academy of Management Review*, **8**, 454–463.

Fagley, N. S. and Miller, P. M. (1987). The effects of decision framing on choice of risky vs certain options. *Organizational Behavior and Human Decision Processes*, **39**, 264–277.

Farris, H. H. and Revlin, R. (1989). Sensible reasoning in two tasks: Rule discovery and hypothesis evaluation. *Memory and Cognition*, **17**, 221–232.

Fauconnier, G. (1985). *Mental Spaces: Aspects of Meaning Construction in Natural Language*. Cambridge, MA: MIT Press.

Felix, W. L. and Kinney, W. R. (1982). Research in the auditor's opinion formulation process: State of the art. *The Accounting Review*, **57**, 245–249.

Fiedler, D. and Beach, L. R. (1978). On the decision to be assertive. *Journal of Consulting and Clinical Psychology*, **46**, 537–546.

Fiedler, D. and Beach, L. R. (1982). The sporting choice—a decision/expectancy model. *Journal of Sport Psychology*, **4**, 81–91.

Fischhoff, B. (1975). Hindsight ≠ foresight: The effect of outcome knowledge on judgment under uncertainty. *Journal of Experimental Psychology: Human Perception and Performance*, **1**, 288–299.

Fischhoff, B., Goitein, B. and Shapira, Z. (1983). Subjective expected utility: A model of decision making. In R. W. Scholz (ed.), *Decision Making Under Uncertainty*. Amsterdam: North-Holland.

Fishbein, M. and Ajzen, I. (1975). *Belief, Attitude and Behavior: An Introduction to Theory and Research*. Reading, MA: Addison-Wesley.

Fishburn, P. C. (1974). Lexicographic order, utilities and decision rules: A survey. *Management Science*, **20**, 1442–1471.

Fishburn, P. C. (1986). Comment. *Statistical Science*, **1**, 492–495.

Fiske, S. T. (1980). Attention and weight in person perception: The impact of negative and extreme behavior. *Journal of Personality and Social Psychology*, **38**, 889–906.

Fodor, J. A. and Pylyshyn, Z. W. (1988). Connectionism and cognitive architecture: A critical analysis. *Cognition*, **28**, 3–71.

Ford, J. K., Schmitt, N., Schechtman, S. L., Hults, B. M. and Doherty, M. L. (1989). Process tracing methods: Contributions, problems, and neglected research questions. *Organizational Behavior and Human Decision Processes*, **43**, 75–177.

Franzoi, S. L., Davis, M. H. and Young, R. D. (1985). The effects of private self-consciousness and perspective taking on satisfaction in close relationships. *Journal of Personality and Social Psychology*, **48**, 1584–1594.

Frederickson, J. W. (1984). The comprehensiveness of strategic decision processes: Extension, observations, future directions. *Academy of Management Journal*, **27**, 445–466.

Frederickson, J. W. and Mitchell, T. R. (1984). Strategic decision processes: Comprehensiveness and performance in an industry with an unstable environment. *Academy of Management Journal*, **27**, 399–423.

Freud, S. (1933). *New Introductory Lectures on Psychoanalysis*. New York: Norton.

Galambos, J. A. (1986). Knowledge structures for common activities. In J. A. Galambos, R. P. Abelson and J. B. Black (eds.), *Knowledge Structures*. Hillsdale, NJ: Erlbaum.

Galambos, J. A., Abelson, R. P. and Black, J. B. (eds.) (1986). *Knowledge Structures*. Hillsdale, NJ: Erlbaum.

Galanter, E. (1962). The direct measurement of utility and subjective probability. *American Journal of Psychology*, **75**, 208–220.

Goffman, E. (1974). *Frame Analysis*. Cambridge, MA: Harvard University Press.

Gollwitzer, P. M. and Heckhausen, H. (1987). *Breadth of Attention and the Counter-Plea Heuristic: Further Evidence on the Motivational vs Volitional Mindset Destruction*. Munich: Max Plank Institute for Psychological Research.

Gollwitzer, P. M., Heckhausen, H. and Ratajczak, H. (1987). *From Weighting to Willing: Approaching a Change Decision through Deliberative or Implemental Mentation*. Munich: Max Planck Institute for Psychological Research.

Gore, W. J. (1964). *Administrative Decision Making: A Heuristic Model*. New York: John Wiley.

Gray, C. A. (1972). *Factors in Students' Decisions to Attempt Academic Tasks* (Technical Report No. 72-1-1). Seattle, WA: University of Washington, Department of Psychology.

Gray, C. A. (1975). Factors in students' decisions to attempt academic tasks. *Organizational Behavior and Human Performance*, **13**, 147–164.

Guyau, J. M. (1902). *La Genèse de l'Idèe de Temps*. Paris: Alcan.

Guzzo, R. A., Wagner, D. B., Maguire, E., Heer, B. and Hawley, C. (1986). Implicit theories and the evaluation of group process and performance. *Organizational Behavior and Human Decision Processes*, **37**, 279–295.

Hacking, I. (1975). *The Emergence of Probability*. New York: Cambridge University Press.

Hage, J. and Dewar, R. (1973). Elite values versus organizational structure in predicting innovation. *Administrative Science Quarterly*, **18**, 279–290.

Hammond, K. (1982). *To whom does the future belong: Is you is or is you ain't my baby?* Paper presented at the third annual meeting of the Judgment and Decision Making Society, Minneapolis, MN.

Hammond, K. R., Hamm, R. M., Grassia, J. and Pearson, T. (1987). Direct comparison of the efficacy of intuitive and analytical cognition in expert judgment. *IEEE Transactions on Systems, Man, and Cybernetics*, **SMC-17**, 753–770.

Harrison, R. (1972, May/June). Understanding your organization's character. *Harvard Business Review*, 119–128.

Hayes, R. H. (1985, November/December). Strategic planning—forward in reverse? *Harvard Business Review*, 111–119.

Heckhausen, H. and Gollwitzer, P. M. (1987). Thought contents and cognitive functioning in motivational and volitional states of mind. *Motivation and Emotion*, **11**, 101–120.

Heckhausen, H. and Kuhl, J. (1985). From wishes to action: The dead ends and short cuts on the long way to action. In M. Frese and J. Sabini (eds.), *Goal Directed Behaviour*. Hillsdale, NJ: Erlbaum.

Hintzman, D. L. (1986). 'Schema abstraction' in a multiple-trace memory model. *Psychological Review*, **93**, 411–428.

Hoffman, L. W. and Hoffman, M. L. (1973). The value of children to parents. In J. T. Fawcett (ed.), *Psychological perspectives on population*. New York: Basic Books.

Hofstatter, P. R. (1939). Über die Schätzung von Gruppeneigenschaften *Zeitschrift für Psychologie*, **145**, 1–44.

Hogarth, R. (1981). Beyond discrete biases: Functional and dysfunctional aspects of judgmental heuristics. *Psychological Bulletin*, **90**, 197–217.

Holmstrom, V. L. and Beach, L. R. (1973). Subjective expected utility and career preferences. *Organizational Behavior and Human Performance*, **10**, 201–207.

Hovland, C. I. and Weiss, W. I. (1953). Transmission of information concerning concepts through positive and negative instances. *Journal of Experimental Psychology*, **45**, 175–182.

Huffman, M. D. (1978). *The Effect of Decision Task Characteristics on Decision Behavior* (Technical Report No. 78–16). Seattle, WA: University of Washington, Department of Psychology.

Isenberg, D. J. (1984, November/December). How senior managers think. *Harvard Business Review*, 81–90.

Isenberg, D. J. (1986). Thinking and managing: A verbal protocol analysis of managerial problem solving. *Academy of Management Journal*, **29**, 775–788.

Jacob, P. E., Flink, J. J. and Shuchman, H. L. (1962). Values and their function in decision making. *American Behavioral Scientist*, **5** (Suppl. 9), 6–38.

James, W. (1890/1950). *The Principles of Psychology* (Vol. 2). New York: Dover.

Janis, I. L. and Mann, L. (1977). *Decision-Making: A Psychological Analysis of Conflict, Choice and Commitment*. New York: Free Press.

Jaques, E. (1982). *The Form of Time*. London: Heinemann.

Jastrow, J. (1927). The animus of psychical research. In C. Murchison (ed.), *The Case For and Against Psychical Belief*. Worcester, MA: Clark University Press.

Johnson, E. J. and Payne, J. W. (1985). Effort and accuracy in choice. *Management Science*, **31**, 395–414.

Johnson-Laird, P. N. (1983). *Mental Models*. Cambridge, MA: Harvard University Press.

Jungermann, H. (1983). The two camps on rationality. In R. W. Scholz (ed.), *Decision Making under Uncertainty*. Amsterdam: North-Holland.

Jungermann, H. (1985). Inferential processes in the construction of scenarios. *Journal of Forecasting*, **4**, 321–327.

Jungermann, H. and Thüring, M. (1987). The use of causal knowledge in inferential reasoning. In J. L. Mumpower, O. Renn, L. D. Phillips and V. R. R. Uppuluri (eds.), *Expert Judgment and Expert Systems*. Berlin: Springer-Verlag.

Jungermann, H., von Ulardt, I. and Hausmann, L. (1983). The role of the goal for generating actions. In P. Humphreys, O. Svenson and A. Vari (eds.), *Analyzing and Aiding Decision Processes*. Amsterdam: North-Holland.

Kahneman, D., Slovic, P. and Tversky, A. (1982). *Judgement Under Uncertainty: Heuristics and Biases*. New York: Cambridge University Press.

Kahneman, D. and Tversky, A. (1972). Subjective probability: A judgment of representativeness. *Cognitive Psychology*, **3**, 430–454.

Kahneman, D. and Tversky, A. (1973). On the psychology of prediction. *Psychological Review*, **80**, 237–251.

Kahneman, D. and Tversky, A. (1979). Prospect theory: An analysis of decision under risk. *Econometrica*, **47**, 263–291.

Kahneman, D. and Tversky, A. (1982a). On the study of statistical intuitions. *Cognition*, **11**, 123–141.

Kahneman, D. and Tversky, A. (1982b). The psychology of preferences. *Scientific American*, **246**, 160–173.

Kahneman, D. and Tversky, A. (1982c). The simulation heuristic. In D. Kahneman, P. Slovic and A. Tversky (eds.), *Judgment Under Uncertainty: Heuristics and Biases*. New York: Cambridge University Press.

Keeney, R. L. (1980). *Siting Energy Facilities*. New York: Academic Press.

Keren, G. B. and Wagenaar, W. A. (1985). On the psychology of playing blackjack: Normative and descriptive considerations with implications for decision theory. *Journal of Experimental Psychology: General*, **114**, 133–158.

Keren, G. B. and Wagenaar, W. A. (1987). Violation of utility theory in unique and repeated gambles. *Journal of Experimental Psychology: Learning, Memory and Cognition*, **13**, 387–396.

Kiyak, H. A. and Beach, L. R. (1983). *Developing and testing a decision aid for orthognathic surgery*. Paper presented at the meeting of the American Association for Dental Research, Cincinnati, OH.

Klayman, J. (1985). Children's decision strategies and their adaptation to task characteristics. *Organizational Behavior and Human Decision Processes*, **35**, 179–201.

Klein, N. M. (1983). Utility and decision strategies: A second look at rational decision-making. *Organization Behavior and Human Performance*, **31**, 1–25.

Kluckhohn, C. (1951). Values and value-orientations in theory of action. In T. Parsons and E. A. Shills (eds.), *Toward a General Theory of Action*. Cambridge, MA: Harvard University Press.

Knudson, R. M. (1985). Marital compatibility and mutual identity confirmation. In W. Ickes (ed.), *Compatible and Incompatible Relationships*. New York: Springer-Verlag.

Kohlberg, L. (1969). Stage and sequence: The cognitive-developmental approach to socialization. In D. A. Goslin (ed.), *Handbook of Socialization Theory and Research*. Chicago: Rand McNally.

Köhler, W. (1925). *The Mentality of Apes*. New York: Harcourt Brace.

Kosslyn, S. M. (1980). *Image and Mind*. Cambridge, MA: Harvard University Press.

Kotter, J. P. (1982, November/December). What effective managers really do. *Harvard Business Review*, 156–167.

Kotter, J. P. and Schlesinger, L. A. (1979, March/April). Choosing strategies for change. *Harvard Business Review*, 106–114.

Kreitler, H. and Kreitler, S. (1979). *Cognitive Orientation and Behavior*. New York: Springer.

Kuhl, J. (1983). *Motivation, Konflikt und Handlungskontrolle*. Heidelberg: Springer.

Kundera, M. (1984). *The Unbearable Lightness of Being*. London: Faber and Faber.

Lachter, J. and Bever, T. G. (1988). The relation between linguistic structure and associative theories of language learning—A constructive critique of some connectionist learning models. *Cognition*, **28**, 195–247.

Laestadius, J. E. (1970). Tolerance for errors in intuitive mean estimations. *Organizational Behavior and Human Performance*, **5**, 121–124.

Laing, R. D., Phillipson, H. and Lee, A. R. (1966). *Interpersonal Perception: A Theory and a Method of Research*. New York: Springer.

Landman, J. (1987). Regret and elation following action and inaction: Affective responses to positive versus negative outcomes. *Personality and Social Psychology Bulletin*, **13**, 524–536.

Larson, J. R. and Reenan, A. M. (1979). The equivalence interval as a measure of uncertainty. *Organizational Behavior and Human Performance*, **23**, 49–55.

Lathrop, R. G. (1967). Perceived variability. *Journal of Experimental Psychology*, **23**, 498–502.

Lee, T. W., Locke, E. A. and Latham, G. P. (in press). Goal setting theory and job performance. In L. A. Pervin (ed.), *Goal Concepts in Personality and Social Psychology*. Hillsdale, NJ: Erlbaum.

Lee, W. (1971). *Decision Theory and Human Behavior*. New York: John Wiley.

Lens, W. (1986). Future time perspective: A cognitive–motivational concept. In D. R. Brown and J. Veroff (eds.), *Frontiers of Motivational Psychology*. New York: Springer.

Leslie, A. M. (1987). Pretense and representation: The origins of 'theory of mind'. *Psychological Review*, **94**, 412–426.

Lewicka, M. (1988). On objective and subjective anchoring of cognitive acts: How behavioral valence modifies reasoning schema. In W. Baker and L. Mos (eds.), *Recent Trends in Theoretical Psychology*. New York: Springer-Verlag.

Lichtenstein, E. H. and Brewer, W. F. (1980). Memory for goal directed events. *Cognitive Psychology*, **12**, 412–445.

Lindblom, C. E. (1959). The science of 'muddling through'. *Administration Review*, **19**, 79–88.

Locke, E. A. (1968). Toward a theory of task motivation and incentives. *Organizational Behavior and Human Performances*, **3**, 157–189.

Loftus, E. F. and Beach, L. R. (1982). Human inference and judgment: Is the glass half empty or half full? *Stanford Law Review*, **34**, 939–956.

Loomis, G. and Sugden, R. (1982). Regret theory: An alternative theory of rational choice under uncertainty. *Economic Journal*, **92**, 805–824.

Lopes, L. L. (1981). Decision making in the shortrun. *Journal of Experimental Psychology: Human Learning and Memory*, **1**, 377–385.

Luchins, A. S. (1942). Mechanization in problem solving: The effect of Einstellung. *Psychological Monographs*, **54**, No. 248.

Machina, M. J. (1982). 'Expected utility' analysis without the independence axiom. *Econometrica*, **50**, 277–332.

March, J. G. (1978). Bounded rationality, ambiguity, and the engineering of choice. *Bell Journal of Economics*, **9**, 587–608.

March, J. G. and Olsen, J. P. (1979). *Ambiguity and Choice in Organizations*. Bergen, Norway: Universitetsforlaget.

March, J. G. and Olsen, J. P. (1986). Garbage can models of decision making in organizations. In J. G. March and R. Weissinger-Baylon (eds.), *Ambiguity and*

Command: Organizational Perspectives on Military Decision Making. Cambridge, MA: Ballinger.

March, J. G. and Shapira, Z. (1987). Managerial perspectives on risk and risk taking. *Management Science*, 33, 1404–1418.

March, J. G. and Simon, H. A. (1958). *Organizations.* New York: John Wiley.

Marken, R. S. (1988). The nature of behavior: Control as fact and theory. *Behavioral Science*, 33, 196–206.

Markus, H. and Nurius, P. (1986). Possible selves. *American Psychologist*, 41, 954–969.

Markus, H. and Wurf, E. (1987). The dynamic self-concept: A social psychological perspective. *Annual Review of Psychology*, 38, 299–337.

Marlatt, G. A. and Gordon, J. R. (eds.) (1985). *Relapse Prevention: Maintenance Strategies in the Treatment of Addictive Behaviors.* New York: Guilford.

Marshall, L. L. and Kidd, R. F. (1981). Good news or bad news first? *Social Behavior and Personality*, 9, 223–226.

Martins, J. (1983). *Reasoning in Multiple Belief Spaces* (Technical Report No. 203). Buffalo, NY: Department of Computer Science, SUNY.

Matlin, M. W. and Stang, D. J. (1978). *The Pollyanna Principle: Selectivity in Language, Memory and Thought.* Cambridge, MA: Schenkman.

Maule, J. and Mackie, P. (1988, August). *The harassed decision maker revisited.* Paper presented at the International Conference on Thinking, Aberdeen, Scotland.

Maybee, J. S. and Voogd, H. (1984). Qualitative impact analysis through sign-solvability: A review. *Environment and Planning B: Planning and Design*, 11, 365–376.

McAllister, D., Mitchell, T. R. and Beach, L. R. (1979). The contingency model for selection of decision strategies: An empirical test of the effects of significance, accountability, and reversibility. *Organizational Behavior and Human Performance*, 24, 228–244.

McCauley, C., Stitt, C. L. and Segal, M. (1980). Stereotyping: From prejudice to prediction. *Psychological Bulletin*, 87, 195–208.

McNamara, R. S. (1989, February). The lessons of October: An insider recalls the Cuban crisis. *Newsweek*, 47.

Meichenbaum, D. (1977). *Cognitive–Behavioral Modification.* New York: Plenum.

Meyer, A. D. (1982). How ideologies supplant formal structures and shape responses to environments. *Journal of Management Studies*, 19, 45–61.

Miller, G. A., Galanter, E. and Pribram, K. H. (1960). *Plans and the Structure of Behavior.* New York: Holt, Rinehart & Winston.

Minsky, M. (1968). *Semantic Information Processing.* Cambridge, MA: MIT Press.

Mintzberg, H. (1975, July/August). The manager's job: Folkore and fact. *Harvard Business Review*, 49–61.

Mintzberg, H. (1978). Patterns in strategy formation. *Management Science*, 24, 934–948.

Mintzberg, H. (1987, July/August). Crafting strategy. *Harvard Business Review*, 66–75.

Mintzberg, H., Raisinghani, D. and Théorêt, A. (1976). The structure of 'unstructured' decision processes. *Administrative Science Quarterly*, 21, 246–275.

Mitchell, T. R. (1974). Expectancy models of job satisfaction, occupational preference and effort: A theoretical, methodological, and empirical appraisal. *Psychological Bulletin*, 81, 1053–1077.

Mitchell, T. R. and Beach, L. R. (1976). A review of occupational preference and choice research using expectancy theory and decision theory. *Journal of Occupational Psychology*, 49, 231–248.

Mitchell, T. R. and Beach, L. R. (in press). '...Do I love thee? Let me count...'
Toward an understanding of intuitive and automatic decision making. *Organizational Behavior and Human Decision Processes.*

Mitchell, T. R., Beach, L. R. and Smith, K. G. (1985). Some data on publishing
from the authors' and reviewers' perspectives. In L. L. Cummings and P. J. Frost
(eds.), *Publishing in the Organizational Sciences.* Homewood, IL: Irwin.

Mitchell, T. R. and Knudson, B. W. (1973). Instrumentality theory predictions of
students' attitudes towards business and their choice of business as an occupation.
Academy of Management Journal, 16, 41–52.

Mitchell, T. R., Rediker, K. J. and Beach, L. R. (1986). Image theory and its
implications for organizational decision making. In H. P. Sims and D. A. Gioia
(eds.), *The Thinking Organization.* San Francisco: Jossey-Bass.

Morris, C. (1956). *Varieties of Human Values.* Chicago: University of Chicago Press.

Mosteller, F. and Nogee, P. (1951). An experimental measurement of utility. *Journal
of Political Economy,* 59, 371–404.

Muchinsky, P. M. and Fitch, M. K. (1975). Subjective expected utility and academic
preferences. *Organizational Behavior and Human Performance,* 14, 217–226.

Mukerjee, R. K. (1965). *The Social Structure of Values.* New Delhi: Chand.

Murphy, A. and Winkler, R. (1977). Experimental point and area precipitation
probability forecasts for a forecast area with significant local effects. *Atmosphere,*
15, 61–78.

Nestor, Inc. (1988). *Nestor Decision Learning System for Mortgage Underwriting and
Delinquency Risk Assessment.* Providence, RI: Nestor.

Newman, S. H. and Thompson, V. D. (eds.) (1976). *Population Psychology: Research
and Educational Issues* (DHEW Publication No. (NIH) 76-574). Bethesda, MD:
National Institutes of Health.

Nichols-Hoppe, K. T. and Beach, L. R. (in press). The effects of test anxiety and
task variables on predecisional information search. *Journal of Research in
Personality.*

Nisbett, R., Krantz, D., Jepson, C. and Kunda, Z. (1983). The use of statistical
heuristics in everyday inductive reasoning. *Psychological Review,* 90, 339–363.

Nisbett, R. and Ross, L. (1980). *Human Inference: Strategies and Shortcomings of
Social Judgment.* Englewood Cliffs, NJ: Prentice-Hall.

Norman, D. A. (1981). Categorization of action slips. *Psychological Review,* 88, 1–15.

Nutt, P. C. (1987). Identifying and appraising how managers install strategy.
Strategic Management Journal, 8, 1–14.

Olshavsky, R. W. (1979). Task complexity and contingent processing in decision
making: A replication and extension. *Organizational Behavior and Human
Performance,* 24, 300–316.

Ortony, A. (1979). Beyond literal similarity. *Psychological Review,* 86, 161–180.

Paquette, L. and Kida, T. (1988). The effect of decision strategy and task complexity
on decision performance. *Organizational Behavior and Human Decision Processes,*
41, 128–142.

Payne, J. W. (1976). Task complexity and contingent processing in decision making:
An information search and protocol analysis. *Organizational Behavior and Human
Performance,* 16, 366–387.

Payne, J. W., Bettman, J. R. and Johnson, E. J. (1988). Adaptive strategy selection
in decision making. *Journal of Experimental Psychology: Learning, Memory and
Cognition,* 14, 534–552.

Peeters, G. (1971). The positive–negative asymmetry: On cognitive consistency and
the positivity bias. *European Journal of Social Psychology,* 1, 455–474.

Peeters, G. (1986). Good and evil as softwares of the brain: On psychological 'immediates' underlying the metaphysical 'ultimates'. *Interdisciplinary Studies in the Philosophy of Understanding*, 9, 210–231.

Pennington, N. and Hastie, R. (1986). Evidence evaluation in complex decision making. *Journal of Personality and Social Psychology*, 51, 242–258.

Pennington, N. and Hastie, R. (1988). Explanation-based decision making: Effects of memory structure on judgment. *Journal of Experimental Psychology: Learning, Memory and Cognition*, 14, 521–533.

Peterson, C. R. (ed.) (1973). Cascaded inference. *Organizational Behavior and Human Performance*, 10 (Special issue).

Peterson, C. R. and Beach, L. R. (1967). Man as an intuitive statistician. *Psychological Bulletin*, 68, 29–46.

Phillips, J. S. and Lord, R. G. (1982). Schematic information processing and perceptions of leadership in problem-solving groups. *Journal of Appied Psychology*, 67, 486–492.

Phillips, L. D. (1985, April). Systems for solutions. *Datamation Business*, 26–29.

Phillips, L. D. (1986, October). Computing to consensus. *Datamation*, 2–6.

Piaget, J. (1929). *The Child's Conception of the World*. New York: Harcourt Brace.

Piaget, J. (1932/1965). *The Moral Judgment of the Child*. New York: Free Press.

Polyani, M. (1966). *The Tacit Dimension*. Garden City, NJ: Doubleday.

Pope, A. (1734/1980). Moral essays, Epistle I. In J. Bartlett (ed.), *Familiar Quotations* (15th edn). Boston: Little, Brown.

Powers, W. T. (1973). *Behavior: The Control of Perception*. Chicago: Aldine.

Pratt, J. W. (1986). Comment. *Statistical Science*, 1, 498–499.

Preston, M. G. and Baratta, P. (1948). An experimental study of the auction-value of an uncertain outcome. *American Journal of Psychology*, 61, 183–193.

Prothero, J. and Beach, L. R. (1984). Retirement decisions: Expectation, intention, and action. *Journal of Applied Social Psychology*, 14, 162–174.

Pruitt, D. G. and Rubin, J. Z. (1986). *Social Conflict: Escalation, Stalemate, and Settlement*. New York: Random House.

Pylyshyn, Z. W. (1973). What the mind's eye tells the mind's brain: A critique of mental imagery. *Psychological Bulletin*, 80, 1–24.

Pylyshyn, Z. W. (1981). The imagery debate: Analogue media versus tacit knowledge. *Psychological Review*, 88, 16–45.

Rayner, S. and Cantor, R. (1987). How fair is safe enough? The cultural approach to societal technology choice. *Risk Analysis*, 7, 3–9.

Raynor, J. O. (1969). Future orientation and motivation of immediate activity. An elaboration of the theory of achievement motivation. *Psychological Review*, 76, 606–610.

Rediker, K. J. (1988). *The influence of strength of culture and decision optionality on strategic decision making: An exploratory application of image theory*. Unpublished doctoral dissertation, University of Washington, Seattle.

Reilly, D. L., Cooper, L. N. and Elbaum, C. (1982). A neural model for category learning. *Biological Cybernetics*, 45, 35–41.

Reilly, D. L., Scofield, C., Elbaum, C. and Cooper, L. N. (1987, June). *Learning system architectures composed of multiple learning modules*. Paper presented at the IEEE International Conference on Neural Networks, San Diego, CA.

Reither, F. and Stäudel, T. (1985). Thinking and action. In M. Frese and J. Sabini (eds.), *Goal Directed Behavior: The Concept of Action in Psychology*. Hillsdale, NJ: Erlbaum.

Rieke, R. and Sillars, M. (1984). *Argumentation and the Decision Making Process*. Glenview, IL: Scott, Foresman.

Rimey, R., Gouin, P., Scofield, C. and Reilly, D. L. (1986). Real-time 3-D object classification using a learning system. In *Intelligent Robots and Computer Vision* (Vol. 726). Bellingham, WA: Society of Photo-Optical Instrumentation Engineers.

Rokeach, M. (1968). *Beliefs, Attitudes and Values*. San Francisco: Jossey-Bass.

Rosch, E. (1976). Classification of real-world objects: Origins and representations in cognition. In S. Ehrlich and E. Tolving (eds.), *La Memoire Semantique*. Paris: Bulletin de Psychologie.

Rosenfeld, E. (1987, June). *Neurocomputing: A new industry*. Paper presented at the IEEE International Conference on Neural Networks, San Diego, CA.

Rumelhart, D. E. (1977). Understanding and summarizing brief stories. In D. LaBerge and S. J. Samuels (eds.), *Basic Processes in Reading: Perception and Comprehension*. Hillsdale, NJ: Erlbaum.

Rumelhart, D. E., Smolensky, P., McClelland, J. L. and Hinton, G. E. (1987). Schemata and sequential thought processes in PDP models. In J. L. McClelland and D. E. Rumelhart (eds.), *Parallel Distributed Processing: Explorations in the Microstructure of Cognition* (Vol. 2). Cambridge, MA: MIT Press.

Ryan, T. A. (1970). *Intentional Behavior: An Approach to Human Motivation*. New York: Ronald.

Samuelson, P. A. (1963). Risk and Uncertainty: A fallacy of large numbers. *Scientia*. **9**, 108–113.

Samuelson, W. and Zeckhauser, R. (1988). Status quo bias in individual decision making. *Journal of Risk and Uncertainty*, **1**, 7–59.

Savage, L. J. (1954). *The Foundations of Statistics*. New York: John Wiley.

Schandl, C. W. (1978). *Theory of Auditing*. Houston: Scholars Book Company.

Schank, R. C. and Abelson, R. P. (1977). *Scripts, Plans, Goals and Understanding*. Hillsdale, NJ: Erlbaum.

Schoenfeld, A. H. (1983). Beyond the purely cognitive: Belief systems, social cognitions, and metacognitions as driving forces in intellectual performance. *Cognitive Science*, **7**, 329–363.

Schwartz, S. H. (1970). Moral decision making and behavior. In J. Macaulay and L. Berkowitz (eds.), *Altruism and Helping Behavior: Social Psychological Studies of Some Antecedents and Consequences*. New York: Academic Press.

Schwartz, S. H. and Bilsky, W. (1987). Toward a universal psychological structure of human values. *Journal of Personality and Social Psychology*, **53**, 550–562.

Selznick, P. (1957). *Leadership in Administration: A Sociological Interpretation*. Evanston, IL: Row, Peterson.

Shafer, G. (1986). Savage revisited. *Statistical Science*, **1**, 463–501.

Shanteau, J. (1974). Component processes in risky decision making. *Journal of Experimental Psychology*, **103**, 680–691.

Shanteau, J. and Anderson, N. H. (1969). Test of a conflict model for preference judgment. *Journal of Mathematical Psychology*, **6**, 312–325.

Silver, W. (1989). Status quo effects on the framing effect. Unpublished manuscript, University of Washington, School of Business, Seattle.

Simon, H. A. (1955). A behavioral model of rational choice. *Quarterly Journal of Economics*, **69**, 99–118.

Simon, H. A. (1945/1976). *Administrative behavior*. New York: Macmillan.

Simon, H. A. (1972). What is visual imagery? An information-processing interpretation. In L. W. Gregg (ed.), *Cognition in Learning and Memory*. New York: John Wiley.

Simon, H. A. (1979). Rational decision making in business organizations. *American Economic Review*, **69**, 493–513.

Simon, H. A. (1987). Making management decisions: The role of intuition and emotion. *Academy of Management Executive*, **1**, 57–64.

Skov, R. B. and Sherman, S. J. (1986). Information-gathering processes: Diagnosticity, hypothesis-confirmatory strategies, and perceived hypothesis confirmation. *Journal of Experimental Social Psychology*, **22**, 93–121.

Sloan, T. S. (1983). The aura of projected personal futures: A neglected aspect of major life decisions. *Personality and Social Psychology Bulletin*, **9**, 559–566.

Slovic, P. (1966). Value as a determiner of subjective probability. *IEEE Transactions on Human Factors in Electronics*, **HFE-7**, 22–28.

Slovic, P. (1987). Perception of risk. *Science*, **236**, 280–285.

Slovic, P., Lichtenstein, S. and Fischhoff, B. (1985). Decision making. In R. C. Atkinson, R. J. Herrnstein, G. Lindzey and R. D. Luce (eds.), *Stevens' Handbook of Experimental Psychology*. New York: John Wiley.

Smith, J. F., Mitchell, T. R. and Beach, L. R. (1982). A cost–benefit mechanism for selecting problem solving strategies: Some extensions and empirical tests. *Organizational Behavior and Human Performance*, **29**, 370–396.

Smyth, A. H. (ed.) (1906). *The Writings of Benjamin Franklin* (Vol. 7). New York: Macmillan.

Snyder, M., Tanke, E. and Berscheid, E. (1977). Social perception and interpersonal behavior: On the self-fulfilling nature of social stereotypes. *Journal of Personality and Social Psychology*, **35**, 656–666.

Sproull, L. S. and Hofmeister, K. R. (1986). Thinking about implementation. *Journal of Management*, **12**, 43–60.

Staw, B. M. (1975). Attributions of the 'cause' of performance: A general alternative interpretation of cross-sectional research on organizations. *Organizational Behavior and Human Performance*, **13**, 414–432.

Staw, B. M. (1981). The escalation of commitment to a course of action. *Academy of Management Review*, **6**, 557–588.

Steinbruner, J. D. (1974). *The Cybernetic Theory of Decision*. Princeton, NJ: Princeton University Press.

Stevens, S. S. (1962). *Handbook of Experimental Psychology*. New York: John Wiley.

Stillars, A. L. (1985). Interpersonal perception in relationships. In W. Ickes (ed.), *Compatible and Incompatible Relationships*. New York: Springer-Verlag.

Suppes, P. (1957). *Introduction to Logic*. Princeton, NJ: Van Nostrand.

Svenson, O. (1979). Process descriptions in decision making. *Organizational Behavior and Human Performance*, **23**, 86–112.

Swann, W. B. (1983). Self-verification: Bringing social reality into harmony with the self. In G. S. Saunders and J. Suls (eds.), *Social Psychology in Health and Illness*. Hillsdale, NJ: Erlbaum.

Swann, W. B. and Predmore, S. C. (1985). Intimates as agents of social support: Sources of consolation or despair? *Journal of Personality and Social Psychology*, **49**, 1609–1617.

Symonds, W. C. and Miles, G. L. (1985, February). The toughest job in business: How they're remaking US Steel. *Business Week*, 50–56.

Teigen, K. H. (1988). When are low-probability events judged to be 'probable'? Effects of outcome-set characteristics on verbal probability estimates. *Acta Psychologica*, **68**, 157–174.

Teigen, K. H., Brun, W. and Slovic, P. (1988). Societal risks as seen by a Norwegian public. *Journal of Behavioral Decision Making*, **1**, 111–130.

Thorngate, W. (1980). Efficient decision heuristics. *Behavioral Science*, **25**, 219–225.

Thüring, M. and Jungermann, H. (1986). Constructing and running mental models for inferences about the future. In B. Brehmer, H. Jungermann, P. Lourens and G. S. Sevòn (eds.), *New Directions in research in Decision Making*. Amsterdam: North-Holland.

Townes, B. D., Campbell, F. L., Wood, R. J. and Beach, L. R. (1980). A social psychological study of fertility decisions. *Population and Environment*, **3**, 210–220.

Turing, A. M. (1950). Computing machinery and intelligence. *Mind*, **59**, 433–460.

Tversky, A. (1967). Additivity, utility, and subjective probability. *Journal of Mathematical Psychology*, **4**, 175–202.

Tversky, A. (1969). The intransitivity of preferences. *Psychological Review*, **76**, 31–48.

Tversky, A. (1972). Elimination by aspects: A theory of choice. *Psychological Review*, **79**, 218–299.

Tversky, A. (1977). Features of similarity. *Psychological Review*, **84**, 327–352.

Tversky, A. and Bar-Hillel, M. (1983). Risk: The long and the short. *Journal of Experimental Psychology: Learning, Memory, and Cognition*, **9**, 713–717.

Tversky, A. and Kahneman, D. (1971). The belief in the law of small numbers. *Psychological Bulletin*, **76**, 105–110.

Tversky, A. and Kahneman, D. (1974). Judgment under uncertainty: Heuristics and biases. *Science*, **185**, 1124–1131.

Tversky, A. and Kahneman, D. (1981). The framing of decisions and the psychology of choice. *Science*, **221**, 453–458.

Tversky, A. and Kahneman, D. (1983). Extensional versus intuitive reasoning: The conjunction fallacy in probability judgment. *Psychological Review*, **90**, 293–315.

Van Zee, E. H., Paluchowski, T. F. and Beach, L. R. (1989). Information use in screening and in choice. Unpublished manuscript, University of Washington, Department of Psychology, Seattle.

Vlek, C. and Stallen, P. J. (1981). Judging risks and benefits in the small and large. *Organizational Behavior and Human Performance*, **28**, 235–271.

Von Neumann, J. and Morgenstern, O. (1947). *Theory of Games and Economic Behavior*. Princeton, NJ: Princeton University Press.

Von Winterfeldt, D. and Edwards, W. (1986). *Decision Analysis and Behavioral Research*. New York: Cambridge University Press.

Voogd, H. (1982). Multicriteria evaluation with mixed qualitative and quantitative data. *Environment and Planning B: Planning and Design*, **9**, 221–236.

Voogd, H. (1983). *Multicriteria Evaluation for Urban and Regional Planning*. London: Pion.

Voogd, H. (1988). Multicriteria evaluation: Measures, manipulation, and meaning—a reply. *Environment and Planning B: Planning and Design*, **15**, 65–72.

Wagenaar, W. A. and Keren, G. B. (1986). The seat belt paradox: Effects of adopted roles on information seeking. *Organizational Behavior and Human Decision Processes*, **38**, 1–6.

Wagenaar, W. A. and Keren, G. B. (1988). Chance and luck are not the same. *Journal of Behavioral Decision Making*, **1**, 65–75.

Wagenaar, W. A., Keren, G. B. and Lichtenstein, S. (1988). Islanders and hostages: Deep and surface structures of decision problems. *Acta Psychologica*, **68**, 175–189.

Wagenaar, W. A., Keren, G. B. and Pleit-Kuiper, A. (1984). The multiple objectives of gamblers. *Acta Psychologica*, **56**, 167–178.

Waller, W. S. and Felix, W. L. (1984). Cognition and the auditor's opinion formulation process: A schematic model of interactions between memory and current audit evidence. In S. Moriarity and E. Joyce (eds.), *Decision Making and Accounting: Current Research*. Norman, OK: University of Oklahoma Press.

Waller, W. S. and Mitchell, T. R. (1984). The effects of context on the selection of decision strategies for the cost variance investigation. *Organizational Behavior and Human Performance*, **33**, 397–413.

Walsh, J. P. and Fahey, L. (1986). The role of negotiated belief structures in strategy making. *Journal of Management*, **12**, 325–338.

Walsh, J. P., Henderson, C. M. and Deighton, J. (1988). Negotiated belief structures and decision performance: An empirical investigation. *Organizational Behavior and Human Decision Processes*, **42**, 194–216.

Wason, P. C. (1960). On the failure to eliminate hypotheses in a conceptual task. *Quarterly Journal of Experimental Psychology*, **12**, 129–140.

Wason, P. C. (1968). Reasoning about a rule. *Quarterly Journal of Experimental Psychology*, **23**, 273–281.

Weick, K. E. (1979). *The Social Psychology of Organizing*. Reading, MA: Addison-Wesley.

Wells, G. L., Taylor, B. R. and Turtle, J. W. (1987). The undoing of scenarios. *Journal of Personality and Social Psychology*, **53**, 421–430.

Wilson, R. and Crouch, E. A. C. (1987). Risk assessment and comparisons: An introduction. *Science*, **236**, 267–270.

Wood, R. J., Campbell, F. L., Townes, B. D. and Beach, L. R. (1977). Birth planning decisions. *American Journal of Public Health*, **67**, 563–565.

Wright, P. (1974). The harassed decision maker: Time pressures, distraction, and the use of evidence. *Journal of Applied Psychology*, **59**, 555–561.

Wright, P. and Weitz, B. (1977). Time horizon effects on product evaluation strategies. *Journal of Marketing Research*, **14**, 429–443.

Yates, J. (1985). The content of awareness is a model of the world. *Psychological Review*, **92**, 249–284.

Zander, A. (1985). *The Purposes of Groups and Organizations*. San Franciso: Jossey-Bass.

Author Index

Page numbers in brackets indicate author is part of an *et al.*

Abbott, V., 35
Abelson, R. P., 17, 29, 33–34, 50, 122
Ajzen, I., 130
Alexander, L. D., 185, 190
Allais, M., 1
Anderson, B. F., 109
Anderson, N. H., 130
Anderson, P. A., 14, 80, 215, 228–229
Anderson, R. C., 52
Ashton, A. H., 200
Axelrod, R., 14

Bandura, A., 42
Baratta, P., 157
Barclay, S., 40, 113–114, 116, [121], 130
Bar-Hillel, M., 117, 166
Barnard, C. I., 124
Barnes, V. E., 53, [116–117], 119–121, [121–122], 123, [123], 170
Bartlett, F. C., 18
Bateson, G., 50, 62
Bazerman, M. H., 13, 53, 56–57, 64, 170
Beach, B. H., 113–114, [121], [170]
Beach, L. R., 24, 26, [26–27], 32, [40], 45, 51, 54, [54], 74, 80–103, 107, 112–114, 116, [116], 117, 121–125, 127–130, [130], 132–133, 143–147, 153, [153], 155, [155], 157, 164, 167, 168, 170, [170], [172], 178–179, 187, 199, 204, [204], 207–209, [209], 210–211, [211], 213
Beck, R. N., 124, 186
Behn, R. D., 54
Bell, D., 164
Ben Zur, H., 80
Berger, P., 213

Berscheid, E., [122]
Bettenhausen, E., 13
Bettman, J. R., [151], 153–155, [156–157], [168]
Bever, T. G., 111
Beyer, J. M., 12, 26
Bilsky, W., 43
Bjork, L. G., 186
Black, C., 41
Black, J. B., 35
Boulding, K. E., 18
Bourgeois, L. J., 33, 87
Bouwman, M. J., 14
Braithwaite, W. P., [40], [116], [130]
Brand, M., 175
Brauers, J., 172
Brewer, W. F., 29, 34, 35
Breznitz, S. J., 80
Brinberg, D., 199
Brown, F., 26, 204
Brun, W., [65]
Burke, P. J., 25
Burke, R. J., 212

Campbell, F. L., [54], [170], [207], 208, [209–211], [213]
Cantor, R., 65
Carter, W. B., 113–114, [121], 170
Casey, J. T., 14
Chapman, J. P., 117
Chapman, L. J., 117
Christensen-Szalanski, J. J. J., 59, 116, [116–117], 121, [121–123], 128, 134–140, 142, 144–145, 146, 153, 155
Cimler, E., 170
Cohen, M. D., 2, 14
Cohen, P., 20

Connolly, T., 133
Coolidge, T., 170
Cooper, L. N., [111]
Crocker, J., 121
Crocker, O. L. K., 114
Crouch, E. A. C., 64
Csikszentmihalyi, I. S., 28
Csikszentmihalyi, M., 28
Cyert, R. M., 1, 29
Czapinski, J., 74

Davidson, A. R., 54, 208, 209
Davidson, D., 157
Davis, M. H., [212]
Dawes, R., 72, 150
Deane, D. H., [109]
Dearborn, D. C., 63
Deighton, J., [13], [64]
Dewar, R., 26
Dinsmore, J., 20, 50–51
Doherty, M. L., 145–146
Dufty, N. F., 71
Dymond, R., 212

Edwards, W., 1, 151, 157, 159, 170
Einhorn, H. J., 17, 38, 72
Elbaum, C., [111]
Ellis, A., 41–42
Ellsberg, D., 1
Englander, T., 65
Erez, M., 46

Fagley, N. S., 57
Fahey, L., 13, 64
Farago, K., [65]
Farris, H. H., 75
Fauconnier, G., 20, 50–51
Felix, W. L., 199–200, 202–203, 207
Fiedler, D., 170
Fiedler, F., [170]
Fischhoff, B., [65], 117, [117], 168
Fishbein, M., 130
Fishburn, P. C., 130, 150, 163
Fiske, S. T., 75
Fitch, M. K., 130
Flink, J. J., [24]
Fodor, J. A., 111
Ford, J. K., 145–146
Franklin, B., 129
Franzoi, S. L., 212
Frederickson, J. R., 199

Frederickson, J. W., 33
Freud, S., 41
Frishkoff, P., [14]
Frishkoff, P. A., [14]

Galambos, J. A. 29, 34–35, 122
Galanter, E., 18–19, 21, [29], [110], 157
Gettys, C. F., [14]
Goffman, E., 50, 62
Goitein, B., [168]
Gollwitzer, P. M., 68, 74
Gordon, J. R., 180
Gore, W. J., 2
Gouin, P., [111]
Grassia, J., [129]
Gray, C. A., 130, 158–162, 165, 168
Guyau, J. M., 31
Guzzo, R. A., 75

Hacking, I., 119
Hage, J., 26
Hamm, R. M., [129]
Hammond, K. R., [109], 119, 129
Harrison, D., [212]
Harrison, R., 12
Hastie, R., 22, 38, 122
Hausmann, L., [7], [28], [31]
Hawley, C., [75]
Hayes, R. H., 183–185
Heckhausen, H., 28, 68, [68], 74
Heer, B., [75]
Henderson, C. M., [13], [64]
Hinton, G. E., [111]
Hintzman, D. L., 51, 61
Hoffman, L. W., 207
Hoffman, M. L., 207
Hofmeister, K. R., 184
Hofstatter, P. R., 113
Hogarth, R. M., 17, 38, 117
Holmstrom, V. L., 130
Hope, A., [54], [170], [209–210]
Hovland, C. I., 75
Huffman, M. D., 140–145
Hults, B. M., 145–146
Hunt, E. B., 86

Inui, T. S., [170]
Isenberg, D. J., 15, 123–124, 126, 165, 172

Jaccard, J., 199

Jacob, P. E., 24
James, W., 69, 134
Janis, I. L., 69
Jaques, E., 30, 36–37
Jastrow, J., 23
Jepson, C., [121]
Johnson, E. J., [151], 153–155, [156–157], [168]
Johnson-Laird, P. N., 17
Jungermann, H., 7, 17, 28, 31, 38–39, 116–117, 122

Kahneman, D., 40, 50, 52–53, 56–59, 62, 105, 116–117, 119–120, 164, 166, 172, 205
Keating, G. W., [170]
Keeney, R. L., 72
Kellner, H., 213
Keren, G. B., 52, 76, 166–167, [167]
Kida, T., 152, 155–157
Kidd, R. F., 80
Kinney, W. R., 207
Kiyak, H. A., 170
Klayman, J., 156
Klein, N. M., 157
Kluckhohn, C., 24
Knudson, B. W., 130
Knudson, R. M., 212
Kohlberg, L., 41
Köhler, W., 44
Kosslyn, S. M., 16
Kotter, J. P., 15, 184–185
Krantz, D., [121]
Kreitler, H., 19
Kreitler, S., 19
Kuhl, J., 28–29
Kunda, Z., [121]
Kundera, M., 25

Lachter, J., 111
Laestadius, J. E., 113–114
Laing, R. D., 212
Landman, J., 59
Larson, J. R., 114–115
Latham, G. P., [46]
Lathrop, R. G., 113
Lee, A. R., [212]
Lee, T. W., 46
Lee, W., 150
Lens, W., 31
Leslie, A. M., 37

Lewicka, M., 40, 75
Lichtenstein, E. H., 29, 34, 35
Lichtenstein, S., [117], [167]
Lindblom, C. E., 2
Linehan, M., [170]
Locke, E. A., 45, [46]
Loftus, E. F., 116
Loomis, G., 164
Lopes, L. L., 165–167
Lord, R. G., 52
Luchins, A. S., 62
Lundell, J., 86–93, [94], [204], [211]

MacCrimmon, K. B., 29
Machina, M. J., 164
Mackie, P., 80
Maguire, E., [75]
Mai-Dalton, R., [170]
Mann, L., 69
Mannix, E. A., [13], [64], 170
March, J. G., 1, [2], [14], 15, 31, 106, 170
Marken, R. S., 35, 174
Markus, H., 18, 21
Marlatt, G. A., 180
Marshall, L. L., 80
Marshall, M., [170]
Martins, J., 20
Matlin, M. W., 75
Maule, J., 80
Maybee, J. S., 73
McAllister, D., 143–144
McCauley, C., 17, 122
McClelland, G. H., [109]
McClelland, J. L., [111]
McNamara, R. S., 230
Mehle, T., [14]
Meichenbaum, D., 180
Meyer, A. D., 26
Miles, G. L., 64
Miller, G. A., 18–19, 21, 29, 110
Miller, P. M., 57
Minsky, M., 50, 62
Mintzberg, H., 2, 15, 44–45, 48–49, 165, 197
Mitchell, T. R., 26, [26], 27, 32, 33, [51], 54, 86–93, [94], 114, 124–125, 127–130, 132–133, 143–147, 153, [153], 155, [155], 157, 164, 187, [204], [211]
Morgenstern, O., 165

Morris, C., 24
Morrison, D., 24, 199
Mosteller, F., 157
Muchinsky, P. M., 130
Mukerjee, R. K., 23
Murnighan, J. K., 13
Murphy, A., 121

Neale, M. A., 56–57
Nestor, Inc., 111
Newman, S. H., 207
Nichols-Hoppe, K. T., 107, 146
Nisbett, R., 117, 121
Nogee, P., 157
Norman, D. A., 175
Nurius, P., 18, 21
Nutt, P. C., 184–185, 191

Olsen, J. P., [2], [14], 15
Olshavsky, R. W., 107
Ortony, A., 111

Paluchowski, T. F., [51], 95–103, [172]
Paquette, L., 152, 155–157
Payne, J. W., 72, 107–108, 146, 151,
    153–157, 168
Pearson, T., [129]
Peeters, G., 75
Pennington, N., 22, 38, 122
Perrault, C. R., 20
Peterson, C. R., 79, 116, 130
Phillips, J. S., 52
Phillips, L. D., 170
Phillipson, H., [212]
Piaget, J., 18
Pichert, J. W., 52
Pleit-Kuiper, A., [167]
Pliske, R. M., [14]
Polyani, M., 125
Pope, A., 40
Powers, W. T., 174
Pratt, J. W., 164
Predmore, S. C., 212
Preston, M. G., 157
Pribram, K. H., 18–19, 21, [29], [110]
Prothero, J., 170
Pruitt, D. G., 13
Pylyshyn, Z. W., 16–17, 111

Raisinghani, D., [2], [15], [165]
Ratajczak, H., [68]

Rayner, S., 65
Raynor, J. O., 31
Rediker, K. J., 30, [54], 94–95, 102
Reenan, A. M., 114–115
Reilly, D. L., 111, [111]
Reither, F., 182–183, 193
Reitzes, D. C., 25
Revlin, R., 75
Rieke, R., 13
Rimey, R., 111
Rokeach, M., 23–24
Rosch, E., 17
Rosenfeld, E., 111
Ross, L., 117
Rubin, J. Z., 13
Rumelhart, D. E., 17, 111
Ryan, T. A., 32

Samuelson, P. A., 165–166
Samuelson, W., 56–57, 205
Savage, L. J., 163–165
Schandl, C. W., 200
Schank, R. C., 17, 33–34, 122
Schechtman, S. L., 145–146
Schlesinger, L. A., 184–185
Schmitt, N., 145–146
Schoenfeld, A. H., 20, 51
Schwartz, S. H., 43
Scofield, C., [111]
Scopp, T. S., 113
Segal, M., [17], [122]
Selznick, P., 28, 165
Shafer, G., 163–165
Shanteau, J., [109], 130
Shapira, Z., [168], 170
Sherman, S. J., 75
Shuchman, H. L., [24]
Siegel, S., [157]
Sillars, M., 13
Silver, W., 56–58
Simon, H. A., 1, 10–11, 16, 29, 31, 63,
    105–107, 109, 124
Skov, R. B., 75
Sloan, T. S., 26, 38
Slovic, P., 64–65, [65], [105], 117, [117],
    165
Smith, B., 86–93, [94], [204], [211]
Smith, J. F., 144–145, 153, 155
Smith, K. G., 26, [27]
Smolensky, P., [111]
Smyth, A. H., 129

Snyder, M., 122
Solak, F., 112–114
Sproull, L. S., 184
Stallen, P. J., 65
Stang, D. J., 75
Stäudel, T., 182–183, 193
Staw, B. M., 52, 206
Steinbruner, J. D., 2, 184
Stevens, S. S., 113
Stillars, A. L., 212
Stitt, C. L., [17], [122]
Strom, E., 74, 80–87
Sugden, R., 164
Suppes, P., 119, [157]
Svenson, O., 146, 149–150, 152–153
Swann, W. B., 212
Symonds, W. C., 64

Tanke, E., [122]
Taylor, B. R., [40]
Taylor, P. M., 71
Teigen, K. H., 65, 170
Théorét, A., [2], [15], [165]
Thompson, L. L., [13], [64]
Thompson, V. D., 207
Thorngate, W., 151–153, 156–157, 168
Thüring, M., 17, 38–39, 122
Townes, B. D., [54], [170], [207], 208–209, [209–211], [213]
Turing, A. M., 86, 92–93
Turtle, J. W., [40]
Tversky, A., 40, 50, 52–53, 56–59, 62, 105, [105], 110–112, 116–117, [117], 119–120, 130, 150–151, 157, 164, 166, 172, 205

van Zee, E. H., [51], 95–103, 172, 199
Vaupel, J. W., 54
Vlek, C., 65, [167], [169]
von Neumann, J., 165
von Winterfeldt, D., 159, 170
von Ulardt, I., [7], [28], [31]
Voogd, H., 73, 110

Wagenaar, W. A., 52, 76, 166–167, [167], [169]
Wagner, D. B., [75]
Waller, W. S., 144–145, 199–200, 202–203, 207
Walsh, J. P., 13, 64
Wason, P. C., 75
Weber, M., 172
Weick, K. E., 2, 14
Weir, T., [212]
Weiss, W. I., 75
Weitz, B., 80
Wells, G. L., 40
Wilson, R., 64
Winkler, R., 121
Wise, J. A., 45, 178
Wolf, G., 133
Wood, R. J., [209], 211
Wright, P., 80
Wurf, E., 18, 21

Yates, J., 21
Young, R. D., [212]

Zander, A., 10, 13
Zeckhauser, R., 56–57, 205
Zidon, I., 46

Subject Index

ability, 134, 138
acceptance threshold, 86
accountability, 133
action theory, 28–29
additive difference model, 130, 151
adoption, 4, 8
affect, 123–126
aided-analytic strategies, 129
aleatory reasoning, 119–123
ambiguity, 132
audit decisions, 199–207
audit evidence, 199
audit principles, 201
audit strategic image, 201
audit trajectory image, 201

base rate bias, 120
Bayesian logic, 204
behavioral accounting, 200
behavioral economics, 164
beliefs, 24
biases (heuristics), 115–123
bounded rationality, 106

causal models, 17, 38
chance, 167
change, 54
    non-optional, 54
    optional, 54
childbearing, 207–214
cognitive images, 16
cognitive structures, 6, 16
compatibility, 105–126
compatibility test, 9, 71–104, 108, 125
    screening 9, 95–103, 108
compensatory strategies, 151
complexity, 132
confidence, 138, 183
confirming information, 75
conflict couples, 210
conjunction fallacy, 120

conjunctive strategy, 150
context evolution, 54
control, 173–175
control theory, 174
Cuban Missile Crisis, 214–229

decision aids, 168–172
decision environment, 132
decision problem, 132
decision rule, 72
decision strategies, 129–147
decision task, 131–133
deliberation, 5, 66–69
desired family size, 208
disjunctive strategy, 150
dominance strategy, 150

effort, 188, 194
elimination by aspects, 150
emotions, 69
environmental stability, 33
episode schemata, 17
epistemic reasoning, 119–123
equivalence interval, 112–115, 203
expected utility, 1, 28, 128, 137
expected value strategy, 151, 157–168

feedback, 174
financial statements, 199
fit, 72, 125
flat maximum, 159
forecasts, 8, 37–40, 115–123
frames, 4, 8, 21–23, 50–66, 215
    conflicting, 63–66
    effects, 52, 56–59
    misframing, 59
    reframing, 59
    representation, 21–23

gamble, 154, 163
gamble equivalences, 171

gambling analogy, 165–168
goal setting, 46
goal-centered thinking, 180
goals, 6, 23–28, 43–47, 220
   origins, 43–47
   packaging, 46
   trajectory image, 6, 23–28
groups, 13

habit, 61
heuristics (biases), 115–123

identification, 51
ideologies, 12
if–then propositions, 38
images, 3, 6–8, 16–49
   mental, 16
   strategic, 7, 30–40
   trajectory, 6, 28–30
   value, 6, 23–28
   visual, 16
implementation, 173–198
   monitoring, 187–198
independence assumptions, 164
instability, 132
intrinsic motivation, 28
intuition, 123–126
irreversibility, 132
iterativity, 133

judgment, 115–123

kitsch, 25
knowledge partitions, 20–21
knowledge representation, 51

law of small numbers, 120
learning, 62, 111
Leiden conference, 168
lexicographic semi-order, 112, 130, 150
luck, 167

markers, 7
material error, 199
memory, 51
mental images, 16
mental models, 17, 38, 175
mental movies, 130
metadecision, 127
missiles, 215–229
money constraints, 133

monitoring, 187–198
moral algebra, 129
motivation, 134

neural network theory, 111
non-analytic strategies, 129
non-compensatory strategies, 150
non-violations, 74–76, 80–86
normative models, 116

optimists' camp, 117
Optional Parenthood Questionnaire, 209
organizational decisions, 2, 10–12, 183,
   183–186

perception, 63
personal decisions, 178–183
pessimists' camp, 117
plan adoption, 61
plans, 7–8, 30–40, 47–49, 180, 221
   origins, 47–49
   strategic image, 7, 30–40
   tactics, 8, 31–33, 180
policy, 8, 33–37, 60–62
possible futures, 38
Principle of Extentionality, 119
principles, 6, 23–28, 40–43, 88
   origins, 40–43
   primary, 88
   secondary, 88
   value image, 6, 23–28
problem solving, 62
process tracing, 146
profitability, 148–172
profitability test, 9, 127– 147
profitable dimensions strategies, 150
progress decisions, 5, 8, 9, 39, 175–178
prospect theory, 164
prototypes, 17

qualitative impact analysis, 72, 110

recognition, 51
regret, 164
rejection threshold, 9, 72, 76–77, 80–86
resistance, 184
risk assessment, 64
risk aversion, 57

satisficing, 105–109
scenarios, 17, 38–40, 175

schemata, 17–23
screening, 9, 95–103, 108
script theory, 17, 33–36
self-concept, 17, 21
significance, 133
similarity theory, 110
simulations, 87, 154–156, 182
social processes, 14
social support, 180
statistical reasoning, 116
status quo, 53–60
stereotype, 17, 122
sterilization, 209
stopping rule, 76
Story Model, 22, 38
strategic image, 7, 30–40
strategies, 8, 148–151
strategy selection model, 127–147
suboptimality, 116

tacit processes, 125

tactical objectives, 229
tactics, 8, 31–33, 180
text anxiety, 146
testimonials, 181
thoroughness, 187, 194
time constraints, 133, 138, 144, 153
time perspective, 31, 36–37
TOTE, 19
trajectory image, 6, 28–30
Turing test, 86

unaided-analytic strategies, 129
unfamiliarity, 132

value image, 6, 23–28
violations, 9, 71, 80–86, 115, 217–219, 221
visual images, 16

'We' frame, 211–214